FOOD VERSUS FUEL

An informed introduction to biofuels

Edited by

Frank Rosillo-Calle
and Francis X. Johnson

Zed Books
LONDON & NEW YORK

Food versus Fuel: An Informed Introduction to Biofuels was first published in 2010 by
Zed Books Ltd, 7 Cynthia Street, London N1 9JF, UK and
Room 400, 175 Fifth Avenue, New York, NY 10010, USA

www.zedbooks.co.uk

Typeset in Dante with Din by Long House, Cumbria
Cover designed by Safehouse Creative
Printed and bound in Great Britain by CPI Antony Rowe,
Chippenham and Eastbourne

Distributed in the USA exclusively by Palgrave Macmillan, a division of St Martin's
Press, LLC, 175 Fifth Avenue, New York, NY 10010, USA.

A catalogue record for this book is available from the British Library.
Library of Congress Cataloging in Publication Data available.

ISBN 978 1 84813 382 2 hb
ISBN 978 1 84813 383 9 pb
ISBN 978 1 84813 384 6 eb

Contents

Tables and Figures

Tables

Abbreviations

APTA	Agency for Agribusiness Technology (Brazil)	FAPRI	Food and Agricultural Policy Research Institute
ARS	Agricultural Research Service (USDA)	GATT	General Agreement on Tariffs and Trade
BMP	Best management practice	GBEP	Global Bioenergy Energy Partnership
BTL	Biomass-to-liquids (technologies)	GEF	Global Environment Facility
CBD	Convention on Biodiversity	Gha	Gigahectares (= 1 billion hectares)
CCS	Carbon capture and storage	GHG	Greenhouse gas
CGE	Computable general equilibrium (research model)	GJ	Gigajoule (= 1 billion joules)
CGIAR	Consultative Group on International Agricultural Research	GJ/ha/yr	Gigajoules/hectare/year
		GMO	Genetically modified organism
CSIR	Council of Scientific and Industrial Research, India	GREET	Greenhouse gases, regulated emissions and energy in transportation
CTC	Sugarcane Technology Center, Brazil		
EBB	European Biodiesel Board	HEC	Herbaceous energy crop
EI	Erosion index	IAC	Agronomic Institute of Campinas, Brazil
EIA	Energy Information Administration	IEA	International Energy Agency
EJ	Exajoule(s) (1 EJ = 1018 joules)	IEO	International Energy Outlook
Eurostat	Statistical Office of the European Union	IISC	Indian Institute of Science (Bangalore)
FAO	Food and Agriculture Organization	IISD	International Institute for Sustainable Development
FAPESP	State of São Paulo Research Foundation	ILUC	Indirect land-use change
FAPESP-BIOEN	FAPESP Research Programme on Bioenergy	IPCC	Intergovernmental Panel on Climate Change

ISO	International Standards Organization	RFA	Renewable Fuels Agency (UK)
LCA	Life cycle analysis	RFA	Renewable Fuels Association (USA)
LCC	Land capability classification		
LE	Lignocellulosic ethanol	RIDESA	Sugar-Ethanol Sector Development Inter-University Network (Brazil)
LUC	Land-use change		
MBTU	Million British thermal units		
MDGs	Millennium Development Goals	RUSLE	Revised Universal Soil Loss Equation
Mdt	Million dry tons	SSURGO	Soil Survey Geographic (database)
Mha	Million hectares (Megahectares)		
		STAP	Science and Technology Advisory Panel (GEF)
MJ	Megajoule(s)		
MT	Mulch/reduced tillage	t/ha	Tonnes per hectare
Mt	Megaton(s) (one million metric tons)	toe	Tonnes of oil equivalent
		UNCTAD	United Nations Conference on Trade and Development
NASS	National Agricultural Statistics Service		
		UNDP	United Nations Development Programme
NIPE	Interdisciplinary Centre for Energy Planning (UNICAMP)		
		UNECA	United Nations Economic Commission for Africa
NLAE	National Laboratory for Agriculture and the Environment		
		UNEP	United Nations Environment Programme
NREL	National Renewable Energy Laboratory, US	UNFCCC	United Nations Framework Convention on Climate Change
NT	No-till(age)		
OECD	Organisation for Economic Co-operation and Development	UNICA	Sugarcane Industry Association (São Paulo)
		UNICAMP	State University of Campinas, Brazil
PRSP	Poverty Reduction Strategy Paper	UNIDO	United Nations Industrial Development Organization
PISCES	Policy Innovation Systems for Clean Energy Security	USDA	United States Department of Agriculture
R$	Real, Brazilian currency	WEMA	Water Efficient Maize for Africa
R&D	Research and Development		
RED	Renewable Energy Directive (European Commission)	WEO	World Energy Outlook
		WEQ	Wind Erosion Equation

About the Contributors

Luís Cortez is a Professor in the Faculty of Agricultural Engineering at the State University of Campinas (UNICAMP), Brazil. He was formerly Coordinator of the Interdisciplinary Center of Energy Planning (NIPE) at UNICAMP, and is an adviser to the Scientific Director of Special Programs at FAPESP, Brazil.

Rocio Diaz-Chavez is a Research Fellow at the Centre for Environmental Policy, Imperial College London. She holds a PhD from the University of Wales on sustainable development and environmental management and has worked as an academic and consultant in Latin America, Europe, Africa, and Asia. Her research interests are sustainability assessment and other environmental management tools for bioenergy projects and policy development.

J. Richard Hess oversees the Biofuels and Renewable Energy Technology Department and Biomass Program at Idaho National Laboratory and serves on US and international teams working towards development of a sustainable bioenergy trade industry.

Jacob J. Jacobson is a staff researcher at Idaho National Laboratory. He has worked in the field of systems analysis for 25 years, and has numerous publications in this area.

Douglas L. Karlen is a research soil scientist with the USDA Agricultural Research Service (ARS) at the National Laboratory for Agriculture and the Environment (NLAE). He uses soil quality assessment and systems approaches to quantify the sustainability of various soil and crop management practices and uses. He has published widely in this field and made several national and international presentations.

C. Sita Lakshmi is a research scientist at the Centre for Sustainable Technologies, Indian Institute of Science (IISC), Bangalore, and has been working on biofuels and climate change.

Ritumbara Manuvie is a research scientist at the Centre for Sustainable Technologies, IISC, Bangalore, and has been working on biofuels and climate change.

David J. Muth Jr is a research engineer at Idaho National Laboratory who provides computational modelling expertise and indigenous agricultural understanding to collaborative research addressing barriers in the development of sustainable bioenergy feedstock systems.

Richard G. Nelson is Associate Professor with the Center for Sustainable Energy at Kansas State University. He has over 20 years' experience in biomass energy assessment, supply, and sustainability issues.

Leslie P. Ovard works at the Idaho National Laboratory. With a background in Environmental Humanities and Communication, he supports research efforts towards sustainable, environmentally responsible energy solutions.

David Pimentel, Professor Emeritus in the Department of Entomology and Ecology and Evolutionary Biology, Cornell University, New York, is a world authority on the production and use of biofuels. He published the world's first comprehensive life cycle analysis of energy use in corn production.

N. H. Ravindranath is Professor at the Centre for Sustainable Technologies, IISC, Bangalore. He has been a contributing author to several IPCC reports on mitigation in the forestry sector and the greenhouse gas inventory in land-use sectors. He has worked extensively on bioenergy and biofuels. He is a member of the Science and Technology Advisory Panel (STAP) of the Global Environment Facility (GEF).

Manoel Regis L. V. Leal, of the Centre for Alternative Energies and Environment, Fortaleza, Brazil, is a world authority on sugarcane.

Erin M. Searcy has a background in techno-economic analyses of biomass-based energy systems.

Thomson Sinkala is Professor at the University of Zambia, Chair of the Biofuels Association of Zambia, and Managing Director of Thomro Investments Limited, which produces biodiesel and other products from jatropha.

Jeff Tschirley is Chief of Humanitarian and Rehabilitation Policies at the FAO.

Thomas H. Ulrich is Bioenergy Advisory Scientist in the Biofuels and Renewable Energy Technologies Department, Idaho National Laboratory. He has worked for more than 25 years in R&D areas of plant science that support the field of bioenergy.

Ivar Virgin is Senior Research Fellow at the Stockholm Environment Institute, with a background in biology. His work focuses on biotechnology and bio-safety, with a geographical emphasis on eastern and southern Africa.

Introduction

Frank Rosillo-Calle and Francis X. Johnson

Biofuels are not new: their use dates back to the early twentieth century. Ethanol, as a transport fuel, has a long and well-documented history going back to the origin of the automobile industry itself.[1] Henry Ford's famous Model T car (or 'quadricycle'), built in 1908, was conceived as an ethanol-powered product. Ford's vision was to 'build a vehicle affordable to the working family and powered by a fuel that would boost the rural farm economy'.[2] Contrary to general belief, appreciable quantities of fuel ethanol were in use throughout the century, particularly in Europe (Germany, France and Italy, for example) and much later in Brazil and the USA (see Kovarik, 1998; Rosillo-Calle and Walter, 2006).

However, the large-scale use of biofuels is a more recent development. The first national-level programme began in November 1975 with Brazil's creation of its National Alcohol Programme, commonly known as ProAlcool, using sugarcane as the prime feedstock. The second big step was taken in the US later in the 1970s, based on a blend of ethanol (10 percent) and gasoline (90 percent). This initiative was reinforced by the introduction of the Clean Energy Act of 1992 and then the Energy Independence and Security Act of 2007, which established the US as the world's largest producer and consumer of biofuels. These two examples were followed by the EU and many other countries around the world, including China and India.

Rising oil prices and increasing evidence of climate change led to greater support for biofuels. With greenhouse gas (GHG) emissions rising fastest in the transportation sector, biofuels appeared to be among the few near-term mitigation options. In addition to addressing climate change and energy security concerns, biofuels were seen to have the political and economic benefit of supporting rural areas and farming regions in developed and developing countries alike. The rationale varies across countries and regions: in Brazil, the main concerns are social and agro-industrial development; in the EU, energy security and climate change are the main drivers; in the US, energy security and support for farmers are prominent; in most other countries, a combination of these various advantages is cited.

Many governments set up biofuels programmes before all the pros and cons were fully assessed; their advantages, perhaps, were overemphasized. What at first were perceived as clear benefits came to be questioned as new studies were carried out that undermined some of the original claims. Now the benefits of biofuels are constantly the subject of claims and counterclaims. This should not be surprising, given the cross-sector nature and complexity of biofuels, and the rapid technological changes in the energy sector; for both fossil fuels and biofuels, energy outputs and GHG emissions are constantly being tweaked and refined.

Inevitably, global interest in biofuels has thus given rise to a legitimate concern about the potential negative impacts of large-scale biofuel production. This came to a head between 2007 and mid-2008 when, boosted by a combination of factors well explained in this book, food prices shot up to alarming levels (see Chapter 1). The consequences for poorer people, particularly in urban areas, became abundantly clear. Biofuels were often portrayed in the media as the culprits; however, as this book also shows, biofuels were actually only a small component of the equation.

Why has there been so much debate, replete with contradictions and lacking in consensus? The reasons are many and varied: the diversity of the feedstocks utilized, with correspondingly diverse potential impacts (positive and negative) in different parts of the world; the sheer range of views taken, and assumptions made, by different actors on issues related to biofuel know-how, the scale of its application, and the availability of technology; and underlying attitudes to climate change, environmental objectives, and economic development priorities, sometimes involving conflicts between rural and urban poverty.

The ensuing political, economic, technological, scientific, and ethical debate often arises from vested interests and lacks a solid scientific basis.

This underinformed public debate has not been assisted by the polarizing role of the media, struggling for headlines in the Internet age; arguably, reporting on biofuels has tended to focus on risks and threats, rather than on economic and development opportunities. Faced by the complex nature of biofuels, the media have tended to simplify the issues rather than conducting deeper analysis. In hindsight, this debate has been rather premature: both the pro- and anti-biofuel lobbies have used arguments that lack solid scientific credibility. This book therefore aims at presenting a balanced and unbiased assessment of the pros and cons of biofuels, in a manner that makes it accessible to a wider audience.

Broadly speaking, there are two main schools of thought. The anti-biofuels lobby argues that 'we do not need biofuels' for many reasons, including moral and ethical ones, citing the presumed competition with food, water, and other scarce natural resources. Prominent among these critics is Professor David Pimentel, our lead author in Chapter 2. In this sector of the debate an obviously sensitive issue arises: it is usually difficult to refute ethical/moral arguments with scientific data. Within the broader 'anti' lobby, technical reasons are sometimes cited, such as difficulties in using biofuels to power existing engines; changes in engine fuel technology that offer better alternatives than biofuels; and the development of electric vehicles.

The pro-biofuels lobby has also gathered substantial arguments in support of its case. The argument is that there is sufficient land available, given modern agricultural management practices, to produce both food and a reasonable portion of biofuels without affecting food supply. Production of biofuels can be complementary to food production, and rural areas stand to benefit substantially from both. The fact that so many people in the world are undernourished is due to many factors (including poverty, inequality, and lack of capital), and has little or nothing to do with biofuels, which presently claim less than 1 percent of agricultural land. The 'pro' lobby argues that the social, economic, and environmental benefits of biofuels outweigh the potential negative impacts.

The debate has concentrated on many issues, but the following have been particularly debated, and are also discussed in considerable detail in this book.

1 *Food prices*. Biofuels are blamed for higher food prices, although there are many factors involved, such as the stage of agricultural development, speculation, inequality, rural poverty, and social injustice.

2 *Land use*. Land-use changes such as deforestation and degradation are attributed to biofuels. However, large-scale land-use change has been under way for several hundred years in most of the world. Some of the issues are controversial and perhaps insoluble: an example is so-called 'indirect land-use change' (ILUC).

3 *Environment/GHG*. Changing estimates of GHG emissions for biofuels and the diversity of impacts across different crops and regions have raised the question of when 'good' reductions become 'good enough' to meet sustainability criteria. The GHG balances are further complicated by the many activities to be assessed, the mountain of data involved, and rapidly changing methods of data collection. For example, estimates of GHG savings for biofuels range from zero to over 80 percent, depending on the source. Further, a recent study credits 123.5 Mt of GHG saved by biofuels globally in 2009; this represents an average reduction of 57 percent when compared to emissions from equal quantities of petroleum fuels (see S & T, 2009). In 2009 biofuel production (bioethanol plus biodiesel) surpassed 100 billion litres, displacing 1.15 million barrels of crude oil per day.[3]

4 *Social and economic impact*. Although ongoing analysis needs to be extended considerably, the use of biofuels seems to have a positive economic result, certainly for rural areas. The rise of biofuels during the past few decades has accompanied the rise of the important concept of *sustainable development*, which has forced us to rethink the modern form of agricultural development previously subsidized by cheap fossil fuels.

5 *Energy balance*. Continuous refinement has altered considerably the energy balance of most feedstocks used in biofuels production; the example of biofuels in Brazil showed that the energy balance could be improved five-fold in just two decades. Less positively, 'first-generation' ethanol from grain crops, such as corn in the US, has failed so far to overcome the drawback of a poor overall energy balance.

6 *Subsidies*. The anti-biofuel lobby claims that subsidies given to bio-fuels distort the market; this argument sometimes ignores the large

subsidies that have been granted to fossil fuels in various forms (a practice that continues in many countries). To put all transport fuels on a more equal footing, all subsidies need to be incorporated into the equation.

Although this book deals primarily with liquid biofuels, we cannot ignore the growing role of energy as a whole, especially since it is precisely the multi-faceted and multi-purpose nature of biomass that makes it important in the long term, as fossil fuels become more costly and scarce. This is why other uses of biomass are also discussed in the book, albeit briefly.

Demand for bioenergy is growing, both in its traditional and modern applications, although fossil fuels dominate the global energy market with an estimated contribution of 500 EJ in 2008 compared to 50–54 EJ from biomass, of which 70–80 percent is represented by traditional applications, primarily in developing countries. In 2007 biomass contributed about 6.4 EJ to power generation and industrial applications and just 2.6 EJ as transportation fuels (Dornburg *et al.*, 2010). The World Bioenergy Association[4] has recently estimated that the potential of bioenergy production ranges from 1,135 EJ to 1,548 EJ by 2050.

This book has brought together experts from many parts of the world to investigate all these issues in a balanced and unbiased manner for the benefit of professionals, students, and the wider public. The recent United Nations Framework Convention on Climate Change (UNFCCC) conference in Copenhagen offered some reminders of why biofuels and bioenergy need to be understood better by the international community. The North–South conflicts that arose in the meeting demonstrate the need to look for areas where mutual opportunities can be exploited. Biomass and bioenergy (both in its solid and liquid forms) represents the area of energy/climate that has special relevance for the developing world, which holds the vast majority of future bioenergy potential. Sustainable exploitation of this potential, coordinated by the UNFCCC process, can proceed to the benefit of North and South alike. This requires broad international cooperation, and the benefits and costs of bioenergy options need to be better incorporated into methodologies related to carbon finance and mitigation strategies.

Chapter 1 sets out the pros and cons of the biofuel arguments, in general terms. Chapter 2 deals with the anti-biofuel argument, particularly from a US perspective. Chapter 3 argues in favour of bio-fuels, particularly from a Brazilian and an African perspective. Chapter 4 investigates land use for agricultural and other purposes in relation to biofuel development. Chapter 5 looks at the social and sustainability arguments. Chapter 6 deals with the potential implications from a climate change perspective. Chapter 7 considers biofuels within the con-text of the ongoing transformation in global use of biomass resources for food, feed, fibre, fuel, fertilizer, and many other needs. Finally, Chapter 8 revisits the main issues raised in the previous chapters with the aim of assisting the independent reader to draw out the key conclusions of the book.

Notes

1   For example, 152 popular and scholarly articles on alcohol as a fuel appeared between 1900 and 1921 alone. See Kovarik, 1998.
2   Quoted in 'History of ethanol production', Report No. 12, Rural Enterprise and Alternative Agricultural Development Initiative, June 2002.
3   Of this, ethanol production in 2009 corresponded to 73.7 billion litres, with a reduction of 87.7 Mt of GHG emissions when compared with its petroleum equivalent. For biodiesel the estimated numbers are 16.4 billion litres and 39.9 Mt, respectively.
4   <www.worldbioenergy.org>.

References

Dornburg, V., D. van Vuuren, G. van de Ven *et al.* (2010) 'Bioenergy re-visited: key factors in global potential of bioenergy', *Energy and Environmental Science*, 3: 258–67.

Kovarik, B. (1998) 'Henry Ford, Charles F. Kettering and the fuel of the future', *Automotive History Review*, 32 (Spring): 7–27.

Rosillo-Calle, F. and A. Walter (2006) 'Global market for bioethanol: historical trends and future prospects', *Energy for Sustainable Development*, 10 (1): 20–32.

S & T (2009) 'GHG emissions reductions from world biofuels production and use', report prepared for Global Renewable Fuels Alliance by S & T Consultants, <www.globalrfa.org>.

1 Food versus Fuel: Setting the Scene

Frank Rosillo-Calle and Jeff Tschirley

As the twenty-first century settles on its course, energy security concerns, high oil prices and growing international commitment to address climate change have sparked significant interest and investment in renewable energy resources. Particular emphasis has been placed on liquid biofuels, which are seen as a means to reduce greenhouse gas emissions from transport, contribute to rural development, and reduce costly dependence on imported oil. Some countries also see biofuels as a way to exploit their comparative advantage in agriculture and increase their export earnings. Needless to say, the demand for bioenergy is likely to influence agriculture strongly in the foreseeable future.

A political and scientific debate, particularly with regard to the potential negative social and environmental impacts of bioenergy production, has been taking place for several years and was intensified during 2008 by spikes in agricultural commodity prices. The areas of greatest concern have been impacts on food security, land competition and indirect land-use change; lower-than-expected greenhouse gas benefits from some biofuel feedstocks; biodiversity and sustainability impacts; and market distortions caused by subsidies.

There is a role for an informed, nuanced and accessible source, grounded in science and economics rather than conjecture and controversy. The aim of this book is to bring a balanced perspective to bear on the major issues affecting the development of biofuels in order to facilitate a more informed debate among academic and professional specialists as well as the general public. This book explores the wider implications associated with the multi-faceted nature of biofuels and the multiple purposes that generally lie behind support for biofuels.

This chapter sets the scene for those that follow by reviewing the major issues in the food versus fuel debate, to be examined later in greater detail. We review the positions of various biofuel interest groups; examine some of the moral dilemmas; and assess how issues such as food prices, land use, subsidies, and greenhouse gases may influence the outcome in the current drive towards greater use of renewable energy sources.

The biofuel debate has centred around three major dilemmas: (1) whether biofuel production and use lead to – or imply – a choice between food and fuel; (2) whether biofuels have positive or negative effects for climate change and the broader environment; and (3) whether biofuels contribute to socio-economic development, wealth generation and distribution.

The 'food versus fuel' debate is not new (e.g. Rosillo-Calle and Hall, 1987; FAO, 1999) but intensified in recent years when a number of factors converged. Among the driving forces were policy decisions in the EU and US to increase their use of biofuels significantly and provide incentives for their production. The response by the private sector and a number of developing countries was strong; the result was an expanding bioenergy market, but environmental and social concerns rapidly emerged. During 2007 and 2008, as the global economy was undergoing significant and widespread changes in the scale and geographical scope of supply and demand, spikes in many commodity markets occurred, including soaring prices for key agricultural commodities such as maize, rice and wheat.

The sharp increase in food prices has been attributed to a combination of factors and the specific influence of biofuel production is widely recognized, even if the magnitude of the impact is still a matter of debate.[1] However, the rapid transition towards biofuel use, primarily in the US and EU, was seen by many as the root of the problem. Growing concern was expressed by some international organizations (FAO, 2007; Royal Society, 2008) as well as non-governmental groups (Doornbosch and Steenblik, 2007);[2] Kutas *et al.*, 2007; Koplow, 2007) over a rapid rush to biofuels that failed to take the full risks into account. Their concern was reinforced by studies that questioned the overall greenhouse gas benefits and the availability of land to support biofuel feedstock production.

Much of the criticism has been focused on 'first-generation' biofuels dependent on technologies likely to be used for at least the next decade, until 'second-generation'[3] technologies start to become more wide-spread. But there has also been a failure to understand fully the potential economic implications that such a significant additional demand for biofuel feedstocks places on agricultural commodity prices and human wellbeing.

Factors such as transport costs of feedstocks, infrastructure require-ments, land availability and rapid growth in demand from some developed countries are significant in economic terms. However, developing countries in the tropics, which have a comparative advantage in producing biomass and biofuels due to favourable climatic condi-tions, face other challenges – land tenure rights, food insecurity and limited infrastructure, to name just a few – that constrain their efforts to enter the biofuel marketplace.

Government policy in a number of OECD countries was imple-mented without sufficient analysis of the environmental, social and economic effects. Furthermore, dialogue between the countries that would import biofuels and those that would produce them was minimal. This led to unrealistic assumptions and expectations. In this sense, the current debate is relevant but somewhat premature – as the world confronts a significant financial downturn and practical reality begins to take hold, the costs and benefits of biofuel production will be seen from a different and more practical perspective than they have to date.

The simplistic manner in which the popular press has portrayed biofuels as a 'food versus fuel' issue has neglected complex interactions with factors such as climate change, livelihoods and development goals;[4] misconceptions and misunderstandings among academics, policy makers and the wider public have flourished.

The benefits and risks of biofuels are highly context-specific – a system that is sustainable in one country does not necessarily work in a neighbouring country. Biofuel systems are as diverse as the feedstocks and agro-ecosystems from which they are produced. Each system has its own pros and cons. It is also essential to recognize that renewable energies will provide only a fraction of global energy needs during the next few decades; the biofuel portion will be even more limited. While bioenergy needs to be produced on a sustainable basis, claims that it can provide the bulk of transport fuel demand lack a solid economic foundation.

Thus it is important neither to overstate the potential contribution of biofuels nor to underestimate the environmental and social impacts. Overestimates of potential create unrealistic expectations and less effective incentives. A misrepresentation of impacts can result in the imposition of stringent requirements that place biofuels at a disadvantage in comparison with fossil fuels, thus hindering rather than enhancing their development.

A stronger link between agriculture and the demand for energy could contribute to higher agricultural prices, output and domestic income. The development of biofuels could also promote access to energy in rural areas, further supporting economic growth and long-term improvements in food security. At the same time, higher food prices could threaten the food security of the world's poorest people in urban areas, many of whom spend more than half of their household incomes on food. Demand for biofuels could place additional pressure on the natural resource base, with potentially harmful consequences, particularly for people who already lack access to energy, food, land and water. These issues are covered in greater detail in Chapters 5 and 6.

The pro- and anti-biofuels arguments

There are two main schools in the biofuels debate, whose arguments we summarize here. The anti-biofuels lobby (see Pimentel *et al.* in Chapter 2) maintains that:

- Large-scale production of biofuels will lead to food insecurity worldwide.
- Increasing food prices will disproportionately affect the poorest people in developing countries.
- Land competition, including indirect land-use change, will increase as competing demands for food and non-food products intensify, leading to deforestation, ecosystem destruction and loss of biodiversity.
- Many of the social and environmental benefits of biofuels are not yet fully proven.
- Large-scale biofuels production will increase soil erosion, putting stress on water resources and other ecosystem services.

The pro-biofuels lobby (see Cortez, Regis and Sinkala in Chapter 3) argues:

- There is sufficient land available to produce both food and a reasonable portion of biofuels (5–20 percent of transport fuels demand) without affecting food supply.
- Food-insecure countries that do not have their own fossil fuel reserves pay a significant portion of their national income in dollars for imported oil. In such cases, biofuels are a good alternative to fossil fuels and would free up foreign exchange for other investments.
- More than 2.5 billion people have little or no access to modern energy systems. Developing-country agriculture and rural areas need more energy in absolute terms; bioenergy availability can actually enhance food production.
- Multi-functional agricultural production systems already exist in many countries; these systems can or do contribute to overall welfare by providing food and non-food products in a sustainable and socially balanced manner.
- The social, economic and environmental benefits of biofuels can thus outweigh potential negative impacts if good management practices are applied.

Produce food or fuel?

Since its inception, modern agriculture has produced a variety of both food and non-food products. Biofuel feedstocks are in many respects simply one more agricultural product. Most farmers seek to maintain a viable livelihood; they are less concerned with what they produce than with whether they can make a reasonable economic return. The production of natural fibres, plant-derived pharmaceuticals and chemicals, non-edible oils, and starches and sugars are further examples of agricultural products (see also Chapter 7).

Biofuels offer qualified farmers[5] the opportunity to produce a new or existing crop for a purpose which can diversify their on-farm income. However, some people find it unethical to use land in food-insecure countries to produce biofuels that benefit mostly wealthy people, when almost one billion of the world's people are chronically undernourished. Leaving aside the issue of whether this ethical position is too simplistic, we need also to recognize that the reasons people go hungry are many and complex; they usually have little to do with food or land availability, but rather with poverty and income inequality. It is also relevant that, given the right conditions (financing, markets, skills, et cetera), farmers can consistently deliver far more food than is generally assumed.

Climate change and greenhouse gases

One of the greatest challenges currently facing humankind is the potential impact of climate change (see Chapter 6). What role might biofuels play, positive or negative, in addressing this challenge? The answers depend upon many factors such as positive contribution to GHG, energy balance, the specific feedstock (such as sugarcane or maize) and the circumstances of production and processing (see Royal Society, 2008).

Some analysts have long questioned the energy balance (Pimental *et al.*, Chapter 2) while the GHG benefits of biofuels have been further questioned by critics who cite the influences of land-use change on carbon benefits (Fargione *et al.*, 2008; Searchinger *et al.*, 2008). However, it is important to distinguish the case for biofuels made from starch and grain crops (such as corn or wheat) in temperate climates from the case of biofuels made from highly efficient tropical crops like sugarcane; the latter have significantly better energy balance and greenhouse gas benefits (see Cortez, Regis and Sinkala in Chapter 3).

It is also important to consider that energy and GHG balances are constantly changing as they are the focus of significant technical efficiency improvement efforts. In the case of corn, a study by Darlington (2009) shows that GHG emission savings from ethanol production and utilization will more than double from 1995 to 2015, based on the projected level. The study indicates that 'there is a danger of making policy decisions based on historical data without taking into account learning experiences and the potential gains that can be expected as industries develop'.

The GHG balance uses life-cycle analysis to measure all emissions of greenhouse gases in a specific biofuel production process against emissions in producing equivalent energy from fossil fuel. GHG balances differ widely among crops and locations, depending on feedstock production methods, conversion technologies and use. Inputs such as nitrogen fertilizer and the type of electricity generation used to convert feedstocks to biofuels yield different balances. Most life-cycle analyses of biofuels to date have been undertaken for cereals and oilseeds in Europe and the US, and for sugarcane ethanol in Brazil. Potentially at least, second-generation biofuels, although not yet widely deployed, could reduce emissions significantly.

Some studies (Fargione *et al.*, 2008, Searchinger *et al.*, 2008) have raised questions and considerable debate by claiming very high impacts on GHG balances from land use and land conversion, although many unanswered questions remain. Some countries, primarily the USA and in the EU, have suggested that biofuels need to offer 40–60 percent GHG savings over fossil fuels in order to qualify for import. A basic climate change principle in producing biofuels would seem to require full accounting for all these factors in providing an energy balance rating for a particular product.

The role of biofuels in wealth creation and distribution

The socio-economic impacts of biofuels are widely debated (see Chapter 5). Some analysis has shown biofuels create and distribute wealth in a fairly efficient and equitable fashion, but other analyses dispute this. This debate is specious in so far as biofuel crops are not *intrinsically* better or worse than any other agricultural crop. Critics of biofuels often cite the difficult working conditions in the Brazilian sugarcane fields; however, such conditions should be compared to those of other agricultural jobs. In fact, wages and to some extent working conditions as well are better than in many other agro-industries. These higher wages are dictated by market forces, not the benevolence of employers.

The land area used for sugarcane has also been misunderstood. In the late 1970s and early 1980s, some biofuel critics claimed Brazil was being covered by sugarcane plantations to produce ethanol so that rich people could drive big cars! Of a land area of 850 million hectares (Mha), approximately 1.7 Mha were planted with sugarcane, and most of the crop was actually part of sugar production (Rosillo-Calle and Hall, 1987).

Nonetheless, the debate on this matter does raise the legitimate issue of whether developing nations should receive fiscal incentives to produce biofuels for export to wealthier countries where energy demand is higher (see Chapters 5 and 7). This question cannot be answered here, though there would be broad agreement that a transition towards greater use of biofuels in the transport sector must be accompanied by commensurate efforts to achieve net reductions in energy consumption and increased efficiency throughout the global economy, and especially in the OECD countries. However, a number of developing countries are projected to increase their energy consumption dramatically during the next 40 years. It is imperative that they emphasize the maximum possible use of renewable energies and efficient production systems. Technology transfer efforts should therefore be emphasized, so as to move best practice options into developing countries at the earlier stages of their growth before inefficient technologies are locked in.

Food prices

The potential impacts of biofuels on food prices came to light dramatically during the commodity price increases from 2007 to 2008, after which food prices decreased almost as sharply as they had risen. There has been sharp criticism from the anti-biofuel lobby, blaming biofuels as a major cause of the price surge. Although it is likely that biofuels contributed to price increases for some crops (especially maize) there were many other causal factors, including the following:

- Changed consumption patterns.[6] Improved living conditions, particularly in developing countries such as Brazil, China and India, result in a higher consumption of meat. Meeting this demand requires more land since, for example, it takes 8 to 10 kg of wheat (for example) to produce 1 kg of meat.
- The historical and continuing effects of distorted agricultural markets, caused by rich countries subsidizing domestic agricultural production and dumping surplus production on the world market.
- Sustained low levels of investment in agriculture. In the 1980s about 17 percent of international development aid was for agriculture, but in 2005 investment from this source had shrunk to just 3 percent. This reduction has been exacerbated in the last decade by low com-

modity prices and the shifting exchange rate of the US dollar; farmers
have struggled to survive.

• Many countries have cut their reserves, making them more vulnerable to temporary market fluctuations and shortages.

• Increased interest from investors and traders in commodities makes
price development much more sensitive to differences in the modes
of market organization in different countries. The price of corn in
the US, widely reported in the media, was blamed for the rapid hike
in the price of tortillas in Mexico, but monopolistic distribution of
tortilla flour was a more telling factor.

• Poverty and unequal income distribution: food is not *unavailable* but
unaffordable for a significant share of the population in the developing
world. There is evidence that 'as a result of agricultural intensification, more food is produced today than [is] needed to feed the entire
world population, and at prices that have never been so low' (Hazel
and Woods, 2008). Thus food has become cheap in wealthy countries
but not in developing countries, where people have very low formal
(cash) incomes.

• Increasing cost of inputs such as fertilizers and pesticides: however,
the cost of raw materials plays a comparatively small role in the retail
food price since price increases are largely determined by commercial
marketing structures. A 50 percent increase in the cost of raw
materials in the US leads to only about a 5 percent increase in the
price of bread and breakfast cereals, while other links in the production chain (processing, packaging and distribution) account for 90
percent. Thus, farmers are often squeezed out by traders, distributors,
marketers, retailers and other middlemen.

Food price increases are therefore the result of a complex web of
factors that need to be incorporated in any debate. Price increases due to
direct land competition are quite unlikely, except in highly isolated con-
texts, since only about 1 percent of global agricultural land area is currently dedicated to biofuels. Furthermore, higher agricultural prices have
both positive and negative impacts. Higher incomes will allow farmers to
invest more in agricultural productivity and/or expansion; rural farmers
will thus tend to benefit from higher prices, though not the urban poor.

It seems clear that the very high food prices of 2008 will not be sustained but that a higher price floor has nevertheless been established. About 70 percent of the world's poor live in rural areas and could therefore benefit from price increases if they are net food sellers. However, urban dwellers and net food buyers will tend to be affected negatively, at least in the short term. Thus, higher food prices will require concerted policy action on the part of governments.

Land use and intensification of production

Many studies have attempted to estimate land requirements (see Chapter 6), but with widely varying results. Thus – after excluding forests, protected areas and land needed to meet increased demand for food crops and livestock – estimates of the amount of land available for expanded cultivation vary from 250 to 800 Mha (see also Chapter 3). Most of it is in tropical Latin America or in Africa.[7]

Some of this land could be used directly for biofuel feedstock production, and there can be direct land-use change impacts, including GHG emissions. Furthermore, additional biofuel production could stimulate expansion of non-biofuel crops elsewhere, causing so-called indirect land-use change (ILUC). Both direct and indirect land-use changes caused by expanded biofuel production need to be considered when assessing the environmental impacts of bioenergy production. One difficulty is that the ILUC methodology is still in its infancy, and so care must be taken with respect to policy decisions. Policy makers must establish an enabling environment to ensure that bioenergy provides positive environmental benefits within a fair playing field for all energy sources.

In 2004, an estimated 14 Mha worldwide were being used to produce biofuels and their by-products, representing about 1 percent of global cropland (IEA, 2006). In 2008 the total land area was approximately 19 Mha. Future estimates of land-use requirements for bioethanol range from 24 Mha for sugarcane to 39 Mha for sweet sorghum and 50 Mha for maize. For biodiesel, the range is from 29 Mha for palm oil or 106 Mha for jatropha and 221 Mha for soybean (see Chapter 6).

The German Advisory Council on Global Change (WBGU, 2009) estimates that in the long term up to 10 percent of the global energy requirement could be met by bioenergy.[8] The WBGU argues that the highest priority should be the use of organic waste and other agroforestry residues, and that generation of heat and electricity rather than liquid biofuels would be the most effective way of utilizing biomass. Although the area expansion for biofuel feedstock production is likely to play a significant role in meeting increased demand for biofuels over the next few years, the intensification of land use through improved technologies and management practices will complement this option.

For example, ethanol experts in Brazil believe that even without genetic improvements in sugarcane, yield increases of around 20 percent could be achieved over the next ten years through improved production chain management. In Brazil ethanol yields have been increasing steadily since 1975, from approximately 2,000 l/ha to 7,000 l/ha in 2009, and even in some cases close to 10,000 l/ha (see also Chapter 3). It has been shown that increases in productivity can boost ethanol output ten-fold without affecting food production (Goldemberg and Guardabassi, 2010).

According to Woods (2007) and Moreira (2006) between 80 Mha and 250 Mha will be sufficient to meet 30 percent of ethanol demand in 2070. This will require selected advanced conventional biofuel production technologies, using sugarcane as the main feedstock. Global average productivity of main sugarcane-growing nations ranges from 60–85 tons/ha/year. The commercial maximum achieved is 148 t/ha/yr and as high as 212 t/ha/yr in experimental plots (Goldemberg and Guardabassi, 2010). The current global planted area for sugarcane is about 25 Mha, while approximately 260–70 Mha were dedicated to wheat in the 2007/08 harvest (see <www.fas.da.gov>). Table 1.1 shows land requirement for biofuels in 2004 and estimates for 2030.

Some crops currently used as biofuel feedstocks require high-quality agricultural land and major inputs in terms of fertilizer, pesticides and water to generate economically viable yields. With second-generation technologies based on lignocellulosic feedstock, this food–fuel competition could be reduced. Over the medium-to-long term (10–15 years), significant efficiency gains in bioenergy system output should alleviate some of the pressure on land resources.

Table 1.1 Land requirements for biofuel production

| | 2004 | | 2030 | | | | | |
| | | | Reference scenario | | Alternative scenario | | Second-generation biofuels case | |
Country Grouping	(million ha)	(% of arable land)	(Million ha)	(% of arable land)	(Million ha)	(% of arable land)	Million ha)	(% of arable land)
Africa and Near East	–	–	0.8	0.3	0.9	0.3	1.1	0.4
Developing Asia	–	–	5.0	1.2	10.2	2.5	11.8	2.8
European Union	2.6	1.2	12.6	11.6	15.7	14.5	17.1	15.7
Latin America	2.7	0.9	3.5	2.4	4.3	2.9	5.0	3.4
OECD Pacific	–	–	0.3	0.7	1.0	2.1	1.0	2.0
Transition economies	–	–	0.1	0.1	0.2	0.1	0.2	0.1
United States of America and Canada	8.4	1.9	12.0	5.4	20.4	9.2	22.6	10.2
World	13.8	1.0	34.5	2.5	52.8	3.8	58.5	4.1

Note: – = negligible
Source: FAO 2008; IEA, 2006.

Additional uncertainties include the long-term productivity and sustainability of energy crop production; the effect of population growth and changing diets; global markets for food and animal feed; efficiency of biomass conversion technology; increased need for water and fertilizers; demand for other non-energy uses of land; and climate uncertainties. But most experts agree that, given current agriculture technology and practices, the most productive land is already in use.

FAO statistics[9] show that there are about 2 Gha of land considered degraded or abandoned which could present an opportunity for re-invigoration.[10] A portion of this land could be brought under cultivation with relatively low investment, as land is often abandoned because of factors other than low productivity – low prices of commodities, and the lack of markets, infrastructure, finance and capital.

A large land area for biofuel production could also come from under-utilized pastures and grasslands (rather than from forested land, as is sometimes feared). A major challenge will be to increase productivity per hectare with low inputs on a sustainable basis. An even greater challenge, and one beset by uncertainty, is how to deal with the potential impacts of climate change, in which limiting factors may be lack of water, soil salinity and erosion, and lack of investment. Clearly, the development of bioenergy must be undertaken in parallel with educational and agricultural modernization and capacity building.

Subsidies

Subsidies given to biofuels have been strongly criticized but need to be examined within a wider context. Government subsidies have supported energy production, both for fossil fuels and renewable energy, for many decades. The size of these subsidies varies considerably from country to country, but historically, government support for fossil fuels and nuclear energy has dwarfed encouragement of biofuels. Larsen and Shah (1992) estimate that fossil fuel subsidies have cost more than $230 billion, and many of these subsidies continue today under various forms. The US General Accounting Office reported that the petroleum industry received $135–50 billion in tax breaks from 1968 to 2000 alone, excluding foreign investment tax credits estimated to cost the Treasury a further $7 billion per year. This should be compared with the $7.7–11.6 billion given to the ethanol industry from 1979 to 2000 (GAO, 2000; Worldwatch Institute, 2007).

A recent study by the Environmental Law Institute (ELI, 2009) shows that fossil fuels benefited from about $72 billion in the fiscal years 2002–08, compared with $29 billion for renewables over the same period (about $16.8 billion of this was for corn-based ethanol). Of the fossil fuel subsidy, $70.2 billion went to oil and coal and just $2.3 billion to carbon capture and storage (CCS).

US subsidies to the petroleum industry equal approximately $0.003 cents per litre, but when indirect subsidies such as military expenditures to ensure secure oil supplies from the Persian Gulf (in 2003 this amounted to about $50 billion) are included, this represents an additional $0.30 cents per litre of gasoline (Worldwatch Institute, 2007), and does not include the environmental damage due to oil spills and other types of pollution.[11] On the other hand, Pimentel *et al.* (Chapter 2) state that current direct subsidies per litre of ethanol-based corn in the US far exceed those for gasoline.

In summary, then, while critics suggest that the subsidies to biofuels distort the market, it should be noted that the subsidies to fossil fuels are estimated as much higher than those for biofuels, and for renewables in general. It is also well established that subsidies may be needed for emerging industries – whereas fossil fuels are a mature industry. Another factor is that diesel and gasoline are still heavily subsidized in many developing countries – especially in oil-producing countries, but even in oil-importing countries where the subsidies are intended to support commerce by making transport more affordable.

Energy balance

The energy balance expresses the ratio of energy contained in a fuel relative to the energy used in its production. A fossil energy balance of 1.0 means that it requires as much energy to produce a litre of fuel as it contains. An energy balance of 2.0 means that a litre of fuel contains twice the amount of energy as that required to produce it. Conventional petrol and diesel have energy balances of around 0.8–0.9, because some energy is consumed in refining and transporting them. If a biofuel has a fossil energy balance exceeding these numbers, it contributes to reducing dependence on fossil fuels; in general, all biofuels today have energy balances that are greater than fossil fuels (although this does not necessarily include land-use impacts). Balances for biodiesel range from 1 to 4 for rapeseed and soybean feedstocks, compared with 9 for palm oil. For crop-based ethanol, balances range from less than 2 for maize to around 2–9 for sugarcane (8 to 10 in the case of Brazil: see Macedo *et al.*, 2004 and Walter *et al.*, 2008). Sugarcane-based ethanol, as produced in Brazil, depends not only on feedstock productivity, but also on the fact that it is processed using biomass residues from the sugar cane (bagasse) as energy input. The energy balances for cellulosic feedstocks will tend to be even higher.

The energy balance of biofuels production is nevertheless still a contentious issue, particularly in the case of ethanol from corn (Wu *et al.*, 2006, Shapouri *et al.*, 1995, Wang, Wu and Huo, 2007). It is also an issue that is often oversimplified, given the complex web of economic, social and political factors that need to be taken into account; different assumptions and calculations can, therefore, lead to different results. One of the difficulties is that old data tend to be used while improvements in biofuels production and land use are not always incorporated into the analyses.

Some authors still argue that more energy is consumed than is produced when producing biofuels. Pimentel *et al.* (Chapter 2) state that to manufacture one litre of ethanol from corn in the USA uses 46 percent more fossil energy than it produces. However, this estimate might not have included improvements in recent years, such as lower inputs, general technical improvements, productivity increases, and increasing use of non-fossil fuels in the ethanol production processes. 'In addition to simply over-counting the energy in producing ethanol, detractors fail to recognize the significant gains in recent years in yields, and energy in processing. Modern ethanol plants are producing 15 percent more ethanol from a bushel of corn, and using 20 percent less energy than five years ago.'[12]

It is important to bear in mind that the energy balance of gasoline is less than one. Sheehan *et al.* (1998) found that the primary energy use for each 1 MJ of petroleum diesel requires 1.2007 MJ, corresponding to 83.28 percent energy efficiency. Petroleum diesel uses 1.1995 MJ to produce 1 MJ of fuel product energy. GREET model[13] calculations indicate that the fossil energy input per unit of ethanol is 0.78 MJ of fossil energy consumed per each MJ of ethanol delivered. This compares with 1.23 MJ of fossil energy consumed for each MJ of gasoline delivered (see EERE, 2007).

Despite ongoing debate, some consensus seems to be emerging on the overall energy balance for several biofuels. US maize is generally accepted to vary from 1.25 to 1.35; this could be improved to 2.9 if fossil fuels in industrial processes are substituted by biomass-based fuels. The energy balance is not static but changing continuously. Major improvements (such as reducing energy consumption, greater energy self-sufficiency, developing new co-products, and so on) will increase the energy balance further. US maize is, however, one of the least efficient feedstocks for ethanol production, especially when compared with sugarcane (see Chapter 3).

Sustainability and certification schemes for biofuels

Since the EU 2003 Directive on Biofuels came into force, there has been growing concern over the availability of energy resources and the development of energy crops to produce them, including imports from developing countries (see Chapters 5 and 7). This crop-based increment is expected to come mainly from sugarcane, soya, palm oil, rapeseed, wood products and other biofuel feedstocks (Walter *et al.*, 2008).

Despite considerable ongoing work to develop sustainability and certification systems for bioenergy, many questions remain to be answered. Principles, criteria and requirements are under consideration among many private and public groups, along with compliance mechanisms to assess performance and guide development of the sector. The Global Bioenergy Partnership's task forces on greenhouse gas methodologies and on sustainability, and the Round Table on Sustainable Biofuels are among other public, private and non-profit efforts. Such diversity suggests that a process for harmonizing the various approaches may eventually be needed, especially in the light of evolving policy mandates and targets (van Dam *et al.*, 2008).

The term 'standards' implies rigorous systems for measuring technical or physical parameters against defined criteria, in which failure to comply could prevent a country from exporting its product; this approach should not be confused with certification. International certification systems already exist for food safety, chemical products and human health, and these existing systems tend to be considered as model frameworks for biofuels.

But is the biofuel sector sufficiently prepared for a certification system? Are the risks sufficiently great that its absence would pose significant, irreversible threats to human health or the environment? Should biofuels be treated more stringently than other agricultural commodities? Given that most environmental impacts of biofuels are indistinguishable from those of increased agricultural production in general, it could be argued that standards should be applied more broadly. Certification systems that restrict land-use change could foreclose legitimate opportunities for developing countries to benefit from increased demand for their agricultural commodities.

Most of the criteria are being developed in industrialized countries and are aimed at ensuring that biofuels are produced, distributed and used in an environmentally sustainable manner before they enter into international trade. However, to date none has been tested – and this is particularly necessary when the criteria are to be used in conjunction with government support schemes such as subsidies, or when biofuels are designated for preferential treatment under international trade agreements (UNCTAD, 2008).

The biofuel sector is characterized by a wide range of stakeholders with diverse interests; this, combined with the rapid evolution of the sector, has led to a proliferation of initiatives to ensure sustainable bioenergy development. New contributions from the International Bioenergy Platform include the development of analytical frameworks to guide countries in assessing their potential bioenergy and food security concerns and accounting for the full range of environmental impacts, including land, water, biodiversity, and greenhouse gases (FAO, 2009). Other work is in progress on social and environmental sustainability criteria, including limits on deforestation, competition with food production, adverse impacts on biodiversity, soil erosion and nutrient leaching.

Solutions will require careful dialogue and negotiation among countries if the combined goals of agricultural productivity growth and environmental sustainability are to be achieved. A starting point might be to establish best practices for sustainable production of biofuels (as some large food companies already do with their contract farmers) which can help transform farming practices for non-biofuel crops. Capacity-building efforts are a necessary platform for more stringent standards and certification systems.

Payments for environmental services in combination with biofuel production could be another option. This mechanism would compensate farmers for providing specific environmental services using production methods that are environmentally sustainable. Payments could be linked to compliance with standards and certification schemes agreed at the international level. Although challenging and complicated to implement, such schemes could help to ensure biofuels are produced in a sustainable manner.

Main conclusions

The biofuel debate has centred on three major dilemmas: (1) Is biofuel production a choice between food or fuel? (2) What is the real potential of biofuels in mitigating climate change and the broader environment?

(3) Do biofuels contribute to socio-economic development, wealth generation and distribution? This chapter has addressed these questions in general terms; the following chapters investigate them in greater detail. Much of the public debate in recent years has focused more on the adverse impacts of bioenergy development rather than the benefits: in particular, food security impacts, higher food prices and environmental degradation have been at the centre of concern. Crucial to the way forward is a balanced debate on the pros and cons of biofuels, which is the main aim of this book.

For example, over the medium-to-longer term, there could be a positive response from agricultural producers towards generating a sustained supply of bioenergy feedstocks not only from industrial producers but also from smallholders, as discussed in Chapter 5. The emergence of biofuels as a new source of demand for agricultural commodities could thus contribute to revitalizing agriculture in developing countries, with positive implications for economic growth, poverty reduction and food security.

However, it is also important to recognize the limitations of bioenergy, particularly liquid biofuels. Bioenergy has an important contribution to make in the global transition to sustainable energy. It is also important to ensure that biomass energy is used in the most suitable way and is based on the most efficient feedstocks – such as organic wastes, agro-forestry residues, and highly efficient crops such as sugarcane. This means that it may make greater sense to use biomass for electricity and heat rather than liquid biofuels. Large-scale dedicated energy crop plantations may be undesirable in some cases, due to the land-use implications.

Depending on how the demand for biofuels develops, many poor countries are well placed, in agro-ecological terms, to produce biomass for liquid biofuel production. However, they will continue to face constraints that have prevented them in the past from promoting agriculture-led growth – such as lack of favourable agricultural policy, availability of capital for investment, and efficient market mechanisms.

On the demand side, there is uncertainty about the pace of expansion of biofuels using agricultural feedstocks. Should Europe and the US modify their current biofuel policy mandates and targets, a moderated but sustained supply response might be the result. This could also serve to reduce some of the price volatility in agriculture commodities. To be competitive, the prices of bioenergy feedstocks cannot rise faster than real energy prices, with some additional allowance for the value of environmental benefits such as GHG savings.

Notes

1　Taken together, most estimates now suggest that 15–20 percent of the surge in food commodity prices was caused by increased production of biofuel feedstocks.

2　Prepared for the OECD and widely attributed to this organization, although it does not necessarily represent the official OECD view.

3　'Second-generation' technologies are generally defined as those that use advanced conversion processes to make better use of the raw biomass supplied; they include lignocellulosic conversion (for ethanol) and Fischer-Tropsch synthesis (for various fuel types). See Chapter 7 for more discussion of advanced biofuels.

4　Media reports on bioenergy, particularly ethanol and biodiesel, are frequently superficial. For example, Jean Ziegler, a former UN special rapporteur on the right to food, referred to the production of fuel rather than food as 'a crime against humanity' in the *International Herald Tribune*, <www.iht.com/bin/8074319>, 1 November 2007. A report in *The Ecologist* on the rapid expansion of biodiesel in Colombia headlined the question posed by its authors: 'Are you driving on blood fuel?'; see Nicholls and Campos, 2007.

5　A 'qualified farmer' might be seen as one who owns or has access to land with the required agro-ecosystem characteristics, market access, and production know-how to produce a sustainable bioenergy crop.

6　See, for example, Rosillo-Calle *et al.*, 2010.

7　On these points, see Fischer (2008).

8　Other estimates put this between 20 and 30 percent, or even 50 percent.

9　See FAOSTAT, the FAO statistical database, <http://faostat.fao.org/default.aspx>.

10　Degraded land poses serious challenges since it is often of lower fertility or affected by climatic conditions, and will involve higher costs and be less productive than other land. This could be counterbalanced by the environmental and ecological benefits of reclamation and sustainable management.

11　For example, environmental damage caused by diesel in the transport sector in 1993 (the year for which data are available) has been estimated at $0.31cents/litre (see Worldwatch Institute, 2007).

12   'Net energy balance of ethanol production, Fall 2004', isssue brief, <www.ethanolacrossamerica.net>.
13   GREET (Greenhouse gases, regulated emissions and energy in transportation) was developed by Dr Michael Wang, of Argonne National Laboratory's Centre for Transportation Research, with support from the United States Department of Energy.

References

Darlington, T. L. (2009) 'Land use effects of US corn-based ethanol', report for Air Improvement Resources, Inc., Novi MI.

Doornbosch, R. and R. Steenblik (2007) 'Biofuels: is the cure worse than the disease?' Report prepared for round table conference on sustainable development, OECD General Secretariat, draft report SG/SD/TR (2007)3, Paris.

EERE (2007) 'Ethanol: the complete energy life cycle picture', (US) Office of Energy Efficiency and Renewable Energy, <www.eere.energy.gov>.

ELI (2009) 'Estimating US government subsidies to energy souces: 2002–2008', Environmental Law Institute and Woodrow Wilson International Centre for Scholars, Washington DC.

FAO (1999) 'The multi-functional character of agriculture and land: the energy function', Background Paper 2, FAO/Netherlands Conference on the Multi-Functional Character of Agriculture and Land, Maastricht, 12–17 September.

—— (2007) 'Recent trends in the law and policy of bioenergy production, promotion and use', Legal Paper No. 68, Rome.

—— (2008) *The State of Food and Agriculture*, Food and Agriculture Organization of the United Nations, Rome.

—— (2009) 'Overview of FAO activities related to bioenergy', Powerpoint presentation by J. B. Tschirley, Rome.

Fargione, J., J. Hill, D. Tilman, S. Polasky and P. Hawthorne (2008) 'Land clearing and the biofuel carbon debt', *Science* 319: 1235–8 <www.scienceexpress.org> (7 February).

Fischer, G. (2008) 'Implications for land use change', paper presented at FAO expert meeting on global perspectives on fuel and food security, Rome, 18–20 February 2008.

GAO (2000) 'Tax incentives for petroleum and ethanol fuels: descriptions, legislative histories, and revenue loss estimates', General Accounting Office of the US, Washington DC.

Goldemberg, J. and P. Guardabassi (2010) 'The potential for first-generation ethanol production from sugarcane', *Biofuels, Bioproducts and Biorefining* 4 (1): 17–24.

Hazel, P. and S. Woods (2008) 'Drivers of change in global agriculture',

Philosophical Transactions of the Royal Society B 363 (1491): 495–515.

IEA (2006) *World Energy Outlook 2006*, International Energy Agency, Paris.

Koplow, D. (2007) 'Biofuels: at what cost? Government support for ethanol and biodiesel in the United States', Global Subsidies Institute, International Institute for Sustainable Development, Geneva, <www.iisd.org>; <www.globalsubsidies.org>.

Kutas, G., C. Lindberg and R. Steenblik (2007) 'Biofuels: at what cost? Government support for ethanol and biodiesel in the European Union'. Global Subsidies Institute, International Institute for Sustainable Development, Geneva, <www.iisd.org>; <www.global subsidies.org>.

Larsen, B. and A. Shah (1992) 'World fossil fuel subsidies and global carbon emissions', World Bank Policy Research Paper, WPS 1002, Washington DC.

Macedo, I. C., M. R. L. V. Leal and J. E. A. R. Silva (2004) 'Assessment of greenhouse gases emissions in the production and use of fuel ethanol in Brazil', report for the Secretariat of the Environment, State of São Paulo.

Moreira, J. R. (2006) 'Global biomass energy potential', *Mitigation and Adaptation Strategies for Global Change* 11: 313–42.

Nicholls, K. and E. Campos (2007) 'Are you driving on blood fuel?', *The Ecologist*, 37 (7): 44–8.

Rosillo-Calle, F. and D. O. Hall (1987) 'Brazilian alcohol – food versus fuel', *Biomass* 12 (2): 97–128.

Rosillo-Calle, F., L. Pelkmans, R. Nelson, M. Cocchi and M. Black (edited by A. Faaij and M. Junginger) (Forthcoming 2010) 'Report on the potential of biofuels in the transport sector', International Energy Agency (IEA) Task 40 Website, <www.bioenergy trade.org>.

Royal Society (2008) 'Sustainable biofuels: prospects and challenges', policy publication, Royal Society, London.

Searchinger, T., R. Heimlich, R. A. Houghton *et al.* (2008) 'Use of US cropland increases greenhouse gases through emissions from land use change', *Science* 319 (5867): 1238–40, <www.scienceexpress.org> (7 February 2008).

Shapouri, H., J. A. Duffield and M. Graboski (1995) 'Estimating the net energy balance of corn ethanol', Agricultural Economic Report No. 721, US Department of Agriculture.

Sheehan, J., V. Camobreco, J. Duffield, M. Graboski and H. Shapouri (1998) 'An overview of biodiesel and petroleum diesel life cycles', National Renewable Energy Laboratory report, NREL/TP-500-24772, Golden CO.

UNCTAD (2008) 'Making certification work for sustainable development: the case of biofuels', study by United Nations Conference on Trade and Development, Geneva, Switzerland.

van Dam, J., M. Junginger, A. Faaij, I. Jürgens, G. Best and U. Fritsche (2008) 'Overview of recent developments in sustainable biomass certification', *Biomass and Bioenergy* 32 (8): 749–80.

Walter, A., F. Rosillo-Calle, D. Dolzan, E. Piacente and K. Borges da Cunha

(2008) 'Perspectives on fuel ethanol consumption and trade', *Biomass and Bioenergy* 32 (8): 730–48.

Wang, M., M. Wu and H. Huo (2007) 'Life-cycle energy and greenhouse gas emission impacts of different corn ethanol plant types', Environmental Research Letters 2: 024001 (13 pp.).

WBGU (2009) 'Bioenergy Factsheet', German Advisory Council on Global Change, <http://69.90.183.227/doc/biofuel/wbgu-factsheet-bioenergy-en-2009-06-03.pdf>.

Woods, J. (2007) 'Sustainable biofuel systems: opportunities and threats', paper presented at the Royal Society International Biofuel Opportunities workshop, London, 23–24 April.

Worldwatch Institute (2007) *Biofuels for Transport: Global Potential and Implications for Sustainable Energy and Agriculture*, Earthscan, London.

Wu, M., M. Wang and H. Huo (2006) 'Fuel-cycle assessment of selected bioethanol production pathways in the United States', Report ANL/ESD/06-7, Argonne National Laboratory, Chicago IL.

2 Why We Should Not Be Using Biofuels*

David Pimentel, Alison Marklein, Megan A. Toth,
Marissa N. Karpoff, Gillian S. Paul, Robert McCormack,
Joanna Kyriazis, and Tim Krueger

Global shortages of fossil energy, especially oil and natural gas, and heavy biomass energy consumption have focused worldwide attention and concern on biofuel production from crops such as corn, sugarcane and soybean (Barbara, 2007). Wood and crop residues are also being used as fuel (Pimentel and Pimentel, 2008). Though it may seem beneficial to use renewable plant materials to address the energy crisis, many environmental and ethical concerns also arise (Pimentel, 2006).

Diverse conflicts exist when land, water, energy and other environmental resources are used in the production of both food and biofuel. In the US, about 19 percent of all fossil energy is utilized in the food system: about 7 percent for agricultural production, 7 percent for processing and packaging foods, and 5 percent for distribution and preparation of food (Pimentel *et al.*, 2008a). In developing countries, about 50 percent of wood energy is used primarily for cooking in the food system (Nonhebel, 2005).

The objective of this chapter is to analyse: (1) the uses and interdependencies among land, water, and fossil energy resources in food and biofuel production; and (2) the characteristics of the resulting environmental impacts.

Food and malnourishment

The UN's Food and Agriculture Organization (FAO) confirms that food available *per capita* worldwide has been declining *continuously* – a conclusion based on the availability of cereal grains during the past

* This chapter was originally published in February 2009 as 'Food versus biofuels: environmental and economic costs', *Human Ecology* 37 (1): 1–12.

23 years (FAO, 1961–2006). Cereal grains make up an alarming 80 percent of the world's food supply (Pimentel and Pimentel, 2008). Although grain yields per hectare in both developed and developing countries are still gradually increasing, the rate of increase is slowing, while the world population and its food needs are rising (FAO, 1961–2006; PRB, 2007). For example, from 1950 to 1980, US grain yields increased at about 3 percent per year. Since 1980, the annual rate of increase for corn and other grains is only approximately 1 percent (USDA, 1980–2006). Thus, worldwide, the rate of increase in grain production is not keeping up with the rapid rate of world population growth, of 1.1 percent (PRB, 2007).

The resulting decrease in food supply results in widespread malnutrition, which claims more lives than any other cause of death in the world today (Pimentel *et al.*, 2007). The latest estimate of the number of malnourished and starving people in the world is 66 percent – the highest proportion in history. We believe that the use of food grains and other foods to produce biofuels is contributing to starvation in the world, and that the increase in world food prices is a direct result. For example, the US Congressional Budget Office estimates that Americans are paying between $6 billion and $9 billion more per year for food because of corn ethanol production.

World cropland and water resources

More than 99.7 percent of human food comes from the terrestrial environment, while less than 0.3 percent comes from the oceans and other aquatic ecosystems (FAO, 2002). Worldwide, of the total 13 billion hectares of land area, the percentages in use are: cropland, 11 percent; pasture land, 27 percent; forest land, 32 percent; urban, 9 percent; and other uses, 21 percent. Most of the remaining land area is unsuitable for crops, pasture, and/or forests because the soil is too infertile or shallow to support plant growth or the climate and region are too harsh, too cold, dry, steep, stony or wet (FAOSTAT, 2001). Most of the suitable cropland is already in use.

As the human population continues to increase rapidly, there has been an expansion of diverse human activities, which have dramatically reduced cropland and pasture land – a good deal of which has been covered by transportation systems and urbanization. In the US, about 0.4 ha (1 acre) of land per person is covered with urbanization and highways (USCB, 2007). In 1960, when the world population numbered only 3 billion, approximately 0.5 ha was available per person for the production of a diverse, nutritious diet of plant and animal products (Giampietro and Pimentel, 1994). It is widely agreed that 0.5 ha is essential for a healthy diet (UN, 1999). China's recent explosion in development provides an example of rapid declines in the availability of *per capita* cropland (Pimentel and Wen, 2004). The currently available cropland in China is only 0.08 ha *per capita*. This relatively small amount of cropland provides the people in China with a predominantly vegetarian diet, which requires less energy, land and biomass than the typical American diet.

In addition to land, water is a vital controlling factor in crop production (Gleick, 1996). The production of 9 tons/ha of corn requires about 7 million litres of water (Pimentel *et al.*, 2004). Other crops also require large amounts of water, much of which reaches them via irrigation: 17 percent of the crops that are irrigated worldwide provide 40 percent of the world's food supply (FAO, 2002). A major concern is that the world's supply of irrigation water is projected to decline further because of global warming (Cline, 2007).

Energy resources and use

Since the industrial revolution of the 1850s, the rate of energy use from all sources has been growing even faster than world population growth. For example, from 1970 to 1995, energy use increased at a rate of 2.5 percent per year (doubling every 30 years) compared with population growth of 1.7 percent per year (doubling every 40 to 60 years) (Pimentel and Pimentel, 2008). Developed nations annually consume about 70 percent of the fossil energy worldwide, while the developing nations, which have about 75 percent of the population, use only 30 percent of fossil energy (International Energy Annual, 2006).

Although about 50 percent of all the solar energy captured by photosynthesis is used by humans for food, forest products, and other requirements, it is still inadequate to meet all of human food production needs (Pimentel, 2001). To make up for this shortfall, about 499 EJ of fossil energy – mainly oil, gas, coal and a small amount of nuclear energy – is utilized each year (International Energy Annual, 2006). Of this, about 106 EJ (22 percent) is consumed in the United States – although only 4.5 percent of the world's population lives there (USCB, 2007).

Each year, the US population uses three times more fossil energy than the total solar energy captured by all harvested US crops, forests and grasses (Table 2.1). Industry, transportation, home heating and cooling, and food production account for most of this consumption (USCB, 2007). *Per capita* use of fossil energy in the United States per year amounts to about 9,500 litres of oil equivalents – more than seven times the *per capita* use in China (Pimentel and Pimentel, 2008). In China, most fossil energy is used by industry, although

Table 2.1 Total amount of above ground biomass[a]

Crops	901 x 106 tons	15.2 EJ
Pasture	600 x 106 tons	10.1 EJ
Forest	527 x 106 tons	8.9 EJ
Total	2,028 x 106 tons	34.2 EJ

a) Except for some crops that include underground biomass and solar energy captured each year in the United States. An estimated 34 EJ of sunlight reaching the US per year suggests that green plants in the US are collecting 0.1 percent of the solar energy (Jölli and Giljum, 2005; Crop Production, 2007; Crop Harvest, 2007; Forest Service, 2007).

approximately 25 percent is now used for agriculture and in the food production system (Pimentel and Wen, 2004).

The earth's natural gas supply is considered adequate for about 40 years and that of coal for about 100 years (BP, 2005; Youngquist, 1997; Lunsford, 2007; Konrad, 2007; IEA, 2007). In the United States, natural gas supplies are already in short supply: it is projected that they will be depleted in about 20 years (Youngquist and Duncan, 2003). Many agree that the world reached peak oil and natural gas in

2007; from this point, these resources have begun a slow and continuous decline (Youngquist and Duncan, 2003; Campbell, 2006; Heinberg, 2007; Lunsford, 2007; Konrad, 2007; IEA, 2007).

Youngquist (1997) reports that earlier estimates based on exploration drilling of the amount of oil and gas to be found in the United States were very optimistic. Both the US oil production rate and existing reserves have continued to decline. Domestic oil and natural gas production have been decreasing for more than 30 years and are projected to continue to decline (USCB, 2004–05). Approximately 90 percent of US oil resources have already been exploited. At present, the United States is importing more than 63 percent of its oil (USCB, 2007); this puts its economy at risk from fluctuating oil prices and difficult international political situations, as was seen during the 1973 oil crisis, the 1991 Gulf War, and the current Iraq War (Mackay, 2002).

Biomass resources

The total sustainable world biomass energy potential has been estimated at 97 EJ per year (Parikka, 2004), which represents 19 percent of global energy use. The total forest biomass produced worldwide is 40 EJ per year (Parikka, 2004), which represents 8 percent of total energy use. In the US, wood fires provide only 1–2 percent of home heating (USCB, 1990).

Global forest area removed each year totals 15 million ha (Forest Degradation Data, 2007). Global forest biomass harvested is just over 1,431 billion kg per year (Mt/yr), of which 60 percent is industrial roundwood and 40 percent is fuelwood (FAOSTAT, 2005). About 90 percent of the fuelwood is utilized in developing countries (Parikka, 2004). A significant portion (26 percent) of all forest wood is converted into charcoal (Arnold and Jongma, 2007), a process that causes between 30–50 percent of the wood energy to be lost (Demirba, 2001) and produces large quantities of smoke. Charcoal is cleaner-burning and thus produces less smoke than burning wood fuel directly (Arnold and Jongma, 2007); it is dirty to handle but lightweight.

Worldwide, most biomass is burned for cooking and heating; however, it can also be converted into electricity. Assuming that an optimal yield globally of 3 dry tonnes per hectare (t/ha) per year of woody biomass can be harvested sustainably (Ferguson, 2001; 2003), this would provide a gross energy yield of 57 GJ/ha (13.5 million kcal/ha). Harvesting this wood biomass requires an energy expenditure of approximately 30 litres of diesel fuel per hectare, plus the embodied energy for cutting and collecting wood for transport to an electric power plant. Thus, the energy input per output ratio for such a system is calculated to be 1:25 (Hendrickson, 1993).

Per capita consumption of woody biomass for heat in the US amounts to 625 kilograms (kg) per year, while the diverse biomass resources (wood, crop residues, and dung) used in developing nations average about 630 kg *per capita* per year (Kitani, 1999). Woody biomass has the capacity to supply the US with about 5 EJ (1.5 x 10^{12} kWh thermal) of its total gross energy supply by the year 2050, provided that the amount of forest land stays constant (Pimentel, 2008). A city of 100,000 people using the biomass from a sustainable forest (3 t/ha per year) for electricity requires approximately 200,000 ha of forest area, based on an average annual electrical demand of slightly more than 1 billion kWh (Pimentel, 2008).

Air quality impacts from burning biomass are less harmful than those associated with coal, but more harmful than those associated with natural gas (Pimentel, 2001). Biomass combustion releases more than 200 different chemical pollutants into the atmosphere, including 14 carcinogens and four co-carcinogens (Burning Issues, 2006). As a result of this, approximately 4 billion people globally suffer from continuous exposure to smoke (Smith, 2006). In the United States, wood smoke kills 30,000 people each year (EPA, 2002), although many of the pollutants from electric plants that use wood and other biomass can be mitigated. These controls include the same scrubbers that are frequently installed on coal-fired plants.

An estimated 2 billion tonnes of biomass is produced per year across the United States (Table 2.1). This translates into about 34 EJ of energy, which means that the solar energy captured by plants equates to only 32 percent of the energy currently consumed as fossil energy (Pimentel *et al.*, 2008b). There is insufficient biomass for ethanol and biodiesel production to make the country oil-independent. This is part of a worldwide scenario in which devoting a portion of presently designated cropland and forest land to biofuel production will stress both ecosystems severely, but still not be sufficient to solve the world fuel problem.

Corn ethanol

In the United States, ethanol constitutes 99 percent of all biofuels (Farrell *et al.*, 2006). In terms of capital expenditure, new plant construction costs $0.28–$0.79 per litre ($1.05–$3.00 per gallon) of ethanol (Shapouri and Gallagher, 2005). Fermenting and distilling corn ethanol requires large amounts of water. The corn is finely ground and approximately 15 litres of water are added per 2.69 kg of ground corn. After fermentation, to obtain a litre of 95 percent pure ethanol from the 10 percent ethanol and 90 percent water mixture, it must be extracted from approximately 10 litres of the ethanol/water mixture. To be mixed with gasoline, the 95 percent ethanol must be further processed and more water removed, requiring additional fossil energy inputs to achieve 99.5 percent pure ethanol (see Tables 2.2 and 2.3). Thus, a total of about 12 litres of waste water must be removed per litre of ethanol produced, and this relatively large amount of sewage effluent has to be disposed of at an energy, economic, and environmental cost.

Manufacture of a litre of 99.5 percent ethanol uses almost half as much *more* energy (from fossil sources) than it produces and costs $1.05 per litre ($3.97 per gallon) (Table 2.3). The corn feedstock alone requires more than 33 percent of the total energy input. The steam energy and electricity used in the fermentation/distillation process are also large input elements in a total per litre of ethanol of 31,294 kJ (7,474 kcal) (Table 2.3). However, a litre of ethanol has an energy value of only 21,479 kJ (5,130 kcal). With a net loss of 9,814 kJ (2,344 kcal) per litre of ethanol produced, 46 percent more energy is expended than is produced as ethanol. The total cost, including the energy inputs for the fermentation/distillation process and the apportioned energy costs of the stainless steel tanks and other industrial materials, is $1,045 per 1,000 litres of ethanol produced (Table 2.3).

Table 2.2 Energy inputs and costs of corn production per hectare in the United States

Inputs	Quantity	Kcal x 1,000	Costs
Labour	11.4 hrs[a]	462[b]	300.00[c]
Machinery	55 kg[d]	1,018[e]	310.00[f]
Diesel	88 L[g]	1,003[h]	500.00[i]
Nitrogen	155 kg[k]	2,480[l]	255.00[m]
Phosphorus	79 kg[n]	328[o]	150.00[p]
Potassium	84 kg[q]	274[r]	78.00[s]
Lime	1,120 kg[t]	315[u]	60.00
Seeds	21 kg[v]	520[w]	230.00[x]
Irrigation	8.1 cm[y]	320[z]	350.00[aa]
Herbicides	6.2 kg[bb]	620[ee]	372.00
Insecticides	2.8 kg[cc]	280[ee]	180.00
Electricity	13.2 kWh[dd]	34[ff]	27.00
Transport	204 kg[gg]	169[hh]	180.00
TOTAL		8,228	$2,992.00
Corn yield 9,400 kg/ha[ii]	33,840	Kcal input:output 1:4.11	

a) NASS, 2003.
b) It is assumed that a person works 2,000 hrs per year and utilizes an average of 8,000 litres of oil equivalents per year.
c) It is assumed that labour is paid $26.32 an hour.
d) Pimentel and Pimentel, 2008.
e) Pro-rated per hectare and 10-year life of the machinery. Tractors weigh from 6 to 7 tons and harvesters 8 to 10 tons, plus ploughs, sprayers, and other equipment.
f) Estimated.
g) Estimated.
h) Input 11,400 kcal per litre.
i) Estimated.
j) Input 10,125 kcal per litre.
k) NASS, 2003.
l) Patzek, 2004.
m) Cost $1.65 per kg.
n) NASS, 2003.
o) Input 4,154 kcal per kg.
p) Cost $1.90 per kg.
q) NASS, 2003.
r) Input 3,260 kcal per kg.

s) Cost $0.93 per kg.
t) Brees, 2004.
u) Input 281 kcal per kg.
v) Pimentel and Pimentel, 2008.
w) Pimentel and Pimentel, 2008.
x USDA, 1997a.
y) USDA, 1997b.
z) Batty and Keller, 1980.
aa) Irrigation for 100 cm of water per hectare costs $1,000 (Larsen et al., 2002).
bb) Larson and Cardwell, 1999.
cc) USDA, 2002.
dd) USDA, 1991.
ee) Input 100,000 kcal per kg of herbicide and insecticide.
ff) Input 860 kcal per kWh and requires 3 kWh thermal energy to produce 1 kWh electricity.
gg) Goods transported include machinery, fuels, and seeds that were shipped an estimated 1,000 km.
hh) Input 0.83 kcal per kg per km transported.
ii) Average. USDA, 2006; USCB, 2004–05.

Table 2.3 Inputs per 1,000 litres of 99.5 percent ethanol produced from corn[a]

Inputs	Quantity	Kcal x 1,000	Costs
Corn grain	2,690 kg[b]	2,355[b]	856.22
Corn transport	2,690 kg[b]	322[c]	21.40[d]
Water	15,000 L[e]	90[f]	21.16[g]
Stainless steel	3 kg[i]	165[p]	10.60[d]
Steel	4 kg[i]	92[p]	10.60[d]
Cement	8 kg[i]	384[p]	10.60[d]
Steam	2,646,000 kcal[j]	2,646[j]	21.16[k]
Electricity	392 kWh[j]	1,01[j]	27.44[l]
95% ethanol to 99.5%	9 kcal/L[m]	9[m]	40.00
Sewage effluent	20 kg BOD[n]	69[h]	6.00
Distribution		331 kcal/L[q] 331	20.00[q]
TOTAL		7,474	$1,045.18

a) Output: 1 litre of ethanol = 5,130 kcal (Low heating value).The mean yield of 9.5 litres (2.5 gal) pure EtOH per bushel has been obtained from the industry-reported ethanol sales minus ethanol imports from Brazil, both multiplied by 0.95 to account for 5% by volume of the #14 gasoline denaturant, and the result was divided by the industry-reported bushels of corn inputs to ethanol plants. (See http://petroleum.berkeley. edu/ patzek/ BiofuelQA/Materials/TrueCostof EtOH.pdf; Patzek, 2006)

b) Data from Table 2.

c) Calculated for 144 km roundtrip.

d) Pimentel, 2003.

e) 15 litres of water mixed with each kg of grain.

f) Pimentel et al., 2004.

g) Pimentel et al., 2004.

h) 4 kWh of energy required to process 1 kg of BOD (Blais et al., 1995).

i) Estimated from the industry-reported costs

of $85 millions per 246 million litres/yr (65 million gallons/yr) dry grain plant amortized over 30 years. The total amortized cost is $43.6/1000L EtOH, of which an estimated $32 go to steel and cement.

j) Illinois Corn, 2004. The current estimate is below the average of 11.2 MJ/litre (40,000 Btu/gal) of denatured ethanol paid to the Public Utilities Commission in South Dakota by ethanol plants in 2005.

k) Calculated based on coal fuel. Below the 1.95 kWh/gal of denatured EtOH in South Dakota, see j).

l) $.07 per kWh (USCB, 2004–05).

m) 95% ethanol converted to 99.5% ethanol for addition to gasoline (T. Patzek, personal communication, University of California, Berkeley, 2004).

n) 20 kg of BOD per 1,000 litres of ethanol produced (Kuby et al., 1984).

o) Newton, 2001.

p) DOE, 2002.

Subsidies for corn ethanol total more than $6 billion per year (Koplow, 2006). This means that the subsidies per litre of ethanol are 60 times greater than the subsidies per litre of gasoline. In 2006, nearly 19 billion litres of ethanol were produced on 20 percent of US corn acreage (USCB, 2007). This represents only 1 percent of total US petroleum use (USCB, 2007).

However, even if we completely ignore corn ethanol's negative energy balance and high economic cost, we still find that it is absolutely not feasible to use ethanol as a replacement for US oil. If all 341 billion kg of corn produced in the US (USDA, 2006) were converted into ethanol at the current rate of 2.69 kg per litre of ethanol, then 129 billion litres of ethanol could be produced. This would provide only 7 percent of total oil consumption in the US. Of course, in this situation there would be no corn available for livestock and other needs.

In addition, the environmental impacts of corn ethanol are enormous:

1 Corn production causes more soil erosion than any other crop grown (NAS, 2003).
2 Corn production also uses more nitrogen fertilizer than any other crop, and is the prime cause of the dead zone in the Gulf of Mexico (NAS, 2003). In 2006, approximately 4.26 million tonnes of nitrogen were used in US corn production (USDA, 2007). Natural gas is required to produce nitrogen fertilizer. The US now imports more than half of its nitrogen fertilizer (Huang, 2004). In addition, the country uses 1.54 million tonnes of phosphorus (USDA, 2007).
3 Corn production uses more insecticides than any other crop (McLaughlin and Walsh, 1998).
4 It also uses more herbicides (Patzek, 2004).
5 More than 6,443 litres of water are required to produce 3.79 litres of ethanol (Pimentel and Patzek, 2008).
6 Enormous quantities of carbon dioxide are produced. This is due to the large quantity of fossil energy used in production, and the immense amounts of carbon dioxide released during fermentation and soil tillage. All this speeds global warming (Socolow *et al.*, 2004).

7   Air pollution is a significant problem (Hodge, 2003; Jacobson, 2007; Pimentel and Patzek, 2007). Burning ethanol emits pollutants such as peroxyacetyl nitrate, acetaldhyde, alkylates, and nitrous oxide (Davis and Thomas, 2006). These can have significant impacts on human health as well as other organisms and ecosystems.

In addition to corn ethanol's intensive environmental degradation and inefficient use of food-related resources, the production of corn ethanol also boosts world food prices. For instance, the use of corn for ethanol production has increased the prices of US beef, chicken, pork, eggs, breads, cereals, and milk by 10–20 percent (Brown, 2008). Corn prices have more than doubled during the past year.

Grass and cellulosic ethanol

Tilman *et al.* (2006) suggest that all 235 million hectares of grassland plus crop residues can be converted into cellulosic ethanol. This suggestion has caused concern among scientists. Tilman *et al.* recommend that crop residues, like corn stover, can be harvested and utilized as a fuel source. This would be a disaster for the agricultural ecosystem, because crop residues are vital for protecting topsoil. Leaving the soil unprotected would intensify soil erosion by ten-fold or more (Rasnake, 1999) and may increase soil loss as much as 100-fold (Fryrear and Bilbro, 1994). Furthermore, even a partial removal of the stover can result in increased CO_2 emissions and intensify acidification and eutrophication due to increased run-off (Lal, 2004; Kim and Dale, 2005). Already, the US crop system is losing soil ten times faster than the sustainable rate (NAS, 2003). Soil formation rates, at less than 1 t/ha/yr, are extremely slow (NAS, 2003; Troeh *et al.*, 2004). Increased soil erosion also facilitates soil-carbon oxidation and contributes to the greenhouse emissions problem (Lal, 2004).

Tilman *et al.* assume about 1,032 litres of ethanol can be produced through the conversion of the 4 t/ha/yr of grasses harvested. However, Pimentel and Patzek (2007) report a negative 50 percent return in ethanol produced compared with the fossil energy inputs in switchgrass conversion (Tables 2.4 and 2.5). Converting all 235 million ha of US grassland into ethanol, even at the optimistic rate

Table 2.4 Average inputs and energy inputs per hectare per year for switchgrass production

Inputs	Quantity	10^3 Kcal	Dollars
Labour	5 hr[a]	200[b]	$65[c]
Machinery	30 kg[d]	555	50[a]
Diesel	150 L[e]	1,500	75
Nitrogen	80 kg[e]	1,280	45[e]
Seeds	1.6 kg[f]	100[a]	3[f]
Herbicides	3 kg[g]	300[h]	30 [a]
TOTAL	10,000 kg yield[i]	3,935	$268[j]
	40 million kcal yield		input/output ratio1:02[k]

a) Estimated.

b) Average person works 2,000 hours per year and uses about 8,000 litres of oil equivalents. Pro-rated this works out to be 200,000 kcal.

c) The agricultural labour is paid $13 per hour.

d) The machinery estimate also includes 25% more for repairs.

e) Calculated based on data from Brummer et al., 2000.

f) Data from Samson, 1991.

g) Calculated based on data from Henning, 1993.

h) 100,000 kcal per kg of herbicide.

i) Samson et al., 2000.

j) Brummer et al. 2000 estimated a cost of about $400/ha for switchgrass production.Thus, the $268 total cost is about 49% lower than what Brummer et al. estimate, and this includes several inputs not included in Brummer et al.

k) Samson et al. (2000) estimated an input per output return of 1:14.9, but we have added several inputs not included in Samson et al.Still the input/output return of 1:11 would be excellent if the sustained yield of 10t/ha/yr were possible.

Table 2.5 Inputs per 1,000 litres of 99.5 percent ethanol produced from US switchgrass[a]

Inputs	Quantity	10^3 Kcal	Dollars
Switchgrass	5,000 kg[b]	1,968[c]	500
Switchgrass transport	5,000 kg[b]	600[c]	30[d]
Water	250,000 L[e]	140[f]	40[m]
Stainless steel	3 kg[g]	165[g]	11[g]
Steel	4 kg[g]	92[g]	11[g]
Cement	8 kg[g]	384[g]	11[g]
Grind switchgrass	5,000 kg	200[h]	16[h]
Sulphuric acid	240 kg[i]	0	168[n]
Steam	8.1 tons[i]	4,404	36
Lignin	1,250 kg[j]	minus 1,500	minus 12
Electricity	666 kWh[i]	1,703	46
95% ethanol to 99.5%	9 kcal/L[k]	9	40
Sewage effluent	40 kg BOD[l]	138[o]	12
Distribution	331 kcal/L[p]	331	20
TOTAL		8,634	$929

a) Output: 1 litre of ethanol = 5,130 kcal.The ethanol yield here is 200 L/t dry biomass (dbm) Iogen suggests 320 L/t dbm of straw that contains 25% of lignin.This yield is equal to the average yield of ethanol from corn, 317 L/t dbm. In view of the difficulties with breaking up cellulose fibres and digesting them quickly enough, the Iogen yield seems to be exaggerated, unless significantly more grinding, cell exploding with steam, and hot sulphuric acid are used.

b) Data from Table 2.4.

c) Calculated for 144 km roundtrip.

d) Pimentel, 2003.

e) 15 litres of water mixed with each kg of biomass.

f) Pimentel et al., 2004.

g) Newton, 2001.

h) Calculated based on grinder information (Wood Tub Grinders, 2004).

i) Estimated based on cellulose conversion (Arkenol, 2004).

j) Wood is about 25% lignin and removing most of the water from the lignin by filtering, the moisture level can be reduced to 200% (Crisp, 1999).

k) 95% ethanol converted to 99.5% ethanol for addition to gasoline (T. Patzek, personal communication, University of California, Berkeley, 2004).

l) 20 kg of BOD per 1000 litres of ethanol produced (Kuby et al., 1984).

m) Pimentel, 2003.

n) Sulphuric acid sells for $7 per kg.

o) 4 kWh of energy required to process 1 kg of BOD (Blais et al., 1995).

p) DOE, 2002.

suggested by Tilman *et al.*, would provide only 12 percent of annual consumption of US oil (USDA, 2006; USCB, 2007). Verified data, however, confirm that the output in ethanol would require 1.5 litres of oil equivalents to produce 1 litre of ethanol (see Tables 2.4 and 2.5).

To achieve the production of so much ethanol, US farmers would have to displace the 100 million cattle, 7 million sheep, and 4 million horses that are now grazing on 324 million hectares of US grassland and rangeland (USDA, 2006). Already, overgrazing is a serious problem on US grassland and a similar problem exists worldwide (Brown, 2002). We can only conclude that the assessment by Tilman *et al.* of the quantity of ethanol that can be produced on US and world grasslands (2006) appears to be unduly optimistic.

Converting switchgrass into ethanol results in a negative energy return of 57 percent (Table 2.5). This is slightly more negative than even corn ethanol production (compare Tables 2.3 and 2.5). The cost of producing a litre of ethanol using switchgrass was 93 US cents (Table 2.5).

Several problems exist in the conversion of cellulosic biomass into ethanol. First, 2–5 times more cellulosic biomass have to be produced and handled to achieve the same quantity of starches and sugars as are found in corn grain (Pimentel and Patzek, 2007). In addition, the starches and sugars are tightly held in lignin in the cellulosic biomass. They can be released using a strong acid to dissolve the lignin. Once the lignin is dissolved, the acid action is stopped with an alkali. Now the solution of lignin, starches, and sugars can be fermented. Some claim that the lignin can be used as a fuel. Clearly, it cannot be used when dissolved in water. The lignin in the water mixture can only be extracted using various energy-intensive technologies, and usually less than 25 percent of it can be recovered (Pimentel and Patzek, 2007).

Soybean biodiesel

Processed vegetable oils from soybean, sunflower, rapeseed, oil palm, and other oil plants can be used as fuel in diesel engines. Unfortunately, this is costly in economic and energy terms (Ozaktas,

Table 2.6 Energy inputs and costs in soybean production per hectare in the US

Inputs	Quantity	Kcal x 1,000	Costs $
Labour	7.1 hrs[a]	284[b]	112.00[c]
Machinery	20 kg[d]	360[e]	181.00[f]
Diesel	38.8 L[a]	442[g]	25.00
Gasoline	35.7 L[a]	270[h]	16.00
LP gas	3.3 L[a]	25[i]	1.00
Nitrogen	3.7 kg[j]	59[k]	28.00[l]
Phosphorus	37.8 kg[j]	156[m]	29.00[n]
Potassium	14.8 kg[j]	48[o]	6.00[p]
Limestone	2000 kg[v]	562[d]	56.00[v]
Seeds	69.3 kg[a]	554[q]	59.00[r]
Herbicides	1.3 kg[j]	130[e]	32.00
Electricity	10 kWh[d]	29[s]	1.00
Transport	154 kg[t]	40[u]	56.00
TOTAL	2,959		$602.00
Soybean yield 2,890 kg/ha[v]	10,404	kcal input:output 1:3.52	

a) It is assumed that a person works 2,000 hrs per year and utilizes an average of 8,000 litres of oil equivalents per year.

b) It is assumed that labour is paid $13 an hour.

c) Pimentel and Pimentel, 2008.

d) Machinery is pro-rated per hectare and a 10-year life of the machinery. Tractors weigh from 6 to 7 tons and harvesters from 8 to 10 tons, plus ploughs, sprayers, and other equipment.

e) College of Agricultural, Consumer and Environmental Sciences, 1997.

f) Input 11,400 kcal per litre.

g) Input 10,125 kcal per litre.

h) Input 7,575 kcal per litre.

i) Economic Research Statistics, 1997.

j) Patzek, 2004.

k) Hinman *et al.*, 1992.

l) Input 4,154 kcal per kg.

m) Cost 77¢ per kg.

n) Input 3,260 kcal per kg.

o) Costs 41¢ per kg.

p) Pimentel *et al.*, 2002.

q) Costs about 85¢ per kg.

r) Input 860 kcal per kWh and requires 3 kWh thermal energy to produce 1kWh electricity.

s) Goods transported include machinery, fuels, and seeds that were shipped an estimated 1,000 km.

t) Input 0.83 kcal per kg per km transported.

u) Mississippi State University Extension Service, 1999.

v) USDA, 2004.

Source: Ali and McBride, 1990

Table 2.7 Inputs per 1,000 kg of biodiesel oil from soybeans

Inputs	Quantity	Kcal x 1,000	Costs $
Soybeans	5,556 kg[a]	5,689[a]	1,157.00[a]
Electricity	270 kWh[b]	697[c]	18.90[d]
Steam	1,350,000 kcal[b]	1,350[b]	11.06[e]
Clean-up water	160,000 kcal[b]	160[b]	1.31[e]
Space heat	152,000 kcal[b]	152[b]	1.24[e]
Direct heat	440,000 kcal[b]	440[b]	3.61[e]
Losses	300,000 kcal[b]	300[b]	2.46[e]
Stainless steel	11 kg[f]	605[g]	18.72[h]
Steel	21 kg[f]	483[g]	18.72[h]
Cement	56 kg[f]	2,688[g]	18.72[h]
TOTAL	12,564		$1,251.74

Note: The 1,000 kg of biodiesel produced has an energy value of 9 million kcal. In addition, 200 ml (2,080 kcal) of methanol must be added to the soy oil for transesterification. With an energy input requirement of 14.7 million kcal, there is a net loss of energy of 63 percent. If a credit of 7.4 million kcal is given for the soy meal produced, then the net loss is less. The cost per kg of biodiesel is $1.25.

a) Data from Table 2.6.

b) Data from Singh, 1986.

c) An estimated 3 kWh thermal is needed to produce a kWh of electricity.

d) Cost per kWh is 7 cents.

e) Calculated cost of producing heat energy using coal.

f) Calculated inputs.

g) Calculated from Newton, 2001.

h) Calculated.

2000; Pimentel and Patzek, 2007) (see Tables 2.6 and 2.7). A slight net return on energy from soybean oil is possible only if the soybean is grown without commercial nitrogen fertilizer. The soybean, since it is a legume, will under favourable conditions produce its own nitrogen. Despite this, soy has a 63 percent net fossil energy loss (Table 2.7).

The US provides $500 million in subsidies for the production of 850 million litres of biodiesel (Koplow, 2006). Proportionally, this rate of subsidy is 74 times greater than for diesel fuel.

The environmental impacts of producing soybean biodiesel are second only to those for corn ethanol:

1   Soybean production causes significant soil erosion, second only to corn production (NAS, 2003).
2   Soybean production uses large quantities of herbicides, again second only to corn production (USDA, 2006). These herbicides cause major pollution problems with natural biota in the soybean production areas (Artuzi and Contiero, 2006; Pimentel, 2006).
3   USDA reports (2005) a soybean yield worldwide of 2.2 tonnes per hectare. With an average oil extraction efficiency of 18 percent (USDA, 1975; 2005), the average oil yield per year would be approximately 0.4 tonnes per hectare. This converts into 454 litres of oil per hectare. Based on current US diesel consumption of 227 billion litres/year (Tickell, 2006), this would require more than 500 million hectares of land – or more than half the US – under soybean! All 71 billion tonnes of soybean currently produced in the US (USDA, 2006) could only supply 2.6 percent of total US oil consumption.

Rapeseed and canola biodiesel

The European Biodiesel Board (EBB) estimates a total biodiesel production of 4.89 million tonnes for the year 2006 (EBB, 2007). Well suited to the colder climates, rapeseed is the dominant crop used in European biodiesel production. Often confused with canola, rapeseed is an inedible crop of the Brassica family yielding oilseeds high in erucic acid. Canola is in the same family, but is a hybrid created to lower saturated fat content and erucic acid content for human consumption in cooking oil and margarine (Tickell, 2006).

Rapeseed-based biodiesel yields in Europe averaged 1,390 litres per hectare in 2005 (Frondel and Peters, 2007). Using the density of biodiesel defined as 0.88 kg/l, it can be estimated that the average annual production of rapeseed biodiesel in Europe is 1.1 million tonnes. Because of its high oil content (30 percent), rapeseed is preferred as a biodiesel feedstock source (Tickell, 2006). While Europe currently dominates world rapeseed production, as the market for high-yield oilseed feedstock for biodiesel grows, interest in canola and rapeseed oil is likely to increase in many northern states of the US and in Canada (Tickell, 2006).

Rapeseed and canola require the application of fertilizers and pesticides in production. The energy required to make these pesticides and fertilizers detracts from the overall net energy produced (Frondel and Peters, 2007). Although soybean contains less oil than canola, about 18 percent for soy compared with 30 percent for canola, soybean can be produced with nearly zero nitrogen inputs (Pimentel *et al.*, 2008b).

The biomass yield of rapeseed/canola per hectare is also lower than that of soybean – about 1,600 kg/ha for rapeseed/canola compared with 2,890 kg/ha for soybean (Pimentel *et al.*, 2008b; USDA, 2004). The production of 1,568 kg/ha rapeseed/canola requires an input of about 18 GJ/ha (4.4 million kcal/ha) and costs about $669/ha (Pimentel *et al.*, 2008b). About 3,333 kg of rapeseed/canola oil is required to produce 1,000 kg of biodiesel (Pimentel *et al.*, 2008b). Therefore, all 333 million tonnes of rapeseed and canola produced in the US in 2006 (USDA, 2007) could be used to make 100 million litres of biodiesel, or 0.005 percent of the total oil used in the US. The total energy input to produce 1,000 litres of rapeseed/canola oil is 54 GJ (13 million kcal). This suggests a net loss of 58 percent of energy inputs (Pimentel *et al.*, 2008b). The cost per kg of biodiesel is also high, at $1.52. We conclude that rapeseed and canola are energy-intensive and economically inefficient biodiesel crops.

Oil palm

A major effort to plant and harvest oil palms for biofuel is under way in some tropical developing countries, especially Indonesia, Malaysia, Thailand, Colombia, and some countries in West Africa (Thoenes, 2007). In the last 20 years, the production of vegetable oil has more than doubled. Palm oil makes up 23 percent of biological oils and fats produced worldwide. In 2003, more than 123.5 million tonnes were produced, with Indonesia and Malaysia leading the way (MPOA, 2005).

Once established, after four years the oil palm will produce about 4,000 kg of oil per hectare per year (Carter *et al.*, 2007). The energy inputs for maintaining the hectare of oil palm are indicated in Pimentel *et al.* (2008b). The data suggest that about 31 kJ (7.4 million kcal) are required to produce 26,000 kg of oil palm nuts, sufficient to produce 4,000 kg of palm oil. A total of 29 kJ are required to process 6,500 kg of palm nuts to produce 1 tonne of palm oil (Pimentel *et al.*, 2008b). Thus, the net return on fossil energy invested in production and processing totals 30 percent. This is clearly a better return than corn ethanol and soybean bio-diesel. However, an estimated 200 ml (equivalent to 8709 kJ or 2,080 kcal) of methanol is required in addition to the 1,000 kg of palm oil, for transesterification, and this brings the overall net energy output down to a negative 8 percent. There are several negative environmental and social issues associated with oil palm plantations. First, the removal of tropical rainforests to plant the oil palm results in an increase in CO_2. Second, the removal of tropical rainforests and the planting of oil palms reduce the biodiversity of the ecosystem. Finally, using oil palm for fuel reduces the availability of palm oil for human use and increases the price of the oil (Thoenes, 2007).

Algae for oil production

Some cultures of algae consist of 30–50 percent oil (Dimitrov, 2007). Thus there is growing interest in using algae to increase the US oil supply, based on the theoretical claim that 47,000–308,000 litres/hectare/year of oil could be produced using algae (Briggs, 2004; Vincent Inc., 2007). The calculated cost per barrel would be $15 (Green Car, 2006). Currently, oil in the US market is selling for over $100 per barrel. If the above estimated production and price of oil-from-algae were correct, US annual oil needs could theoretically be met if 100 percent of all US land were in algal culture. Despite all the algae-related research and claims dating back to 1970s, none of the projected algae and oil yields has been achieved (Dimitrov, 2007). To the contrary, one calculated estimate based on all the included costs would be $800 per barrel, not $15 per barrel as mentioned. Algae, like all plants, require large quantities of nitrogen and water in addition to significant fossil energy inputs for the production system (Goldman and Ryther, 1977).

Conclusion

A rapidly growing world population and rising consumption of fossil fuels is increasing demand for both food and biofuels. This will exaggerate both the food and fuel shortages. Producing biofuels requires huge amounts of both fossil energy and food resources, which will intensify conflicts among these resources. Using food crops to produce ethanol raises major nutritional and ethical concerns. Nearly 60 percent of humans in the world are currently malnourished, so the need for grains and other basic foods is critical (WHO, 2005). Growing crops for fuel squanders land, water and energy resources vital to the production of food for people. Using food and feed crops for ethanol production has brought 10–20 percent increases in the prices of US beef, chicken, pork, eggs, breads, cereals, and milk (Brown, 2008). In addition, Jacques Diouf, Director-General of the UN Food and Agriculture Organization, reports that using food grains to produce biofuels already is causing shortages for the poor of the world (Diouf, 2007). Growing crops for biofuel not only ignores the need to reduce natural resource consumption, but exacerbates the problem of malnourishment worldwide by turning food into fuel. Recent policy decisions have mandated increased production of biofuels in the United States and worldwide. For instance, in the Energy Independence and Security Act of 2007, President Bush set 'a mandatory renewable fuel Standard (RFS) requiring fuel producers to use at least 36 billion gallons of biofuel in 2022'. This would require 1.6 billion tonnes of biomass harvested per year and would require harvesting 80 percent of all biomass in the US, including all agricultural crops, grasses, and forests (Table 2.1). Harvesting nearly all the country's biomass would decimate biodiversity and food supplies. Increased biofuel production could also threaten the quality of food plants in the US crop system. The release of large quantities of carbon dioxide, associated with the planting and processing of plant materials for biofuels, is reported to reduce the nutritional quality of major world foods, including wheat, rice, barley, potatoes, and soybean (Southwestern University, 2008). When crops are grown under high levels of carbon dioxide, protein levels may be reduced as much as 15 percent. Many problems associated with biofuels have been ignored by some scientists and policy makers. The biofuels that are being created in order to diminish the dependence on fossil fuels actually depend on fossil fuels. In most cases, more fossil energy is required to produce a unit of biofuel than that unit delivers (Tables 2.1–2.7). Furthermore, the US is importing oil and natural gas to produce biofuels, thus increasing oil dependence. Publications promoting biofuels have used incomplete or insufficient data to support their claims. For instance, claims that cellulosic ethanol provides net energy (Tilman *et al.*, 2006) have not been experimentally verified because most of their calculations are *theoretical*. Finally, environmental problems including water pollution from fertilizers and pesticides, global warming, soil erosion and air pollution are intensifying with biofuel production. It is difficult not to conclude there is simply not enough land, water and energy to produce biofuels. Most conversions of biomass into ethanol and biodiesel result in a negative energy return based on careful, up-to-date analysis of all the fossil energy inputs. Four of the negative energy returns are: corn ethanol at minus 46 percent; switchgrass at minus 50 percent; soybean biodiesel at minus 63 percent; and rapeseed at minus 58 percent. Even palm oil production in Thailand results in a minus 8 percent net energy return, when the methanol requirement for transesterification is considered in the equation.

References

Ali, M. B. and W. D. McBride (1990) 'Soybeans: state level production costs, characteristics, and input use, 1990', Economic Research Service, Stock No. ERS SB873, 48pp.

Arkenol (2004) 'Our technology: concentrated acid hydrolysis', <www.arkenol.com/Arkenol%20Inc/tech01.html>, 2 August 2004.

Arnold, J. E. M. and J. Jongma (2007) 'Fuelwood and charcoal in developing countries: an economic survey', <http://www/fap/o.org/docrep/12015e01.htm>, 29 January 2008.

Artuzi, J. P. and R. L. Contiero (2006) 'Herbicides applied in soybean and the productivity of corn in succession', *Pesquisa Agronpecuaria Brasilera* 41 (7): 1119–23.

Barbara, J. S. (2007) 'The false promise of biofuels', special report from the International Forum on Globalization and the Institute for Policy Studies, 30 pp.

Batty, J. C. and J. Keller (1980) 'Energy requirements for irrigation', in D. Pimentel (ed.), *Handbook of Energy Utilization in Agriculture.*, CRC, Boca Raton, FL.

Blais, J. F., K. Mamouny, K. Nlombi, J. L. Sasseville and M. Letourneau (1995) 'Les mesures d'éfficacité énergétique dans le secteur de l'eau', in J. L. Sassville and J. F. Balis (eds), *Les mesures d'éfficacité énergétique pour l'épuration des eaux usées municipales*, Scientific Report 405, Vol. 3. INRS-Eau, Quebec.

BP (2005) 'BP statistical review of world energy', British Petroleum, London, 41 pp.

Brees, M. (2004) 'Corn silage budgets for northern, central and southwest Missouri', <http://www.agebb.missouri.edu/mgt/budget/fbm-0201.pdf>, 1 September 2004.

Briggs, M. (2004) Widescale biodiesel production from algae', <http://unh.edu/p2/biodiesel/article_algae.htm>, 24 January 2008.

Brown, L. R. (2002) "World's rangelands deteriorating under mounting pressure', <http://www.earthpolicy.org/Updates/Updates6.htm, 24 January 2008.

—— (2008) 'Why ethanol production will drive world food prices even higher in 2008', Earth Policy Institute, <http://www.earthpolicy.org/Updates/2008/Update69.htm>, 24 January 2008.

Brummer, E. C., C. L. Burras, M. D. Duffy and K. J. Moore (2000) 'Switchgrass production in Iowa: economic analysis, soil suitability, and varietal performance', research report, Iowa State University, Ames IA.

Burning Issues (2006) 'What are the medical effects of exposure to smoke particles?', <http://burningissues.org/health-effects.html>, 7 December 2007.

Campbell, C. (2006) 'Excel spread sheets of oil and gas of production and discovery', Oil Depletion Analysis Centre, London.

Carter, C., W. Finley, J. Fry, D. Jackson and L. Willis (2007) 'Palm oil markets and future supply', *European Journal of Lipid Science and Technology* 109 (4): 307–14.

Cline, W. R. (2007) 'Global warming and agriculture: impact estimates by country', Peterson Institute for International Economics, <http://www.petersoninstitute.org/publications/briefs/cline4037.pdf>, 5 November 2008.

College of Agricultural, Consumer and Environmental Sciences (1997) 'Machinery cost estimates: summary of operations', research report, University of Illinois at Urbana-Champaign, <www.aces.uiuc.edu/~vo-ag/custom.htm>, 8 November 2001.

Crisp, A. (1999) 'Wood residue as an energy source for the forest products industry', research report, Australian National University, <http://sres.anu.edu.au/associated/fpt/nwfp/woodres/ woodres.html>, 10 July 2006.

Crop Harvest (2007) 'Biological system engineering: crop systems. 2007', research report, Washington State University, 19 September, <http://www.bsyse.wsu.edu/cropsyst/manual/parameters/crop/harvest.htm>, 29 January 2008.

Crop Production (2007) Report, National Agricultural Statistical Services, 7 September 2007, United States Department of Agriculture, 8 September 2007, <http://www.usda.gov/nass/ PUBS/TODAYRPT/crop0907.txt>, 29 January 2008.

Davis, J. M. and V. M. Thomas (2006) 'Systematic approach to evaluating trade-offs among fuel options: the lessons of MTBE', *Annals of the New York Academy of Sciences* 1076: 498–515.

Demirba, A. (2001) *Biomass Resource Facilities and Biomass Conversion*, Elsevier, Amsterdam.

Dimitrov, K. (2007) 'GreenFuel Technologies: a case study for industrial photo-sythetic energy capture', research study, Australian Institute for Bio-engineering and Nanotechnology, Brisbane, <http://moritz. botany.ut.ee/~oilli/b/Dimitrov.pdf>, 11 March 2008.

Diouf, J. (2007) 'Biofuels a disaster for world food', in EU Coherence, <http://eucoherence.org/renderer.do/clearState/false/menuld/227351/return>, 31 October 2007.

DOE (2002) 'Review of transport issues and comparison of infrastructure costs for a renewable fuels standard', US Department of Energy, Washington DC, <http://tonto.eia.doe.gov/FTPROOT/service/question3.pdf>, 8 October 2002.

EBB (European Biodiesel Board) (2007) 'European biodiesel production doubles in two years; EBB warns on need to eliminate "legislative and standards desert"', <http://www.greencarcongress.com/2007/07/european-biodie.html>, 29 January 2008.

Economic Research Statistics (1997) 'Soybeans: fertilizer use by state, 1996', <http://usda.mannlib.cornell.edu/data-sets/inputs/ 9X171/97171/agch0997.txt>, 11 November 2001.

EPA (2002) 'Wood smoke', report by US Environmental Protection Agency <http://www.webcom.com/-bi/brochure.pdf+wood+smoke+pollution-hl=ene=UTF-8>, 20 October 2002.

FAO (1961–2006) Annual reports, Food and Agriculture Organization, Rome.
—— (2002) Food balance sheets, Food and Agriculture Organization, Rome.

FAOSTAT (2001) Statistical report, Food and Agriculture Organization, Rome.
—— (2005) Statistical report, Food and Agriculture Organization, Rome.

Farrell, A. E., R. J. Plevin, B. T. Turner, A. D. Jones, M. O. O'Hare, and D. M. Kammen (2006) 'Ethanol can contribute to energy and environ-mental goals', *Science* 311: 506–8.

Ferguson, A. R. B. (2001) 'Biomass and energy', *Optimum Population Trust* 4 (1): 14–18.
—— (2003) 'Implications of the USDA 2002 update on ethanol from corn', *Optimum Population Trust* 3 (1): 11–15.

Forest Degradation Data (2007) Report, <http://home.alltel.net/ bsundquist1/ df4.html>, 21 January 2008.

Forest Service (2007) 'The Forest Inventory and Analysis RPA Assessment Tables', Forest Service, US Department of Agriculture, Washington DC.

Frondel, M. and J. Peters (2007) 'Biodiesel: a new Oildorado?', *Energy Policy* 35: 1675–84.

Fryrear, D. W. and J. D. Bilbro (1994) 'Wind erosion control with residues and related practices', in P. W. Unger (ed.), *Managing Agricultural Residues*, Lewis Publications, Boca Raton FL.

Giampietro, M. and D. Pimentel (1994) 'Energy utilization', in C. J. Arntzen and E. M. Ritter (eds), *Encyclopedia of Agricultural Science* (Vol. 2), Academic Press, San Diego CA.

Gleick, P. H. (1996) 'Basic water requirements for human activities: meeting basic needs', *Water International* 21: 83–92.

Goldman, J. C. and J. H. Ryther (1977) 'Mass production of algae: engineering aspects' in A. Mitsui *et al.* (eds), *Biological Solar Energy Conversion*, Academic Press, New York NY.

Green Car (2006) Green Car Congress, <http://www.greencarcongress. com/2006/07/malaysia_and_in.html>, 7 January 2008.

Heinberg, R. (2007) 'Oil apocalypse: what happens when demand for oil out-strips supply?', <http://www.richardheinberg.com/>, 29 January 2008.

Hendrickson, O. Q. (1993) 'Residential wood heating: forest, the atmosphere and public consciousness', paper for the Air and Waste Management Association Conference on 'The Emission Inventory: Living in a Global Environment', New Orleans LA.

Henning, J. C. (1993) 'Big bluestem, Indiangrass and switchgrass', Agricultural Publication G04673, Department of Agronomy, University of Missouri, Columbia MO.

Hinman, H., G. Pelter, E. Kulp, E. Sorensen and W. Ford (1992) 'Enterprise budgets for fall potatoes, winter wheat, dry beans and seed peas under rill irrigation', Farm Business Management Reports, Columbia County, Washington State University, Pullman WA.

Hodge, C. (2003) 'More evidence mounts for banning, not expanding, use of ethanol in gasoline', *Oil and Gas Journal* (6 October): 20–5.

Huang, Wen (2004) 'US increasingly imports nitrogen fertilizer', *Amber Waves*, (e-magazine of the Economic Research Service, US Department of Agriculture) February 2004, <http://www.ers.usda.gov/amberwaves/ February04/Findings/USIncreasinglyImports.htm>, 6 November 2008.

IEA (2007) 'Medium-Term Oil Market Report' (July 2007), International Energy Agency, <http://online.wsj.com/public/resources/documents/iea2007 0707.pdf>, 5 November 2008.

Illinois Corn (2004) 'Ethanol's energy balance', <http://www.ilcorn.org/ Ethanol/Ethan_Studies/Ethan_Energy _Bal/ethan_energy_bal.html>, 10 August 2004.

International Energy Annual (2006) Published by the US Department of Energy, Washington DC.

Jacobson, M. Z. (2007) 'Effects of ethanol (E85) versus gasoline vehicles on cancer and mortality in the United States', *Environmental Science and Technology* 41 (11): 4150–7.

Jölli, D. and S. Giljum (2005) 'Unused biomass extraction in agriculture, forestry and fishery', SERI Studies No. 3, Sustainable Europe Research Institute, Vienna.

Kim, S. and B. E. Dale (2005) 'Life cycle assessment of various cropping systems utilized for producing biofuels: bioethanol and biodiesel', *Biomass Engineering* 29: 426–39.

Kitani, O. (1999) 'Biomass resources', in O. Kitani, T. Jungbluth, R. M. Pearth and A. Ramdani (eds), *CIGAR Handbook of Agricultural Engineering*, American Society of Agricultural Engineering, Joseph MI.

Konrad, T. (2007) 'International Energy Agency wakes up and smells the peak oil', <http://seekingalpha.com/article/40617-international-energy-agency-wakes-up-and-smells-the-peak-oil>, 5 November 2008.

Koplow, D. (2006) 'Biofuels – at what cost? Government support for ethanol and biodiesel in the United States', Global Studies Initiative (GSI) of the International Institute for Sustainable Development (IISD), <http://www.globalsubsidies.org/IMG/pdf/biofuels_subsidies_us.pdf >, 16 February 2007.

Kuby, W. R., R. Markoja and S. Nackford (1984) 'Testing and evaluation of on-farm alcohol production facilities', Acures Corporation, Industrial Environmental Research Laboratory, Office of Research and Development, US Environmental Protection Agency, Cincinnati OH, 100 pp.

Lal, R. (2004) 'Soil carbon sequestration impacts on global climate change and food security', *Science* 34 (2004): 1623–7.

Larsen, K., D. Thompson and A. Harn (2002) 'Limited and full irrigation comparison for corn and grain sorghum', <http://www.colostate.edu/Depts/SoilCrop/extension/Newsletters/2003/Drought/sorghum.html>, 2 September 2002.

Larson, W. E. and V. B. Cardwell (1999) 'History of US corn production', <http://citv.unl.edu/cornpro/html/history/ history.html>, 2 September 2004.

Lunsford, P. (2007) 'Is the IEA admitting the peak has been reached?', <http://www.relocalize.net/is_the_iea_admitting_the_peak_has_been_reached>, 5 November 2008.

Mackay, N. (2002) 'Official: US oil at the heart of the Iraq crisis', *Sunday Herald* (Scotland), 6 October 2002.

McLaughlin, S. B. and M. E. Walsh (1998) 'Evaluating environmental consequences of producing herbaceous crops for bioenergy', *Biomass and Bioenergy* 14 (4): 317–24.

Mississippi State University Extension Service (1999) 'Agronomy Notes'

<http://msucares.com/newsletters/agronomy/ 1999/199910.html>, 10 July 2006.

MPOA (2005) 'Roundtable on Sustainable Palm Oil (RSPO) Public Forum on Sustainable Palm Oil, Mont Kiara Business Centre, Kuala Lumpur, January 2005', available from Malaysia Palm Oil Association, Kuala Lumpur, Malaysia.

NAS (2003) *Frontiers in Agricultural Research: Food, Health, Environment, and Communities*, National Academy of Sciences, Washington DC, <http://dels.nas.edu/rpt_briefs/frontiers_in_ag_final%20for% 20print. pdf>, 5 November 2004.

NASS (2003) National Agricultural Statistics Service (US), available online from <http://usda.mannlib.cornell.edu>, 5 November 2004.

Newton, P. W. (2001) 'Human Settlements Theme Report', in 'Australian State of the Environment Report 2001', <http://www.deh.gov.au/soe/2001/ settlements/acknowledgement.html>, 6 October 2005.

Nonhebel, S. (2005) 'Renewable energy and food supply: will there be enough land?' *Renewable and Sustainable Energy Reviews* 9 (2): 191–201.

Ozaktas, T. (2000) 'Compression ignition engine fuel properties of a used sunflower oil-diesel fuel blend', *Energy Sources* 22 (4): 377–82.

Parikka, M. (2004) 'Global biomass fuel resources', *Biomass Bioenergy* 27: 613–20.

Patzek, T. W. (2004) 'Thermodynamics of the corn-ethanol biofuel cycle', *Critical Review in Plant Sciences* 23 (6): 519–67.

—— (2006) 'The real corn-ethanol transportation system', <http://petroleum. berkeley.edu/patzek/BiofuelQA/Materials/TrueCostofEtOH.pdf>, 28 March 2008.

Pimentel, D. (2001) 'Biomass utilization, limits of', in R. A. Meyers (ed.), *Encyclopedia of Physical Science and Technology*, third edition, Vol. 2, Academic Press, San Diego CA.

—— (2003) 'Ethanol fuels: energy balance, economics, and environmental impacts are negative', *Natural Resources Research* 12 (2): 127–34.

—— (2006) 'Soil erosion: a food and environmental threat', *Environment, Development and Sustainability* 8 (2006): 119–37.

—— (2008) 'Renewable and solar energy: economic and wildlife conservation aspects', in J. E. Gates, D. Trauger and B. Czech (eds), *Peak Oil, Economic Growth and Wildlife Conservation*, Island Books, in press.

Pimentel, D. and T. W. Patzek (2007) 'Ethanol production: energy and economic issues related to US and Brazilian sugarcane', *Natural Resources Research* 16 (3): 235–42.

—— (2008) 'Ethanol production using corn, switchgrass and wood; biodiesel production using soybean', in D. Pimentel (ed.), *Biofuels, Solar and Wind as Renewable Energy Systems: Benefits and Risks*, Springer, Dordrecht.

Pimentel, D. and M. Pimentel (2008) *Food, Energy and Society*, third edition, CRC Press, Boca Raton FL.

Pimentel, D. and D. Wen (2004) 'China and the world: population, food and resource scarcity', in T. C. Tso and K. He (eds), *Dare to Dream: Vision of 2050 Agriculture in China*, China Agricultural University Press, Beijing.

Pimentel, D., R. Doughty, C. Carothers, S. Lamberson, N. Bora and K. Lee (2002) 'Energy inputs in crop production in developing and developed countries', in R. Lal, D. Hansen, N. Uphoff and S. Slack (eds), *Food Security and Environmental Quality in the Developing World*, CRC Press, Boca Raton FL.

Pimentel, D., B. Berger, D. Filberto, M. Newton, B. Wolfe, E. Karabinakis, S. Clark, E. Poon, E. Abbett and S. Nandagopal (2004) 'Water resources: current and future issues', *BioScience* 54 (10): 909–18.

Pimentel, D., S. Cooperstein, H. Randell, D. Filiberto, S. Sorrentino, B. Kaye, C. Nicklin, J. Yagi, J. Brian, J. O'Hern, A. Habas and C. Weinstein (2007) 'Ecology of increasing diseases: population growth and environmental degradation', *Human Ecology* 35 (6): 653–68.

Pimentel, D., J. B. Gardner, A. J. Bonnifield, X. Garcia, J. Grufferman, C. M. Horan, E. T. Rochon, J. L. Schlenker and E. E. Walling (2008a) 'Energy efficiency and conservation for individual Americans', *Environment, Development and Sustainability* 11 (3): 523–46.

Pimentel, D., A. Marklein, M. Toth, M. N. Karpoff, G. S. Paul, R. McCormack, J. Kyriazis and T. Krueger (2008b) 'Biofuel impacts on world food supply: use of fossil fuel, land, and water resources', *Energies* 1: 41–78.

PRB (2007) 'World population data sheet', Population Reference Bureau, Washington DC.

Rasnake, M. (1999) 'Tillage and crop residue management', <www.ca.uky.edu/agc/pubs/agr/agr99/agr99.htm>, 31 January 2008.

Samson, R. (1991) 'Switchgrass: a living solar battery for the prairies', Ecological Agriculture Projects, McGill University.

Samson, R., P. Duxbury, M. Drisdale and C. Lapointe (2000) 'Assessment of pelletized biofuels', PERD Program (Contract 23348-8-3145/001/SQ), Natural Resources Canada.

Shapouri, H. and P. Gallagher (2005) 'USDA's 2002 ethanol cost-of-product survey', Agricultural Economic Report Number 841, US Department of Agriculture, Washington DC.

Singh, R. P. (1986) 'Energy accounting of food processing' in R. P. Singh (ed.), *Energy in Food Processing*, Elsevier, Amsterdam.

Smith, K. R. (2006) 'Health impacts of household fuelwood use in developing countries', <http://ehs.sph.berkeley.edu/krsmith/publications/2006%20pubs/Uasylva.pdf>, 29 January 2008.

Socolow, R., R. Hotinski, J. B. Greenblatt and S. Pacala (2004) 'Solving the climate problem', *Environment* 46 (10): 8–19.

Southwestern University (2008) 'Biology research finds rising CO_2 levels could decrease the nutritional value of major food crops', <http://www.blackwell-synergy.com/doi/full10.1111/j.1365-2486.2007.01511.x>, 15 February 2008.

Thoenes, P. (2007) 'Biofuels and commodity markets – palm oil focus', study for

FAO Commodities and Trade Division, Food and Agriculture Organization, Rome.

Tickell, J. (2006) *Biodiesel America: How to Achieve Energy Security, Free America from Middle-East Oil Dependence, and Make Money Growing Fuel* (edited by Meghan Murphy and Claudia Graziano), Yorkshire Press, Ashland OH.

Tilman, D., J. Hill and C. Lehman (2006) 'Carbon-negative biofuels from low-input high-diversity grassland biomass', *Science* 314: 1598–600.

Troeh, F. R., A. H. Hobbs and R. L. Donahue (2004) *Soil and Water Conservation*, Prentice Hall, Upper Saddle River NJ.

UN (1999) 'The world at six billion', Part 1, Population Division, Department of Economics and Social Affairs, United Nations Secretariat, <http://www.un.org/esa/population/publications/sixbillion/sixbilpart1.pdf>, 4 November 2007.

USCB (1990) 'Home heating fuels', United States Census Bureau, <http://www.census.gov/apsd/cqc/cqc.27.pdf>, 7 December 2007.

—— (2004–05) *Statistical Abstract of the United States 2004–2005*, US Census Bureau, Government Printing Office, Washington DC.

—— (2007) *Statistical Abstract of the United States 2007*, US Census Bureau, Government Printing Office, Washington DC.

USDA (1975) 'Nutritive value of American foods', Agriculture Handbook No. 456, Agricultural Research Service, US Department of Agriculture, Washington DC.

—— (1980–2006) *Agricultural Statistics*, US Department of Agriculture, Washington DC.

—— (1991) 'Corn-State. Costs of production', Economic Research Service, Economics and Statistics System, Stock No. 94018, US Department of Agriculture, Washington DC.

—— (1997a) 1997 Census of Agriculture, US Department of Agriculture, <http://www.ncfap.org>, 28 August 2002.

—— (1997b) Farm and Ranch Irrigation Survey, 1997 Census of Agriculture, Volume 3, Special Studies, Part 1, 280 pp.

—— (2002) *Agricultural Statistics, 2002*, US Department of Agriculture, Government Printing Office, Washington DC.

—— (2004) *Agricultural Statistics, 2004* (CD-ROM), US Department of Agriculture/National Agriculture Statistics Service, Washington DC (Reference A1.47/2:2004).

—— (2005) 'Statistics of oilseeds, fats, and oils', Chapter III, *USDA-NASS Agricultural Statistics*,<http://www.usda.gov/nass/pubs/agr05/ acro05.htm>, 20 October 2007.

—— (2006) *Agricultural Statistics, 2006*, US Department of Agriculture, Government Printing Office, Washington DC.

—— (2007) 'Major land uses', study by Economic Research Services (9 June 2006), published by United States Department of Agriculture (9 September 2007), <http://www.ers.usda.gov/ data/majorlanduses>, 29 January 2008.

Vincent Inc. (2007) 'Valcent Products: intial data from the vertigro field test bed plant reports average production of 276 tons of algae bio mass on a per acre/per year basis', <http://money.cnn.com/ news.newsfeeds/ articles/ marketwire/ 0339181.htm>, 7 January 2008.

WHO (2005) 'Malnutrition worldwide', report, World Health Organization, <http://www.mikeschoice.com/reports/malnutrition_worldwide.htm>, 7 December 2007.

Wood Tub Grinders (2004) <http://p2library.nfesc.navy.mil/ P2_Opportunity_ Handbook/7_III_13.html>, 3 August 2004.

Youngquist, W. (1997) *GeoDestinies: the Inevitable Control of Earth Resources over Nations and Individuals*, National Book Company, Portland OR.

Youngquist, W. and R. C. Duncan (2003) 'North American gas: data show supply problems', *Natural Resources Research* 12 (4): 229–40.

3 Why Biofuels are Important

Luís Cortez and Manoel Regis L. V. Leal with Thomson Sinkala

The growing interest in biofuels stems from a combination of factors including climate change, rapid increase in oil prices, security of supply, and provision of rural jobs. This interest is supported by evidence that the greenhouse gas (GHG) benefits of biofuels outweigh their potential negative carbon effects. Many studies conclude that when all co-products are internalized – taken into account in an assessment of all the analysable social and environmental costs and benefits of the process under study – biofuels can cut down significantly on GHG emission. In any case, whatever the shortcomings, the general consensus is that biofuels are much more climate-friendly than fossil fuels.

The earth's land availability is sufficient to provide a good proportion of biofuels (10 to 20 percent) without affecting food production – provided suitable policies are adopted, such as the modernization of agriculture and support for farmers in developing countries. But often the pro-biofuels lobby has been too optimistic, underestimating the complexity of biofuels. This chapter will consider the benefits of biofuels and provide justifications for their use. The main areas to be covered are: (1) overall benefits; (2) land use; (3) land-use policies and impacts on food prices; (4) why biofuels are the most urgent alternative to fossil fuels; (5) the complex nature of biofuels; (6) the broad impacts on agriculture and rural development; (7) the impacts of subsidies; (8) the potential of ethanol from sugarcane in Brazil; and (9) jatropha cultivation in Zambia (the last two topics are case studies).

Overall benefits of biofuels

The first question to be asked is: what are the intended objectives when initiating or expanding biofuel production? The main ones are: to reduce GHG emissions; to ensure energy security; and to promote socio-economic development.

In terms of large scale and market volume, the main global experiences with biofuels are: ethanol from sugarcane in Brazil; ethanol from corn in USA; and biodiesel from rapeseed in various European countries such as Germany. The reasons why these countries have supported the production of biofuels vary considerably.

Brazil has been producing ethanol from sugarcane since the beginning of the twentieth century, but intensified its production after the oil crisis of the 1970s. The main driving force was to reduce oil dependence using the already well-established sugar industry. In 1973, nearly 80 percent of oil consumed in the country was imported, and represented nearly 50 percent of all imports. The Brazilian government also intended to use the ethanol program (ProAlcool) to alleviate economic inequalities between the poorer (north-east) and richer (south-central) regions in the country. At that time, there was no specific intention to look at the benefits of GHG mitigation, although it later turned out that ethanol also presented very positive environmental benefits.

Ethanol from corn in the US had a different background. The United States is a very large corn-producing country, responsible for nearly 50 percent[1] of the world output. During recent decades the US government found it difficult to guarantee price stability for cereals, and resorted to controversial policies such as high subsidies to farmers, tariff protection, and even the implementation of the set-aside land policy. These policies were increasingly difficult to sustain at international negotiating forums such as the GATT, where new agricultural powers such as Brazil demanded elimination of protection and more freedom for trade in agricultural commodities. The US has also faced energy security issues, with its dependence on imported oil increasing steadily from 35 percent in 1973 to 45 percent in 1979 and 60 percent in 2006.[2]

Increasing dependence on foreign oil led to decisions to increase imports from outside the Middle East and to implement efficiency and renewables measures to reduce the amount of imported oil. (It is worth mentioning that in recent years rapidly increasing demand in China has made this country the second major buyer in the international oil market.) One of the important measures undertaken by the US government was to encourage the expansion of the already large production of ethanol from corn. Thus, for the US, the objectives of biofuels production were, primarily, to ensure higher energy security and to promote better economic conditions for its farmers.

In most European countries – as in the German case – the driving force was a combination of the three motivations listed above, although there has been more concern over GHG emissions than in Brazil and the US. Europe also seeks to reduce oil dependence and at the same time create another economic opening for its agricultural sector. In many ways it can be said that biofuels fulfilled the goal of improving farm revenues without harming commodities trade.

We can now review the three overall objectives, the first of which was *reducing GHG emissions*. Using this criterion to discuss benefits, it can be said that not all biofuels, particularly when it comes to raw materials, are equal. For example, a general consensus today is that ethanol from sugarcane in Brazil is better than ethanol produced from corn and other cereals in the US and Europe, and also better than biodiesel produced from rapeseed.

Ensuring energy security, the second criterion, applies with varying relevance from case to case. It can be said that for the three cases discussed above (Brazil, the United States and Europe), biofuels contribute to reducing energy dependence. For example, today sugarcane ethanol provides 50 percent of liquid fuels (by volume) to Brazil's light vehicle fleet. If it was not for sugarcane ethanol, Brazil would not have achieved self-sufficiency in liquid fuels, as it did in 2008.

Using the criterion of *promoting socio-economic development*, we can say that these benefits are more important for developing countries, such as Brazil, that are in need of jobs to guarantee social stability. Although the majority of jobs generated by ethanol production are associated with manual labour in agriculture, this situation is rapidly changing following the introduction of a new law which bans canefield burning in São Paulo, where about 60 percent of the production takes place. According to the Brazilian Association of Vehicle Manufacturers, an ethanol-fuelled car generates 22 more jobs than a gasoline-fuelled vehicle.

The overall benefit analysis is therefore rather dependent on the socio-economic perspective. Another important question concerns the market to which production is oriented, and how large a programme is envisaged. In the case of Brazil, it is becoming clear that the country has the capacity to satisfy domestic needs and also to contribute on a global scale. Although this privileged situation is not necessarily encountered elsewhere, the Brazilian experience remains very valuable for setting up biofuel projects in other countries.

Can biofuels really help to reduce CO_2 emissions?
We have seen that one of the main justifications for the promotion of renewable energy technologies is their capacity to mitigate CO_2 emissions. When it comes to substitution for fossil-derived liquid fuels, the alternatives are very few, to say the least. If we are serious about reducing CO_2 emissions, we need to analyse which ones are the best alternatives for large-scale substitution, considering their cost as well as their environmental and other impacts.

Table 3.1 Ethanol and biodiesel GHG emission reduction for selected paths[a]

Biofuel and path	GHG emission reduction (%)
Sugar beet ethanol	52
Wheat ethanol (process not specified)	16
Wheat ethanol (natural gas in CHP plant)	47
Wheat ethanol (straw as fuel in CHP plant)	69
Corn ethanol (natural gas in CHP plant)	49
Sugarcane ethanol	71 [b]
Rapeseed biodiesel	38
Sunflower biodiesel	51
Soybean biodiesel	31
Palm oil biodiesel (process not specified)	19
Palm oil biodiesel (with methane capture at oil mill)	56
Hydro-treated vegetable oil from rapeseed	47
Lignocellulosic ethanol	70–85 [c]
Fischer-Tropsch diesel	93–5 [c]

a) Renewable Energy Directive default values (land-use change emissions not included).

b) Includes transport emissions from Brazil to EU.

c) Range for different feedstocks.

Source: EC, 2009.

Table 3.1 provides default values for reduction of greenhouse gas emission through the use of several types of biofuels, feedstocks and processing technology, as suggested by the EU Directive (EC, 2009). It is evident that in some cases, depending on the feedstock and process, biofuels production is not primarily motivated by its CO_2 mitigation potential – this is clear in the cases of US and EU options for corn ethanol and rapeseed biodiesel, respectively. Fortunately, the most recent regulations on biofuels, such as the EU Renewable Energy Directive and USA Energy Independence and Security Act of 2007, are emphasizing GHG emission reduction potential.

As can be seen, the GHG mitigation capacity of ethanol and biodiesel varies considerably with the feedstock and processing path; therefore it is not possible to generalize about GHG benefits. Table 3.1 shows that sugarcane and lignocellulosic ethanol are the most efficient options to reduce GHG emissions. Larson (2006) has made a comprehensive review of 42 published life cycle analyses (LCAs) of bio-fuels and found wide variation in the results, even for the same biofuel and feedstock. The four most important parameters contributing to the spread of the results were: (1) climate active species included in the calculation; (2) assumptions related to N_2O emissions; (3) co-product credits allocation methods and values; and (4) soil carbon dynamics. Clearly, LCA methodology needs to be improved and standardized, with a better knowledge of more complex phenomena such as nitrogen soil chemistry for N_2O emission and soil carbon dynamics; without this, results from specific LCAs for a biofuel will be subject to criticism and confusion.

Recently the scientific literature has produced various criticisms of claims made for the potential environmental benefits of biofuels. For example, critics have noted that the GHG reduction potential of sugarcane ethanol was partly due to the fact that sugarcane expansion in Brazil was occurring in pasture land; the land-use change would in the end emit almost as much CO_2 as was saved, considering its life cycle. Such generalizations are misleading, especially in view of of the varying amounts of organic matter stored in the soil. In fact, most of the pasture land taken up by sugarcane is degraded and of low productivity, and therefore has a low level of organic matter.

More effort is required to map pasture land in Brazil, particularly in the central-south area where sugarcane expansion is taking place. For example, Macedo and Seabra (2008) have estimated the effects on soil carbon stocks of both direct and indirect land-use change for different crops displaced by sugarcane in the recent past in Brazil, based on published literature results. Considering the sugarcane-induced LUC profile in the past few years (representative of the fast growth period of ethanol production) an average value was estimated and included in the GHG emission LCA, indicating a negative value (carbon storage) of -0.7 t CO_2/ha, quite different from the value suggested by Fargione *et al.* (2008) of +165 t CO_2/ha (carbon loss); the ILUC-derived GHG emissions for sugarcane ethanol were also estimated to be negative for green harvested sugarcane. However, a strong criticism has been that the authors failed to indicate the strong uncertainties involved in their calculations and simulations. In the case of sugarcane ethanol in Brazil, the authors (Fargione *et al.*, 2008) seem to have used inadequate data on land-use dynamics to prove their points.

Another example is palm oil. In Indonesia from 1990 to 2005 a total of 28.1 Mha were deforested. But oil palm expansion in those areas occupied an area of no more than 1.7–3 Mha in the same period, of which only a very small proportion was dedicated to biodiesel production – since nearly all palm oil is for food or cosmetics markets (Kline *et al.*, 2009). Taking the case of Brazil from 2004 to 2007, when the fastest increase (from 381 to 488 million tons) in sugarcane production took place, it is interesting to note that the rate of deforestation in the Amazon decreased from 2.7 Mha/year to 1.1 Mha/year in the same period (Nogueira, 2008).

In the case of sugarcane, the low use of fossil fuel during the production process makes it very attractive to advocates of strong policies to accelerate fossil fuel substitution and emissions reductions. Not only is sugarcane ethanol probably the best biofuel alternative for mitigating CO_2 emissions (see Table 3.1), but it is also a well-tested alternative in Brazil, where bioethanol has been mixed with gasoline in a wide proportional range (from E5 to E100), and a 'flex(ible)-fuel' engine has been developed and is now extensively used; currently around 90 percent of new cars sold in Brazil (about 3 million) are flex-fuel.

Table 3.2 Energy balance in ethanol production

Process	Maize[a] (GJ/ha/yr)	Switchgrass[a] (GJ/ha/yr)	Cane[b] (GJ/ha/yr)
Energy consumption in agriculture	18.9	17.8	13.9
Biomass energy	149.5[c]	220.2	297.1[d]
Energy ratio in agriculture[e]	7.9	12.3	21.3
External energy consumption in distillery[f]	47.9	10.2	3.4
Ethanol energy content	67.1[g]	104.4	132.5[h]
Total energy ratio	1.21	4.43	8.32

a) Shapouri et al., 2002.

b) Macedo et al., 2004.

c) Corn stover not included.

d) Tops and leaves not included.

e) Energy ratio calculated as row 2 over row 1.

f) External energy input coming from outside the system production boundaries.

g) Does not include credit for co-products.

h) Includes credit for 8 percent bagasse surplus.

In part, the positive indicators of sugarcane ethanol are due to the sugarcane plant itself. When ethanol production from three different crops (corn, switchgrass and sugarcane) is compared, it is clear that sugarcane presents the best energy balance (Table 3.2). The main reason for this is that sugarcane does not need external fuel to provide energy for the process, relying instead on the fibrous residue (known as bagasse) of the plant itself.

Sugarcane is basically composed of sugars (one third) and fibres (two thirds). Today only sugars are utilized to produce ethanol. However, if a second-generation technology – such as hydrolysis, gasification or pyrolysis – is commercialized, a better use of the fibres would further enhance the advantages of sugarcane for bioenergy, since surplus bagasse and some recovered tops and leaves could be used as feedstock for these advanced processes (so-called 'energy cane'). Estimates for the future of sugarcane have indicated that the present efficiency of conversion of the total primary energy of sugarcane can increase from about 30 percent (the present value) to about 50 percent, with a significant increase of ethanol production per ton of sugarcane (up to

50 percent more) and of the distillery gross annual revenues (Leal, 2009).

Land use

Land is becoming a scarce resource on our planet. Fertile land is mainly used for agriculture, pasture and forests. Great efforts are being made by agronomists, geneticists and other professionals to increase agricultural productivity – a higher yield from the same land. Population increase and higher living standards, with greater protein consumption, are among the main causes of the growing demand for more fertile land.

First, it is important to understand that there is still land globally available to produce biofuels on a large scale without jeopardizing food production and biodiversity (see Table 3.3). However, only South America, Central America and Africa have the potential for large-scale production of biofuels, approximately 430 Mha by 2050 (Doornbosch

Table 3.3 Land use for agriculture in selected countries

	(1) Land in agriculture Mha	(2) Arable land Mha	1 : 2 %	1 : total land %
India	170	180	94	54
France	20	30	67	34
Germany	12	17	71	34
Spain	18	29	62	27
Netherlands	0.9	1.9	47	27
Italy	11	15	73	26
UK	6	17	35	24
USA	179	415	43	19
China	135	555	24	11
Argentina	27	129	21	10
Zimbabwe	3,3	21	16	8
Brazil	65	264[a]	25	7
Canada	46	67	69	7
Mozambique	4.1	49	8	5.5
Angola	3.3	58	6	2.6
Colombia	4.5	43	10	1.8

a) Excludes all Amazon Region and Pantanal. Brazil has a total land area of 851 Mha, of which 360 Mha are native Amazon; 210 Mha are pasture lands. The rest has various uses (see Caldas, 2008).

Source: FAO, 2008a.

and Steenblik, 2007). The additional land required between now and 2050 for food production, urban development, and infrastructure to cope with the expected world population growth (estimated at 300 Mha) has already been discounted from this total. It is worth pointing out, however, that around 50 percent of the additional available land is concentrated in just seven countries: Angola, Democratic Republic of Congo, Sudan, Argentina, Bolivia, Brazil and Colombia (Table 3.3). Nevertheless, the International Energy Agency (IEA) estimates that by 2030 most biofuel production, and land use for this purpose, will take place in the United States and Europe (IEA, 2006)

A further point is that countries such as the US and Brazil have been criticized for expanding their occupied land to produce biofuels. To address this issue it is important to look at how much of their land is devoted to producing food crops and how much is available for agricultural expansion. Table 3.3 presents figures on arable land and land already dedicated to agriculture in selected countries. It can be seen that some countries, such as India, have almost reached their full potential. European countries such as France, Germany and Italy are ranked close to a critical level and are also in no position to significantly increase their biofuel production without threatening food crops. Some other European countries – including the Netherlands, the United

Table 3.4 Displacement of 10 percent of world gasoline and diesel consumption (2005)

Biofuel	Feedstock	Yield (litres/ha)	Land requirement (Mha)
Ethanol[a]	Sugarcane	6,000	25
	Maize	3,750 [c]	40
Biodiesel[b]	Soybeans	550 [c]	245
	Castor beans	500	270
	Oil palm	4,700 [d]	45

a)   150 billion litres (120 billion litres of gasoline).

b)   135 billion litres (120 billion litres of diesel).

c)   USA conditions (FAO, 2008a).

d)   Malaysia conditions (FAO, 2008a).

Source: Authors' estimate.

Kingdom, and Spain – already utilize nearly a third of their territory for agriculture. On the other hand, countries such as Brazil, Colombia, Mozambique and Angola, large countries in surface area with relatively small populations, use less than 10 percent of their land for agriculture.[3]

The use of pasture land in Brazil is important because this is where sugarcane expansion is taking place. For example, the national cattle herd numbers about 200 million head, a population density of just one head per hectare (see also Chapter 7). If Brazil aims to substitute 10 percent of world gasoline consumption with sugarcane ethanol, it will need just an additional 25 Mha, mainly from low-productivity degraded pasture land, as is currently happening.

Land use is crucial when biofuels are considered. As emphasized already, the choice of the correct crop will have a tremendous effect on the land required for biofuels production. This is because agricultural productivity needs also to be combined with industrial productivity. This overall yield, expressed in Table 3.4 in terms of litres of biofuel per hectare, gives a good indication. It can be seen that the higher the overall yield, the smaller the land required for a certain level of gasoline or diesel substitution.

It seems clear from the table that biodiesel from soybeans, castor beans (the Brazilian government's feedstock of choice) and other low-yield oil seeds cannot be considered seriously as a long-term solution. Palm oil and maize can only be considered a medium-term solution, taking into account the land requirements and GHG abatement potential.

Land-use policies and impacts on food prices

Land use has been the subject of discussion throughout the world for many years. In several countries land has been seen as a strategic resource not only to increase food production but also to reduce social inequalities through agrarian reforms. Land is also a main condition of biodiversity, particularly in tropical countries where rainforest still remains.

Throughout past centuries humankind has been responsible for large-scale deforestation. For example, of the original forests in the United States and Europe, less than 10 percent remain. Both Europe and the US have achieved a level of high economic development and no longer depend on forest-based extractive activities, unlike many developing regions. These countries are in a good position to implement rational planning and establish a policy to regulate land use. Although such land-use planning is under way in many developing countries today, most have not achieved the level of economic and political development necessary to implement and enforce new land-use legislation.

For example, in Brazil a series of federal and state decrees and laws have been enacted in recent decades in order to organize and create clearer rules for Indian reserves (the first to be established was Xingu National Park in 1954), environment protection areas (more than 100 Mha in the Amazon region), and minimum areas reserved for natural forests, varying from 20 to 80 percent of the total land set aside for any agricultural development project. Another law has been passed to phase out sugarcane burning in São Paulo by 2017.[4]

More recently, land use became a concern for several institutions such as the Brazilian Enterprise for Agricultural Research that have introduced a regime known as 'agricultural zoning' – a first mapping

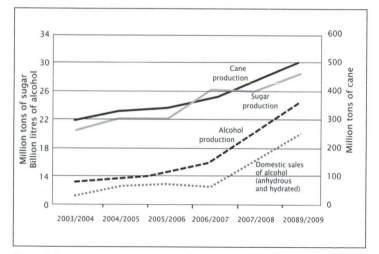

Figure 3.1 Evolution of Brazilian sugarcane, sugar, and ethanol production
Source: Based on data from UNICA (www.unica.com.br)

exercise when new areas of sugarcane are being considered (Caldas, 2008). It is interesting to note that the total area considered adequate for sugarcane production with low environmental and social impacts, including food security and low economic risks, amounts to 64 Mha, about 8 percent of the country's total land area.

During the past 35 years, Brazil has been able to develop the so-called 'Brazilian Ethanol Model' which involves simultaneous production of sugar and ethanol (Figure 3.1). Yet areas of high sugarcane concentration, such as the Ribeirão Preto region in São Paulo, are also the mainstay of crops such as peanuts. So, in the case of Brazil, it cannot be said that overall agricultural production has been negatively influenced by sugarcane. On the contrary, the country has never produced the volume of cereals, meat, coffee and oranges that it does today.

Indeed, sugarcane has helped to modernize the whole Brazilian agriculture sector, introducing new technologies and requiring more and better human resources to manage them. A good example is the dynamic interaction between private (CTC), public (APTA/IAC) and public-private (RIDESA) institutions in the development of new varieties. Another example is the recently created FAPESP-BIOEN research programme and the new Bioethanol Science and Technology National Laboratory. Both initiatives contribute to improving future prospects both for sugarcane ethanol and the modernization of Brazilian agriculture.

In the case of the US, ethanol production has accelerated in the last ten years. The US is a traditional producer and exporter of corn, harvesting about 300 Mt every year (FAO, 2008b). Many countries, such as Mexico, are heavily dependent on US corn exports either for food or animal feed. Most of the corn converted to ethanol is derived from existing production, and little if any additional land has been used except that derived from the 'set-aside policy'. Thus, as ethanol production expanded in the US, less corn was available in the international market up to the middle of 2008 – and this created a measure of volatility.

However, as discussed in Chapter 1, when cereal prices started to fall in the second quarter of 2008, it became clear that the main factor causing high commodity prices (not only cereals, but also minerals and vegetable oils) was the hike in the cost of petroleum driven by demand from emergent countries led by China, and by speculation. Oil prices rose from US$50 to US$140 in 2007 before recoiling to US$40 in 2008.

Why biofuels are the most urgent alternative to fossil fuels

During the last quarter of the twentieth century, concerns increased over the continuing availability of cheap fossil fuels and the threat this posed to economic progress worldwide. Two crises (1973 and 1979) involving Middle East countries suggested that the world should look for alternatives such as energy saving and greater use of renewable energy resources. Various countries implemented measures to reduce energy consumption, and many studies were conducted to analyse the possible role of renewable energies – including the direct use of sunlight, wind and biomass, among others.

However, the resulting introduction of renewable energy in most developed countries was very small-scale. Only a few countries, Brazil being the best example, adopted long-term strategies to create substitutes for fossil fuels. This situation persisted until the end of the century when, in addition to the energy agenda, climate change became a major driver.

Many studies have been carried out over the past decades to simulate and make projections for temperature increase in the atmosphere during this century, and a considerable number of simulations and scenarios have been put forward by the scientific community. The challenge now is to find an effective substitute mechanism to reduce GHG emissions. Many countries are adopting different policies to tackle these issues.

Of the many alternatives to fossil fuel put forward globally, no one seems to be capable of satisfying the demand – particularly in the transport sector, which is still, except in Brazil, almost totally dependent on oil. To generate electricity in large amounts from wind or solar power is still too expensive, although costs are coming down rapidly. For liquid fuels there are no short- or medium-term alternatives to ethanol and biodiesel; electric vehicles and hydrogen-powered cars are still too far off in commercial terms.

The complex nature of biofuels

The benefits of biofuels vary widely according to the feedstock used, local conditions, and the end use: each situation presents its peculiarities. For example, ethanol and biodiesel in Brazil serve different purposes and have different characteristics compared to the same biofuels in the US. The Brazilian government initially promoted biodiesel production in pursuit of social goals and to reduce regional inequalities. The programme has faltered because, in contrast to the ethanol programme, there is no real involvement of the private sector. Planning was shaky, and so was the agricultural base of some of the oil crops grown as feedstock.

The nature of biofuels is also complex because of the many variables involved, including social, economic and technical aspects. A successful biofuels programme has several components:

- availability of good land, rainfall, and sunshine;
- due regard (nationally and locally) for food production, forests, and biodiversity;
- technology and R&D;
- existing infrastructure (roads, communication);
- human capacity (skills) at all levels;
- availability of capital and financial resources.

Of course, not all countries will have, or be able to satisfy, all of these conditions. In reality, as stated, there are drawbacks to each energy resource, and biofuels are not an exception. One can only analyse how biofuels compare with the alternatives.

Broad impacts on agriculture and rural development

Rural areas and biofuels go hand in hand. We shall see that the introduction of energy crops will generate long-term impacts affecting land rights, income distribution, availability of finances, skills, and other aspects of rural life (see the case studies in this chapter and Chapters 4 and 5). First, however, it is important to remember that the main objective is to substitute biofuels for fossil fuel, particularly gasoline and diesel, and so biofuels need to be competitive with what they are replacing. For some feedstocks, biofuel production therefore cannot offer the prospect of high returns per hectare in certain locations, as might be the case for other agricultural activities. Indeed, the direct economic benefits of biofuels are rather small and very much a function of good management, particularly in agriculture, since the raw material production cost usually accounts for 60–70 percent (in the case of ethanol) and 70–90 percent (in the case of biodiesel) of the total cost.

While rural development is certainly a major objective of developing biofuels, there are some pragmatic factors that need to be considered:

- biofuels depend on economies of scale – the larger the agricultural and industrial production, the easier the management and the greater the potential profits – and so agricultural production is usually extensive;
- biofuels are extremely dependent on raw material availability and cost;
- biofuels require the use of raw material with a good energy balance (low inputs and high outputs) such as sugarcane;
- to develop large-scale biofuels commercially requires continuous research and development – with a focus, for example, on better varieties.

The impact of subsidies

Subsidies are in general necessary for the production of biofuels in the early stages so that they can reach market maturity, as pointed out in Chapter 1. It should be borne in mind that the oil industry reached maturity over many decades during which huge subsidies were expended worldwide. Initial dependence on subsidies has also been the experience of Brazil with sugarcane ethanol. At the beginning of the ProAlcool project, when production costs were relatively high, heavy subsidies were applied in various ways. Implementation of new agricultural areas and distilleries was subsidized during the first decade (1975–85), but in the early 1990s all subsidies were phased out as a deregulation policy was introduced in the sector.

However, even with low oil prices during the 1980s and 1990s, the sugarcane ethanol sector in Brazil learned to lower its production costs by introducing new varieties, combining sugar and ethanol production, and steadily improving its overall productivity and management practices. It is difficult to say whether US or European ethanol will follow the same path, because feedstocks, economics and policies are quite different.

As for biodiesel, particularly from crops such as oil palm, there are reasons to believe that a substantial improvement and adaptation is possible in tropical countries. Biofuels obtained from second-generation technologies also are promising, but to develop these pathways subsidies will still be necessary in the early years until they reach commercial maturity. Much depends on the development of these second- and third-generation technologies (fuel from algae, for example) that are expected to reduce costs and pollution considerably once they reach maturity (see Chapter 7).

CASE STUDY

The potential of ethanol from sugarcane in Brazil

Brazil has cultivated sugarcane for nearly 500 years and is the world's largest producer (7.8 Mha), followed by India (4.2 Mha), China (1.2 Mha), Thailand, Pakistan and Mexico. Although sugarcane is cultivated

Table 3.5 Biofuels production costs

Biofuel/Feedstock		US$/litre gasoline or diesel equivalent
Ethanol	Sugarcane	0.25 - 0.50
	Maize	0.50 - 0.80
	Sugar beet	0.63 - 0.83
	Wheat	0.70 - 0.95
	Lignocellulose	0.80 - 1.10
Biodiesel	Animal fat	0.40 - 0.55
	Vegetable oil	0.70 - 1.00
	Lignocellulose (FT)	0.90 - 1.10
Gasoline/Diesel[a]		0.16 - 0.50

a) Oil price US$20–70/barrel.
Source: Doornbosch and Steenblik, 2007.

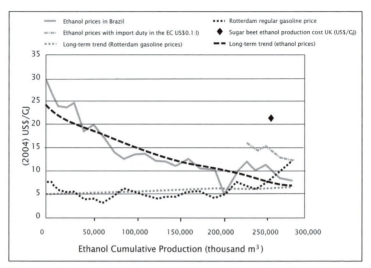

Figure 3.2 Cost learning curve for sugarcane ethanol in Brazil

Source: Adapted from Goldemberg et al., 2008.

in 101 tropical zone countries, the total cultivated area is no more than 25 Mha. An advantage of sugarcane is a robustness that provides potential for increasing productivity at relatively low cost – and in Brazil an important indicator of the successful production of ethanol has been the low production cost illustrated in Table 3.5 and Figure 3.2. This has been achieved by an emphasis on agricultural productivity, flexibility in combining sugar and ethanol production, scaling up, and technological development.

A comprehensive multi-disciplinary study by Leite *et al.* (2009) examined in depth the challenges posed by increasing the sustainable production of sugarcane ethanol in Brazil by a factor of ten in relation to the present output (already sufficient to substitute for 50 percent of the country's gasoline requirement). Some of the main findings of this study inform the discussion that follows.

Areas protected in the national interest for environmental and social reasons – the Amazon, Pantanal, Atlantic Forest, and the Indian reserves

– and those areas currently occupied by food crops were not considered in the study. In the case of the areas under agricultural food crops, the study also estimated a provision for their future growth. In addition, existing mechanization is not permitted in fields where the slope is above 12 percent. Such areas were also excluded.

In cooperation with the privately owned Sugarcane Technology Centre (CTC) located in Piracicaba, São Paulo, a comprehensive survey of new areas for sugarcane development was conducted. However, the study excluded the state of São Paulo and areas located in the south and south-east where expansion is already taking place. The potential for expansion is very large, particularly in the north-eastern region (see Table 3.6). This region is geographically closer to future markets, and has good soils, but present varieties of sugarcane could not be planted unless some irrigation is used and/or varieties resistant to water stress are planted.

Table 3.6 Potential of sugarcane production in Brazil

Potential	Expected Productivity (t/ha/year)	Potential Area (Mha)		Potential Production of Sugarcane per year (Mt)	
		Without irrigation	With irrigation	Without irrigation	With irrigation
High	81.4	7.9	37.9	643	3,090
Average	73.1	113.9	98.0	8,326	7,165
Low	64.8	149.2	167.6	9,670	10,863
Inadequate	0.0	90.6	58.0	0	0
TOTAL		361.6	361.6	18,640	21,115

Source: Leite *et al*. (2009a, 2009b)

Conventional sugarcane breeding
Even before ProAlcool was set up in 1975, there was a considerable awareness of the importance of developing new varieties better suited to local conditions, and for ethanol production rather than sugar. But early sugar and ethanol production depended on a handful of varieties, whereas today more than 500 varieties of sugarcane are available, although many of them are not necessarily produced on a commercial scale.

Table 3.7 Productivity in 2005 and expected gains for 2015 and 2025

Year	2005	2015	2025
Cane productivity, t/ha/yr	70	82	96
Pol (sugar content) of cane (%)	14.5	15.9	17.3
Industrial efficiency, %	85.5	90.0	90.0
Litres ethanol/ha	6,000	8,200	14,400

Source: Leite *et al.* (2009a, 2009b)

Sugarcane breeding in Brazil took place under three main programmes: (1) the Sugar-Ethanol Sector Development Inter-University Network (RIDESA, formerly the Planalsucar Programme, established in 1972); (2) the Sugarcane Technology Centre (CTC) (formerly the Copersucar Technology Center in Piracicaba); and (3) the Agronomic Institute of Campinas (IAC), in Campinas, São Paulo. Productivity in Brazil varies significantly from region to region – 84 tonnes/hectare (t/ha) in São Paulo, 78 t/ha in the centre-south and 56 t/ha in the northeast, for the 2005/6 season – but the above programmes have laid the foundations for significant improvements overall, as illustrated in Table 3.7.

Much still has to be done, however, to increase feedstock production: the genetics of sugarcane and the photosynthesis involved in growing the biomass are key research areas. Essentially, a trial-and-error method was used as a breeding method in the past, but this can hardly be justified in future large-scale ethanol production. Good examples are the work being carried out in Brazil by Alellyx and CanaVialis, owned by Monsanto, who investigate sugarcane genomics with the aim of producing genetically modified sugarcane varieties. It is also important to mention the pioneer genetic engineering programme developed by CTC, involving 12 countries (Macedo, 2005).

Challenges

The future of biofuels, and bioethanol in particular, depends on the capacity to produce feedstock sustainably and to undertake massive industrial production that also satisfies environmental, economic and social criteria. The research mentioned above is therefore fundamental:

understanding the genetics and metabolism of sugarcane is necessary to enhance sustainable future productivity.

Another important area of research is the need to change the paradigm from 'sugar cane' to 'energy cane' (see p. 64): at stake is an increase in energy production from about 520 GJ/ha/yr (12.5 toe) in 2005 to about 1,100 GJ/ha/yr (26 toe) by 2025 (Leite *et al.* 2009). Answers to several research questions, however, are still coming in:

- What are the limits for traditional sugarcane breeding?
- What is the productivity potential of sugarcane?
- Is sugarcane productivity close to its theoretical potential?
- Does natural selection really optimize sugarcane productivity or is there a way to make it better?
- Is energy cane possible?

CASE STUDY (by Thomson Sinkala)

Jatropha cultivation in Zambia

The food vs fuel debate is perhaps nowhere of greater concern than in sub-Saharan Africa, given the significant levels of poverty and hunger. However, food security is really a subset of household security within a national economy. There is a significant population that is able to feed itself in Africa, but yet is unable to pay for education or health care, and unable to participate in the formal economy. Similarly, some nations are able to feed their populations, but lack sufficient disposable national income to develop infrastructure and social services.

The overwhelming proportion of the sub-Saharan African population lives in poverty despite the large amount of land *per capita* and the rich resources that the subcontinent possesses. Agriculture remains Africa's economic backbone, employing 60 percent of the labour force and responsible for 20 percent of GDP. Although many rural areas are self-sufficient in food, they remain trapped in poverty. Seventy percent of the African population living on less than US$1 per day can be found in rural areas (UN, 2009).

Poorly developed infrastructure causes the costs of farming inputs (other than labour) to increase with distance away from urban centres, while the prices of rural agricultural produce decrease with distance away from these centres (Sinkala, 2008). The fuel price, for instance, increases as one moves away from the centre. Consequently fuel and many other commodities are unaffordable for rural populations. There is a contrast with industrialized countries, where it does not matter where foods and other goods and services are produced – they will generally reach the rest of the country efficiently at comparable country-wide prices. This is an important factor which makes the biofuels alternative a location-specific issue.

There are two basic ways that benefits from the biofuels industry can reach poor households. One way is through well-planned and efficiently applied taxes collected from the biofuels industry, and another is through the direct participation of nationals in the biofuels industry value chain. Experience shows that the former avenue of deriving benefits is largely elusive in sub-Saharan Africa due to mismanaged economies and corruption. The second avenue – nationals directly participating in the biofuels value chain – is thus more promising. It in turn depends on the type(s) of feedstocks used for liquid biofuels.

The liquid fuel budgets in each of these countries represent an enormous share of disposable income and of foreign exchange. The money spent on importing fossil fuels, if spent instead on locally produced liquid biofuels, would significantly uplift not only rural economies but also national economies at large.

The case of Zambia

Zambia, with a population of about 11.2 million people, occupies a near-central position on the Southern Africa subcontinent, 10–18 degrees south of the equator. The country has 75.2 million hectares of land mass of which 70 percent is under customary tenure, making it easy for local people to access land. There are 42 million ha of arable land, of which only 6 million ha are currently used, leaving 36 million ha available for agricultural development. There are 900,000 farm families, of whom 75 percent are small-scale farmers, 17 percent medium-scale and 8 percent large-scale.

To maximize benefits from the liquid biofuels industry, Zambia in developing its policies has applied a number of criteria to seek out biofuel feedstocks that will allow maximum participation throughout the value chain of the industry. Participation in the value chain is seen as a direct means of distributing wealth in the country through production. The parameters that Zambia has considered include: scope of ownership of the biofuels wealth at national and individual levels; production technology; job creation; resilience against external disturbances; diversity of products; size of investment; market scope; land requirements; water requirements; food security impacts; geographical coverage of ownership in the country; and environmental concerns (Sinkala, 2009).

These parameters determine to what extent the biofuels industry would be sustainable in Zambia and have a significant bearing on the development of the remaining sectors of the national economy. Using these parameters, the preferred feedstocks identified in the Zambian case include jatropha, palm and castor (for oil/biodiesel) and sweet sorghum, sugarcane and cassava (for bioethanol). To illustrate how the liquid biofuels industry would enhance household economy – food security included – the case of jatropha is considered below.

Jatropha as a liquid biofuel feedstock
Jatropha curcas, a drought-resistant plant reported to come from central-south America and spread to Africa by Portuguese travellers, has been known in Zambia for more than 300 years. The plant is now being promoted for propagation as a source of feedstock for oil/biodiesel production in the country. Jatropha is 100 percent participatory (with respect to poor farmers in rural areas) in its value chain, and is relatively easy to grow. Plant establishment takes several forms, but the major and most common one is the plantation; alternatively, and at a smaller scale, it is planted as a living hedge around other crops.

The technology for extracting jatropha oil and, if need be, converting it into biodiesel ranges from simple to very complex processes. The same wide range of options applies to the production of biogas and organic fertilizer from jatropha press cake (Sinkala, 2008).

Jatropha products have four market levels, the first of which is *the grower's own domestic consumption*. Experience shows that the grower will be more productive if he/she is food-secure. One cannot engage in labour-intensive work on a hungry stomach. The availability of affordable food also contributes significantly to stabilizing and even lowering the production cost of liquid biofuels. Jatropha growers who are producing their own fuel as well as their own organic fertilizer are likely to be the cheapest food producers for the plantation workforce in the same location.

At the second market level *the grower's biofuel products become inputs into commercial activities*. These products include oil/biodiesel, charcoal, biogas and organic fertilizer – all soon produced in larger quantities than growers need for their own use. There is considerable flexibility at this level. If, for instance, the food market is more attractive than selling oil/biodiesel and organic fertilizer on the commercial market, the grower may use these products as inputs into food production for the commercial market. This has the further benefit of adding to national food security.

Beyond these two market levels lie a third level, *the national market*; and a fourth, *the international market*. Clearly, a picture is emerging here: a biofuels grower will increasingly gain capacity to produce for needs beyond just 'food on the table'. Increasingly, the producer will be able to manage other needs by accessing services such as health care, education and communications.

Net conservation of forestry and agricultural land quality as measures of food security

According to the United Nations Economic Commission for Africa (UNECA, 2009):

- Currently, Africa accounts for 27 percent of the world's land degradation and has 500 million hectares of moderately or severely degraded land.
- Degradation affects 65 percent of cropland and 30 percent of pasture land.
- Soil degradation is associated with low land productivity.

- It is mainly caused by loss of vegetation and land exploitation, especially overgrazing and shifting cultivation.
- Insecurity of land ownership has been blamed for accelerated land degradation and lack of long-term investment in sustainable land management and stewardship of natural resources.

It is important to note that, since Africa currently produces almost no biofuel, all of the above changes can be attributed to agricultural activities for food production, along with other rural and peri-urban activities such as subsistence use of wood-based fuel for households and industry. Thus overgrazing, shifting cultivation, fuelwood and charcoal emerge as the main agents of land degradation. In Zambia, for instance, 95 percent of rural people depend on fuelwood and 90 percent of urban households depend on charcoal (Chileshe, 2001). Zambia is losing more than 450,000 hectares of forest every year (Conservation Farming Unit, 2007). One advantage of a crop like jatropha is its ability to reverse these trends and to restore degraded land through careful management and intercropping.

Electricity can be generated with the oil and biodiesel derived from jatropha, while biogas and charcoal briquettes can be produced from the press cake. After jatropha cake is used as biogas, the residue can be applied to crops as organic fertilizer. Since seed production is renewable and increases with the age and size of the plant, growing fuel requirements can be met, while the net effect would be to reduce deforestation and therefore land degradation, as well as improving soil quality.

A household example
In a developing country like Zambia, the grower often becomes the first market for his/her own products. Some basic requirements of a family farm household (two parents and six children), as shown in Table 3.8, provide an example. The amount of fertilizer shown in the table is for growing maize and vegetables for the family and other workers. The need for charcoal has risen significantly during the past year, during which there has been a national power shortage. Electricity is not available constantly as in European countries, and the amount given is what is needed to generate electricity for lights for a few hours in the evenings.

Table 3.8 The value of the jatropha industry to a household economy[a]

Household requirements	Litres	Kg	Cost (US$/Yr)
Fuel (diesel/year)	4,224		9,051.43
Soap (equivalent oil per year)	24		288.00
Charcoal		4,800	1,097.14
Fertilizer		1,000	1,142.86
Mosquito repellant (equivalent oil per year)	3		102.86
Electricity generation	1,095		2,346.43
TOTAL	5,346	5,800	14,028.71

a) The household consists of two parents and six children.

The annual cost of supplying these requirements from sources other than jatropha is about US$14,030. By Zambian standards, this is a very significant economy. Since all these requirements can be addressed by the use of jatropha oil and cake, the family becomes the first customer of its own production. Given a jatropha plantation of 1,000 plants per hectare, a constant yield of 4 kg/plant, and an oil extraction ratio of 30 percent, the requirements shown in the table require a land size of 4.5 hectares. There would even be 10 tons left over to sell as organic fertilizer.

The jatropha cake that remains after pressing out the oil is rich in nitrogen, phosphorus and potassium, and can be used as organic manure. It has been shown to be far superior to cowdung. Analyses have shown that nutrient content is relatively high compared to standard inorganic (fossil-based) fertilizers for Zambian conditions. Thus rural communities can produce organic fertilizer that is not only readily available in their backyards, but also contributes to a reduction of production costs in rural-based farming systems. Both reliability and economy are improved, with positive benefits for food security.

Main conclusions

Our chapter has argued that biofuels can play an important role in reducing GHG, and in contributing to social, economic and technical development. Many of our arguments have drawn on the Brazilian experience. However, such benefits depend on many varying factors, among which the types of feedstock, costs, and local conditions loom large. Although Brazil has been successful in developing and implementing a biofuels programme, the present world energy and environment situation demands a new strategy. It is a measure of Brazilian success that its domestic need for gasoline is already 50 percent fulfilled with bioethanol from sugarcane. However, when world gasoline demand is analysed (about 1.2 trillion litres per year), it is clear that a major global effort will be required in different areas.

Much of the criticism levelled against biofuels is not backed up by solid scientific evidence. For example, land availability is not the fundamental issue. We need to look, rather, at how land is managed, at the availability of investment, at skills, inequalities, markets and so forth. These are the main barriers and impediments to food and fuel production. Overall, it has to be conceded, and should be remembered, that biofuels are far more environmentally friendly than fossil fuels.

The threat to energy security from costly fossil fuels and the impacts of energy poverty in hindering rural development pose especially serious concerns in landlocked, poor countries like Zambia. Jatropha appears to have the potential to reduce energy insecurity, improve rural livelihoods, and enhance the agricultural sector. Zambia has abundant land and food security, and is not threatened by the biofuels industry. On the contrary, when using energy crops such as jatropha, biofuels can protect land from degradation and provide valuable products to the farmer and the local community.

Notes

1   <http://www.nationmaster.com/graph/agr_gra_cor_pro-agriculture-grains-corn-production>.
2   <http://www.publicintegrity.org/investigations/broken_government/articles/entry/1002/>.

3   These figures are, of course, not strictly comparable, since in many coun-
     tries agriculture remains highly undercapitalized and productivity is
     extremely low.
4   São Paulo State Law No. 11.241.

References

Caldas, C. (2008) 'Ordenamento territorial para expansão da cana de Açúcar no
     Brasil: zoneamento agroecológico da cana de Açúcar', Power Point
     presentation at the International Symposium and Technology Exhibition
     for the Sugarcane Agroindustry (SIMTEC), Piracicaba, Brazil, 1 July.
Chileshe, A. (2001) 'A brief on the forestry outlook study in Zambia', Forestry
     Department, Ministry of Environment and Natural Resources, Lusaka,
     <http://www.fao.org/forestry/FON/FONS/outlook/Africa/AFRhom-e.stm>.
Conservation Farming Unit (2007) 'Reversing environmental degradation
     through conservation farming and conservation agriculture',
     <http://www.conservationagriculture.org/assets/images/media/200703
     29_104941_Brief2-CAandtheEnvironment.pdf>.
Doornbosch, R. and R. Steenblik (2007) 'Biofuels: is the cure worse than the
     disease? Round table on sustainable development', draft report SG/SD/TR
     (2007) 3, OECD General Secretariat, Paris.
EC (2009) 'Directive 2009/28/EC of the European Parliament and of the
     Council of 23 April 2009 on the promotion of the use of energy from
     renewable sources, and amending and subsequently repealing Directives
     2001/77/EC and 2003/30/EC', <http://eur-lex.europa.eu/LexUriServ/
     LexUriServ.do?uri=OJ:L:2009:140:0016:0062:en:PDF>.
FAO (2008a) Agricultural Statistics, <http://www.nationmaster.com/graph/
     agr_agr_lan_sq_km-agriculture-agricultural-land-sq-km>.
—— (2008b) *The State of Food and Agriculture – Biofuels: Prospects, Risks and Oppor-
     tunities*, Food and Agriculture Organization of the United Nations, Rome.
Fargione, J. *et al.* (2008) 'Land clearing and the biofuel carbon debt', *Science* 319
     (29 February): 1235–8, <www.scienceexpress.org>.
Goldemberg, J. *et al.* (2008) 'Food security versus energy security', presentation
     at the Gallagher Review Seminar, São Paulo, 13 May.
IEA (International Energy Agency) (2006) 'Biofuels in the European Union – a
     vision for 2030 and beyond', <http://ec.europa.eu/research/energy/pdf/
     biofuels_vision_2030_en.pdf>.
Kline, K., V. H. Dale, R. Lee and P. Leiby (2009) 'In defense of biofuels, done
     right', *Issues in Science and Technology* 25 (3): 75–84, <http://www.issues.
     org/25.3/kline.html>.
Larson, E. D. (2006) 'A review of life-cycle analysis studies on liquid biofuel sys-
     tems for the transport sector', *Energy for Sustainable Development* 10 (2):
     109–26.
Leal, M. R. L. V. (2009) 'Use of sugarcane bagasse and straw for ethanol and

energy production', paper presented (in Portuguese) at the F. O. Licht Ethanol Production Workshop, 23 March 2009, São Paulo.

Leite, R. C. *et al.* (2009a) 'Study of large-scale production of ethanol, its possibilities and impacts, aiming the partial substitution of world gasoline' Report to the Brazilian Ministry of Science and Technology-MCT. <http://www.cgee.org.br>.

Leite, R. C., M. R. L. V. Leal, L. A. B. Cortez, W. M. Griffin, M. I. G. Scandiffio (2009b). 'Can Brazil replace 5 percent of the 2025 gasoline world demand with ethanol?' *Energy* 34: 655–61 (article in journal).

Macedo, I. C. (ed.) (2005) *Sugarcane's Energy: Twelve Studies on Brazilian Sugarcane Agribusiness and Its Sustainability*, União da Agroindústria Canavieira do Estado de São Paulo (UNICA), São Paulo.

Macedo, I. C. and J. E. A. Seabra (2008) 'Mitigation of GHG emissions using sugarcane ethanol', in P. Zuurbier and J. van de Vooren (eds), *Sugarcane Ethanol*, Wageningen Academic Publishers, Wageningen, pp. 95–110, <http://www.scribd.com/doc/9316701/Sugarcane-Ethanol-Contributions-to-climate-change-mitigation-and-the-environment>.

Macedo, I. C., M. R. L. V. Leal and J. E. A. R. Silva (2004) 'Assessment of greenhouse gas emissions in the production and use of fuel ethanol in Brazil', report prepared for the State of São Paulo Secretariat of the Environment, Piracicaba.

Nogueira, L. A. H. (2008) *Sugarcane-Based Bioethanol: Energy for Sustainable Development*, Brazilian Development Bank (BNDES) and Centre for Strategic Studies, Management Science, Technology and Innovation (CGEE), Rio de Janeiro, < http://www.sugarcanebioethanol.org>.

Shapouri, H., J. A. Duffield and M. Wang (2002) 'The energy balance of corn ethanol: an update', Agricultural Economic Report No. 814, US Department of Agriculture, July.

Sinkala, T. (2008) 'Liquid biofuels as a viable alternative to fossil fuels', Working Paper prepared for the Global Renewable Energy Forum, Foz do Iguaçu, Brazil, 18–21 May.

—— (2009) 'Development of next generation biofuels in Africa', paper presented at the Expert Group Meeting, AREA Science Park, Trieste, Italy, 16 November.

UN (2009) 'Regional perspectives on policy priorities and practical measures to expedite implementation in agriculture, rural development, land, drought, and desertification in Africa', statement by the Economic Commission for Africa on behalf of the UN Regional Commissions at the Intergovernmental Preparatory Meeting for CSD-17, 23–27 February, New York, <http://www.un.org/esa/dsd/resources/res_pdfs/csd-17-ipm/26february/PM/UN_Regional_Commissions.pdf>.

UNECA (UN Economic Commission for Africa) (2009) 'Challenges to agricultural development in Africa', Chapter 4 in *Economic Report on Africa, 2009*, <www.uneca.org/era2009/ >.

4 Agriculture and Land Use Issues

J. Richard Hess, Jacob J. Jacobson, Douglas L. Karlen,
David J. Muth Jr, Richard G. Nelson, Leslie P. Ovard,
Erin M. Searcy, and Thomas H. Ulrich

Large-scale biofuels development as a source of renewable energy will shift current dynamics in the agricultural sector that deliver food, feed and fibre. This shift will challenge highly productive, specialized systems to provide services for which they may not be optimized. Sceptics of the biofuel industry cite inadequate agricultural lands to support food, feed, fibre, *and* fuel. Throughout human history, civilization has continuously pushed the productive capacity of the landscape to provide greater amounts of food, feed and fibre per unit area, and serious questions remain about the sustainability of pushing land resources further to produce significant quantities of fuel.

Assessing resource potential

Determining the productive capacity of the world's agricultural sector requires addressing a complex and dynamic set of issues. Very simply, the first and most basic question becomes: what is the aggregate productive capacity of agricultural lands under existing agronomic management scenarios? Of the world's 13.5 billion hectares of land surface area, roughly 61 percent is currently in grassland or forest and 12 percent is in cropland (Fischer, 2008). An additional 14 percent is considered potentially suitable for rain-fed crop production, although this figure should be treated with considerable caution. Much of the land in forests, wetlands and other uses provides valuable environmental services, including carbon sequestration, water filtration and bio-diversity preservation; thus, expansion of crop production in these areas could be detrimental to the environment. After excluding forest land, protected areas and land needed to meet increased demand for food crops and livestock, estimates of the amount of land potentially available for expanded crop production lie between 250 and 800 million hectares (Mha), most of which is found in tropical Latin America or Africa (Fischer, 2008).

The data suggest that overall there may be enough agricultural land to support a growing biofuels industry; however, actual availability of agricultural land is very regionally dependent. There may, in fact, be a substantial discrepancy between the available agricultural land and the demand for biomass for biofuel development. Additionally, the availability of biomass depends on the supply systems and economic viability of accessing the biomass resource. Another important component of economic viability is the purchase cost: agroeconomics indicates that increasing the purchase cost increases the availability.

Agricultural residues: food crops
In the Billion Ton Study, Perlack *et al.* (2005) estimate that the amount of biomass that can be removed from agricultural lands in the United States alone, without impacting current agricultural markets or crop production sustainability, is currently about 194 million dry tons (Mdt) per year. With technology advancements, adapted tillage practices and carefully orchestrated land-use change, they project that within 35 to 40 years this amount can be increased five-fold to nearly 1.36 billion dry tons, while still meeting food, feed, fibre and export demands (Fischer, 2008). The study estimates that 446 Mdt would come from annual crop residues, 377 Mdt from perennial crops, 87 Mdt from grains used for biofuels, and 87 Mdt from animal manures, process residues and other miscellaneous feedstocks (Fischer, 2008). While the actual make-up of the billion-plus tons is under debate, other studies cite similar US biomass total potential (Smith *et al.*, 2004).

The largest agricultural source of biomass for biofuel development is estimated to come from annual crop residues (Perlack *et al.*, 2005). Corn stover resources provide 75 percent of total annual crop residues currently available for biofuel production (Nelson, 2002). Most of the stover supply is concentrated in the Midwest region, where approximately 21 Mha of corn are cultivated, producing an estimated 180 million tons of residue (USDA-NASS, 2008).

Current residue collection technology is capable of recovering about 40 percent of the residue (Patterson, 2003; Hess *et al.*, 2006; Shinners and Binversie, 2007), but foreseeable single-pass harvest technologies will be capable of greater than 70 percent residue removal (Shinners *et al.*, 2007). However, studies have shown that sustainable residue removal rates are extremely site-sensitive, often needing to be kept below 40 percent removal to maintain soil organic carbon and plant nutrients, as well as to prevent erosion, excessive soil compaction and other environmental degradation (Johnson *et al.*, 2006; Wilhelm *et al.*, 2004; Nelson, 2002; Sheehan *et al.*, 2004).

Global potential: the impact of changing diets
The previous discussion suggests that there is sufficient land available to increase biofuel production without reducing the quantity or quality of food production, particularly if marginal lands are the primary target for biofuel production. However, some researchers project that changing food consumption patterns will increase demand, and thus competition, for available production land. Gerbens-Leenes and Nonhebel (2002) estimate that as the standard of living of developing nations increases, their food consumption patterns will change. For example, in the Netherlands, a rise in *per capita* income has resulted in a nearly three-fold increase in meat consumption from 1950 to 1990 (Gerbens-Leenes and Nonhebel, 2002). Figure 4.1 shows a similar increase in the consumption of livestock products as countries become more industrialized (from data in WHO/FAO 2002).

An increased standard of living does not necessarily promote an increase in food consumption, but rather a shift towards more expensive foods that frequently require larger land areas to produce, such as higher-value meats, oils, cheese, and other dairy products, and beverages such as beer, wine, coffee, and tea (Grigg, 1994). Tea, beef, and butter have a specific land requirement of 35.2, 20.9, and 13.8 m² year kg⁻¹, respectively, whereas cereals, potatoes, and pork have a specific land requirement of 1.4, 0.2, and 8.9 m² year kg⁻¹, respectively (Gerbens-Leenes and Nonhebel, 2002). Increased consumption of higher-value foods will have an impact on the amount of land available for biofuels production.

There is a strong positive relationship between the level of income and the consumption of animal protein, with the consumption of meat,

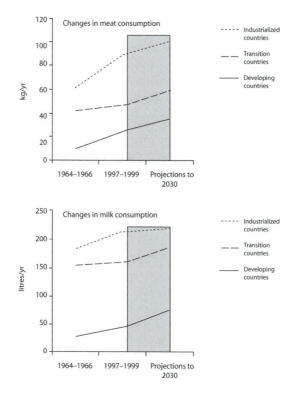

Figure 4.1 Comparison of meat and milk consumption changes over the last 40 years and projected changes according to similar rates for the next 20 years

milk, and eggs increasing at the expense of staple foods. Because of the recent steep decline in prices, developing countries are embarking on higher meat consumption at much lower levels of gross domestic product than the industrialized countries did some 20 to 30 years ago (WHO/FAO, 2002).

Lester Brown brought this issue to the forefront in 1995 in the book *Who Will Feed China? Wake-up Call for a Small Planet*:

If industrialization is rapid, the loss of cropland quickly overrides the rise in land productivity, leading to a decline in grain production. The same industrialization that shrinks the cropland area also raises income, and with it the consumption of livestock products and the demand for grain. Ironically, the faster industrialization proceeds, the more rapidly the gap widens between rising demand and falling production.

There are many factors that make the quantification of the impact of dietary shifts on land availability difficult: for example, a decreasing birth rate with increasing standard of living. Also, the extent to which different cultures integrate different foods into their diet will vary, and different regions will be able to produce higher-value goods using various amounts of resources (WHO/FAO, 2002). As the demand for foods with a higher land requirement increases, sustainable and efficient land use systems will become increasingly important.

Emerging resources: dedicated energy crops
Dedicated energy crops capable of producing high yields per unit area, as well as growing on marginal or currently underutilized lands, can potentially play a key role in providing bioenergy feedstocks that minimize negative impacts to worldwide food supplies. The US Department of Energy (DOE) Regional Biomass Feedstock Partnership has assembled a network of researchers and field trials that focus on developing and commercializing these dedicated energy crops. The partnership includes land grant universities through the Sun Grant Initiative, USDA-ARS researchers and DOE national laboratories. The specific feedstocks of interest include energycane, miscanthus, switchgrass and sorghum herbaceous species, as well as hybrid popular and willow woody species.

Coordinated field trials have been under way since 2008 for the herbaceous species mentioned previously. Early yield results are encouraging. Switchgrass field trial yields have ranged from over 14 dry tonnes per hectare (Heaton, 2009; Owen, 2009) to greater than 24 dry tonnes per hectare (Baldwin, 2009). Miscanthus field trials yielded over 46 dry tonnes per hectare in Illinois (Heaton, 2009). For energycane, a range of 49 to 62 dry tonnes per hectare was achieved (Rainbolt and

Gilbert, 2008), and 54 dry tonnes per hectare were achieved for a selected F_1 wild cane x sugar cross tested in Starkville, Mississippi during the 2008–09 growing season (Baldwin, 2009). Photoperiod sensitive energy sorghum field trials yielded 30 to 37 dry metric t/ha (Rooney *et al.*, 2007). However, sugarcane is perhaps the crop having the largest potential, with productivity of 98 dry t/ha/yr achieved in experimental trials.

These herbaceous species, along with dedicated woody species, provide an opportunity to minimize negative impacts to food supplies by producing bioenergy feedstocks at large volumes per unit area, and by growing feedstock on marginal or underutilized lands.

Framing the challenge
The research community is beginning to agree that biofuels production offers a viable path forward, but there is a difficult balance between food, energy and the environment. Tilman *et al.* (2009) state that:

> In a world seeking solutions to its energy, environmental, and food challenges, society cannot afford to miss out on the global greenhouse-gas emission reductions and the local environmental and societal benefits when biofuels are done right. However, society also cannot accept the undesirable impacts of biofuels done wrong. [See also Chapters 5 and 7.]

With a significant potential resource base established, the following discussion looks at two primary challenges within the agriculture sector for supporting 'biofuels done right'. These challenges are (1) implementing production systems that are sustainable over the long term; and (2) creating accessible markets that provide economic viability while maximizing the quantity of resource that enters the system.

Meeting the challenge: sustainable agricultural systems

The concept of sustainable agriculture has been debated for several decades. For the purposes of this discussion, the 1990 US Farm Bill definition is used: sustainable agriculture is

> an integrated system of plant and animal production practices having a site-specific application that will, over the long term

- Satisfy human food and fibre needs
- Enhance environmental quality and the natural resource base upon which the agricultural economy depends
- Make the most efficient use of non-renewable resources and on-farm resources and integrate, where appropriate, natural biological cycles and controls
- Sustain the economic viability of farm operations, and
- Enhance the quality of life for farmers and society as a whole. (FACTA, 1990)

The first step: second-generation biofuels feedstocks

The social, economic and environmental effects of domestic biofuels have been mixed (Fargione *et al.*, 2008; Searchinger *et al.*, 2008). Diverting corn, soybean oil or other food crops to biofuel production has been seen by some critics as inducing competition between food, feed, fibre and fuel. However, the increases in crop prices that result from increased demand have helped revive rural economies. From the perspective of farmers and small rural communities, development of ethanol plants has created greater local demand for commodity crops and higher prices (see Chapter 1) for corn and soybean. Local investment and control of ethanol and biodiesel plants has invigorated many small US communities by providing well-paid employment opportunities. For example, in 2003 alone the US ethanol industry helped create more than 238,000 jobs in all sectors of the American economy, created billions in both state and federal tax revenues, and boosted household income by over \$12 billion (Urbanchuk, 2007). Proposed expansion of the biofuels industry would deliver a twenty-fold increase in the annual production recorded in 2003. Some argue, however, that the number of jobs added to the local economy is overestimated (Low and Isserman, 2009).

The premise of this discussion is that sustainable feedstock supplies for biofuel production cannot be achieved simply by expanding corn grain and soybean production (Keeney, 2008). Rather, we suggest developing lignocellulosic feedstocks and conversion processes that will have numerous advantages, including their availability from sources that do not compete with food and feed production. Biomass can be reclaimed from municipal solid waste streams and residual products of forestry and farming operations. It can also be grown on marginal or underused cropland, minimizing competition with food, feed and fibre production. Plant biomass also has the potential to play an important role in the global energy future because it can be grown in a sustainable manner and converted into liquid transportation fuels using either biochemical or thermochemical conversion processes.

The next step: sustainability in modern agricultural systems

To foster development of biomass feedstock operations, a good course of action is to develop a landscape or agro-ecoregion approach that capitalizes on soil and plant diversity. To fully grasp our sustainable landscape-management vision, it is helpful to review some of the agricultural changes that have occurred around the world during the past 75 years. Technological advances have resulted in greater crop yields, highly efficient animal production enterprises, new products and global marketing systems. But these advances have also created many new concerns. There has been a consistent, steady decline in the number and diversity of crops being grown in most watersheds. This has resulted in longer periods when precipitation gradually fills up available soil pore space, and biological processes such as nitrogen (N) mineralization occur in the absence of living plants needed to capture sunlight, fix carbon, and accumulate available water and nutrients.

In addition, many wetlands were artificially drained, streams straightened, and riparian vegetation removed to allow for increased areas of row crop production and to ease machinery operations. With regard to hydrology, these changes reduced residence time for surface and near-surface water. This increased the speed of water movement from land to streams and resulted in 'flashier' stream flows that subsequently led to more frequent and greater flood events. It also increased transport of sediment, nutrient, and chemical contaminants to water resources, thus contributing to eutrophication and problems such as Gulf hypoxia, a process in which low dissolved oxygen concentration makes water uninhabitable for aquatic organisms.

The contrast between positive benefits and negative consequences of technological advances is often at the heart of sustainability debates.

With this in mind, we are optimistic that increased demand for feedstock used in producing biofuels and bioproducts will offer many opportunities to increase the net environmental benefits of agriculture, especially if improved management practices are implemented using site-specific technologies, including:

- Erosion
- Soil, water, and air quality
- Carbon sequestration
- Rural community employment and out-migration
- Transportation corridors
- Wildlife habitat
- General aesthetics in rural areas.

CASE STUDY

Implementing sustainabilty criteria to guide resource access

Assessing agricultural sustainability hinges on the identification of key measures that account for the interplay among such agricultural practices as crop rotations, soil type, fertilizer applications and water use, as well as measures that account for both market factors and producer viability. The challenge, of course, is identifying measures effective in assessing sustainability and then understanding what these measures mean over time so that they can be deployed in tools useful to practitioners and policy makers alike.

Background
Agricultural residues such as corn stover and wheat straw play an important role in maintaining/improving sustainability of soil tilth, protecting the soil surface from water and wind erosion, and helping to maintain nutrient levels. The limits that must be set for their removal from cropland for bioenergy use is directly influenced by a number of factors mentioned previously. This context is the focus of the analysis performed in this case study.

Approach

Estimates were made of removable corn and sorghum stover, wheat straw, and/or herbaceous energy crop quantities (dry tonnes) at the individual field level (considering, for example, soil type) for seven counties in south-central Kansas. The overall approach involved applying certain physical and geoclimatic sustainability criteria at the individual soil-type level to estimate residue retention levels as a function of soil erosion, which directly affect residue removal levels. The major criteria involved (1) the slope and erodibility of individual soils within a county; (2) land base classification with respect to four geoclimatic parameters; (3) the level of rainfall and/or wind erosion force present; and (4) the type of crop, yield and rotation. In testing the Uniform-Format biomass supply systems (Hess *et al.*, 2009a), south-central Kansas was the location chosen for analysis of sustainable levels of residue removal. This choice was influenced by the presence of significant differences in types and acreages of crops, yields, rotations, and soils, as well as a combination of rainfall and wind-induced soil erosion forces.

Land base characterization

To predict the amount of soil erosion and obtain estimates of required residue retention rates and removable residue quantities, the physical characteristics of each cropland soil must be known. The Soil Survey Geographic (SSURGO) database provides the most detailed level of information (data at the individual field level) regarding the physical characteristics (soil erodibility [K], field slope, land capability class, tolerable soil loss limits, etc.) of all cropland soils.

Land capability classifications

All individual soils in each county of the United States are grouped into separate land capability classifications (LCCs) that are directly used in planning conservation measures and indirectly used to measure or demonstrate the suitability of a particular soil for producing most kinds of agricultural field crops. Soils are grouped mainly by their ability to sustainably produce common cultivated crops and pasture plants (Helms, 1992). Each soil is assigned an LCC ranging from 1 to 8, with

Class 1 and 2 soils being prime farmland and having low erosion rates. Class 5, 6, and 7 soils have a much higher propensity to erode and be less productive; in some cases they are used as pasture and rangeland. Class 8 soils are primarily non-agricultural.

Kansas analysis

Two previous analyses used the Revised Universal Soil Loss Equation (RUSLE) and the Wind Erosion Equation (WEQ) to estimate quantities of crop residues (corn stover, wheat straw) throughout the United States that need to remain at the individual field level (residue retention rate) to maintain soil loss at or below USDA-imposed tolerable soil-loss levels (Nelson, 2002; Nelson *et al.*, 2003). The tolerable soil loss (T) is defined as the maximum rate of soil erosion that will not lead to prolonged deterioration and/or loss of productivity. Residue retention rates are a function of field physical characteristics (slope, soil type), geoclimatic

Table 4.1 Variation in required residue retention for continuous corn (Sumner County, Kansas) on select soils subject to rainfall and wind forces and two different field management practices (tillage)

Soil type	LCC	Soil erodibility (K)[a]	Average field slope (%)	Tolerable soil loss (t/ha/yr)	Residue remain (rainfall erosion) (t/ha/yr)		Residue remain (wind erosion) (t/ha/yr)	
					Reduced tillage	No-till	Reduced tillage	No-till
Crisfield	1	0.20	1	12.2	0.13	0.00	6.20	4.48
Farnum	1	0.28	0.5	12.2	0.02	0.00	4.88	3.61
Shellabarger	2	0.20	2	12.2	1.63	0.25	6.20	4.48
Pratt	4	0.17	5.5	12.2	5.08	1.75	7.50	5.73
Owens	4	0.32	2	12.2	8.22	3.92	8.15	5.73
Rosehill	4	0.32	4.5	12.2	9.59	5.06	7.50	5.33
Kirkland	4	0.43	2	12.2	5.17	1.79	4.23	3.18
Renfrow	4	0.43	3.5	12.2	7.68	3.49	4.23	3.18
Elandco	5	0.43	0.5	12.2	0.25	0.02	4.23	3.18
Drummond	6	0.43	0.5	4.5	2.80	0.63	5.55	4.03

a] Soil erodibility factor, a dimensionless value, representing both susceptibility of soil to erosion and rate of run-off. A lower value indicates lower susceptibility.

variables (precipitation, wind), and field management practices (tillage).

Table 4.1 provides an example of residue retention rates for select soils with respect to rainfall and wind erosion forces for continuous corn production in Sumner County, Kansas, subject to mulch/reduced tillage (MT) and no-till (NT) field management scenarios. While not all soils in a county would be used to grow any one crop, these analyses show the magnitude of residue needed to protect against erosion if they were produced on any one of them.

Sustainability criteria hierarchy for crop assignment on individual soils
For Kansas and the rest of the United States, no accurate and consistent data exist concerning which crops are grown in individual soils within a county. Crop planting selection is primarily based on market conditions with the assumption that certain crops and field management practices will not be employed to protect soil sustainability (productivity). In general, feed-based grains (corn and grain sorghum) tend to be more erosive than small grains (wheat, barley, oats, et cetera) on the same soil subject to the same erosion forces. Therefore, feed grains would possibly be produced on LCC 1 and 2 soils, and small grains, while suitable to LCCs of 1 and 2, may be produced on LCCs of 3 to 5. National Agricultural Statistics Service (NASS) crop yields were used to provide average annual production levels (tonnes per hectare) for corn, grain sorghum, soybeans and winter wheat to determine corn stover and winter wheat straw quantities. A majority of the cropping rotations in this area are continuous wheat and a feed grain (corn or sorghum)-soybean-winter wheat rotation. Higher yields for all crops within the county were assigned to LCC soils of 1 and 2, while lesser yields were assigned LCCs of 3 to 5.

In addition, for those soils deemed highly erodible, it is probable that they would not be in crop production and could be in pasture or grassland. These lands may also be candidates for production of herbaceous energy crops (HECs) depending upon a number of physical/topological factors (slope, for example) that could affect herbaceous energy crop establishment and sustained production.

One important agriculturally based sustainability parameter is the erosion index (EI), which is a measure of the propensity of a particular soil to erode given a number of physical and geoclimatic factors. EI is created by dividing potential rainfall and wind-induced erosion, calculated from the RUSLE or WEQ equations, by the tolerable soil loss: soils classified as highly susceptible to rainfall and/or wind erosion forces have an EI greater than 8.

In addition, individual field slope and LCC can affect whether commodity crops are produced and, if so, which field managements (tillage) are employed. These agricultural and geoclimatic attributes were used to develop a possible 'sustainability-based' hierarchy for assigning crops, rotations and yields to individual soils within the seven-county region in south-central Kansas.

For each individual soil type with an EI equal to or greater than 8, slope equal to or greater than 6 percent, or LCC equal to or greater than 5, the acres were assigned to prairie (PR), meaning that, from a soil sustainability perspective, they were in native pasture or grassland. If these conditions were not met, the soil type was assigned to a commodity crop or for possible herbaceous energy development. If the soil physical parameters allowed for possible commodity crop production or the possibility of herbaceous energy crop development, the determination of which crops or HEC was made according to the following criteria:

1) If $T < 4$, then assigned to herbaceous energy crop development
2) If $K > 0.43$, then assigned to pasture
3) If $LCC = 1$, then assigned to corn, grain sorghum, and wheat rotation
4) If $LCC > 2$, then assigned to continuous wheat.

From previous analyses, the amount of residue that must remain on the field for the individual soil type in each of the seven counties with respect to rainfall and wind erosion forces is known as a function of tillage practice. In south-central Kansas, no dominant erosion force between rainfall and wind exists, so an average value for remaining residue for corn, grain sorghum and wheat was calculated for each individual soil type. Table 4.2 presents data on the assignment, based on the above criteria, of commodity crop, HEC, and prairie to select soils in Reno County in south-central Kansas. The residue that could be removed is the difference in the last two columns of Table 4.2. For prairie (PR) and HEC, the residue quantity columns are held at zero. For the corn, grain sorghum, and wheat (C GS W) rotation, and the continuous wheat management, this technique is used to demonstrate sustainable residue removal based on existing yield data.

Table 4.2 Cropping practice, yield assignment, and residue production

Soil type – component name	LCC	Cropping rotation[a]	Hectares	Ave. annual agr. crop residue produced (dry tonne/ha)	Residue that needs to remain (dry tonne/ha)	Residue to remove, (dry tonne/ha)
Avans	1	C GS W	6255	6.90	2.51	4.39
Ost	2	Wheat	1365	5.85	0.60	5.22
Clark	2	PR	899	0.00	0.00	0.00
Clark	2	PR	4275	0.00	0.00	0.00
Solvay	2	Wheat	2785	5.85	0.60	5.24
Zellmont	2	HEC	1978	0.00	0.00	0.00
Nalim	2	Wheat	7573	5.85	0.60	5.24
Nalim	2	PR	324	0.00	0.00	0.00
Avans	2	Wheat	523	5.85	0.87	4.97
Piedmont	2	HEC	681	0.00	0.00	0.00
Smolan	2	PR	592	0.00	0.00	0.00
Kaskan	2	HEC	212	0.00	0.00	0.00
Tobin	2	Wheat	137	5.85	0.43	5.40
Buhler	2	HEC	797	0.00	0.00	0.00
Dillhut	3	PR	584	0.00	0.00	0.00
Saxman	3	Wheat	196	3.78	0.60	3.20
Imano	3	PR	230	0.00	0.00	0.00
Jamash	4	HEC	681	0.00	0.00	0.00
Piedmont	4	PR	379	0.00	0.00	0.00
Piedmont	4	HEC	477	0.00	0.00	0.00
Longford	4	Wheat	464	3.78	0.87	2.91
Dillwyn	4	PR	1261	0.00	0.00	0.00
Ninnescah	5	PR	1034	0.00	0.00	0.00
Lucien	6	PR	185	0.00	0.00	0.00

a) C GS W = corn, grain sorghum, and wheat rotation; HEC = energy crop, PR = prairie

Residue required to be left on site and removable residue quantities were calculated for all individual soils in each of the counties. These data were employed to generate supply curves (quantities of biomass available at specific edge-of-field costs).

Case study conclusions
This case study demonstrates a solid understanding and capability of determining and implementing sustainable practices relative to agricultural residue removal. The challenging reality is that implementing these criteria to determine good practices within current management scenarios generally leads to less resource available for biofuels production. Maximizing the productive capacity of the land, while adhering to sustainability and ecosystem service constraints, will require a new approach to landscape management. This approach will advance a modern and dynamic agricultural sector that assembles the most advanced science and technologies to utilize each feature of the landscape in its most productive capacity.

Introducing the landscape management vision
By incorporating annual, perennial and intercropping mixtures into future farming operations, a diversified landscape can help address a number of the previously discussed interrelated land management concerns. Implementing this type of landscape-scale vision will also address many concerns regarding productive capacity to support a biofuels industry (see, for example, Doornbosch and Steenblik, 2007; Ernsting and Boswell, 2007; Fargione *et al.*, 2008; Searchinger *et al.*, 2008).

To understand the sustainable landscape vision, it is important to recognize that agriculture is more than farms, farmers and commodity crops (corn, soybean, wheat, cotton, rice and sugarcane). Developing lignocellulosic feedstocks and biofuel enterprises within definable watersheds could provide several unique opportunities to more fully integrate economic, environmental and social aspects of agriculture into integrated systems. By planning to harvest only in areas where the amount of crop residue exceeds that required to maintain soil resources (Lal, 2006) and striving to develop dedicated bioenergy crops, agriculture as a system could help mitigate increased nitrate (NO_3-N)

Figure 4.2 Landscape management vision to more fully integrate economic, environmental, and social aspects of agriculture into integrated systems to produce food, feed, fibre, and fuel sustainably (Photo courtesy of USDA-NRCS)

concentrations in streams and groundwater, the need for dredging of sediments, and potential hypoxia problems.

By using biofuel feedstock production as the economic driver, many ecosystem services could be captured through implementation of a landscape management plan that includes establishing woody species as buffers near streams and long-term perennial biomass crops at slightly higher landscape positions (NAS, NAE, NRC, 2009). These vegetative buffers could reduce leaching of NO_3-N and run-off of soluble phosphorus (P) while sequestering carbon (C) for several months, before being harvested as feedstocks during their dormant period. Slightly higher on the landscape, diverse perennial mixtures of warm season grasses and cool season legumes could produce biomass and store organic carbon in soils. In autumn, these perennials would provide a source of biomass, providing at least three landscape management benefits (biomass production, C sequestration, and water quality). Further up the landscape, a diversified rotation of annual and perennial crops would be used to meet food, feed and fibre needs. Erosion could be partially mitigated by using cover crops and/or living mulches. Intensive row crop production areas could be established using best management practices (BMPs); if fertilizer recovery was less than desired, there would be substantial buffer areas at lower landscape positions to capture residual nutrients and sediment.

Currently, our landscape vision is conceptual, but calculations based on a recent US study in Iowa suggest that converting just 10 percent of a watershed from no-tillage corn and soybean to strips of herbaceous perennial plants could decrease water run-off by 49 percent and soil erosion by 96 percent, while simultaneously increasing native plant, bird and beneficial insect populations (Liebman, 2009). This confirms that understanding complex interactions between economics, soil and crop management decisions, productivity and environmental consequences can result in agricultural systems that would meet global food, feed, fibre and fuel demands in a truly sustainable manner.

Meeting the challenge: engineering accessible markets

Available resources are not just those that can be sustainably grown, but also those that can be economically collected and transported to the conversion facility. Ensuring that diverse and integrated biomass production systems can economically integrate with existing commodity markets, as well as an emerging biofuels industry, will require a fundamental shift in current biorefinery supply systems concepts.

Conventional systems: the current dynamic

The feedstock supply system encompasses all operations necessary to format and move biomass from the location of production (field) to the biorefinery (Hess *et al.*, 2003). The logistics of biomass collection, storage, preprocessing, handling and transportation represent one of the largest challenges to this industry, and the supply system logistics associated with these activities can make up 40 to 60 percent of total ethanol production costs (Fales *et al.*, 2007). These designs do work

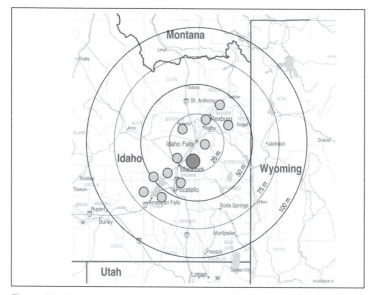

Figure 4.3 Typical sugar beet distribution system. (The smaller pale circles represent sugar beet dump sites, and the larger darker circle represents the processing facility.)

today because they adapt to the local available biomass resources and facilitate producer participation by minimizing perturbations to their present operations, and by reducing the investment risks associated with new and unproven supply system equipment. However, the conventional supply systems do not scale up economically to the scales envisioned in the future.

A production analogy: sugar beets vs grain
The limits of conventional biomass refinery systems can be demonstrated using the analogy of sugar beets. Fewer than 30 sugar beet processing factories are operating in the US, all located in or near production areas to minimize transport costs and reduce sugar losses (Ali, 2004). This makes the processing operation vulnerable to local weather conditions, disease and pests, as well as constraining market access for producers not currently in the contracting regions of the existing processing facilities.

According to a report issued by the University of Wisconsin and University of Minnesota (UW/UM, 2000), sugar beet production should not be initiated without first securing a market, as market access may be the greatest obstacle facing sugar beet farmers in the northern US. Existing processing facilities do not have excess capacity, as they are farmer-owned cooperatives. If the opportunity arises to accept more sugar beets at the refinery, the existing suppliers (that is, the owners) have the option to grow and supply the feedstock, and a new grower must purchase shares or an existing contract from the cooperative. A typical sugar beet distribution system is shown in Figure 4.3.

The sugar beet system would present several challenges as a model for emerging bioenergy-based production and supply systems. A primary limitation is effectively providing accessible markets across the productive landscape. Potentially highly productive land will fall outside of the contracting region for facilities, thus stranding significant production capacity. Maximizing the landscape's ability to produce bioenergy resources will require providing accessible markets to all capable regions. This leaves grower production decisions to funda-mental economics and creates an environment where bioenergy systems can integrate into the landscape.

Contrary to the sugar beet supply system, grain commodity markets effectively move billions of tons of aerobically stable, dense, flowable bulk-solid biomass to biorefineries around the globe. Storage and handling systems for grain are highly replicable, scalable, and optimized for cost-effective performance. The grain system storage tanks and their loading/unloading systems are typically sold and constructed as 'turnkey' systems that are assembled with common interchangeable and replicable components to meet a customer's performance specification. This dynamic provides an opportunity for highly efficient and economical implementation. Consistent, uniform material properties of grain allow trucks and trains to seamlessly move biomass large distances to terminals or destination markets.

Another important consequence of grain's material characteristics is the ability to blend, grade and efficiently track material throughout trading within the supply system. In the case of corn grain, distributors employ fast screening methods to test and blend feedstock to stringent specifications of individual biorefineries, as well as maintaining the integrity of the food supply for non-genetically modified organism (GMO) consumers. This is possible by working with a uniform-format material with adequate bulk density and flowability performance that allows a common, replicable set of high-capacity bulk-solids handling equipment to be employed throughout the supply system.

On-farm storage, depots or elevators, blending terminals and biorefineries all work together to create a local, regional, national and even worldwide set of markets for grain commodities. These markets are highly efficient and effective at connecting the resource with end users within tight specifications. These connections are not limited by distance and mitigate local production risks for all uses of grain commodities by allowing wider access to resources.

The uniform-format solution: biomass as a corollary to grain commodities
While national US assessments identify sufficient biomass resource to supply the biomass volume required to meet national fuel production goals, much of that resource is inaccessible using current biomass supply systems because of unfavourable economics. Increasing the demand for lignocellulosic biomass introduces many logistical challenges to providing an economic, efficient and reliable supply of quality feed-stock to the biorefineries.

One strategy to address these logistic challenges is the gradual transition from existing biomass supply systems to an economic and reliable commodity-scale supply system that provides uniform, aerobically stable, quality-controlled feedstocks to biorefineries (Hess *et al.*, 2009a). This uniform-format strategy takes advantage of the highly efficient, scalable, and economic bulk solids handling infrastructure that is used today for grain.

Hess *et al.* (2009a) detail two feedstock supply system designs: the Conventional Bale Feedstock Supply System Design ('Conventional Bale'), which reflects current practice, and the Uniform-Format Supply System Design ('Uniform-Format'), which locates the preprocessing unit operation as early in the supply system as practically possible, minimizing logistical issues arising from transporting and handling dispersed, low-density, often aerobically unstable biomass. The

Uniform-Format system is presented in two implementations: (1) a Pioneer Uniform system that uses current or very near-term technologies and offers incremental improvements over the Conventional Bale system and (2) an Advanced Uniform system that meets all cost and supply targets and requires some conceptual equipment, such as advanced processing systems, to provide a commodity-scale bulk solid feedstock. The Advanced Uniform system is demonstrated using a pellet

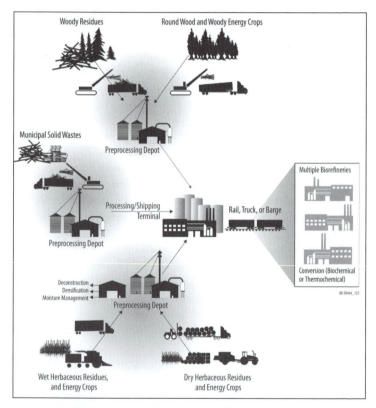

Figure 4.4. The Advanced Uniform-Format feedstock supply system emulates the current grain commodity supply system, which manages crop diversity at the point of harvest and at the biomass depot/elevator, allowing subsequent supply system infrastructure to be similar for all biomass resources

(Hess *et al.*, 2009a). (Image courtesy of Idaho National Laboratory)

format; however, there are many possible bulk solid formats that could be implemented (such as granules, powder, or briquettes).

The Pioneer Uniform design enables the transition from the Conventional Bale to the Advanced Uniform supply system by developing the supply chain infrastructure required for forward-deployed preprocessing. The Advanced Uniform system formats biomass of various types (such as corn stover or switchgrass) and physical characteristics (bulk densities, moisture content and so on) into a standardized format early in the supply chain. This uniform material format allows biomass to be handled as a commodity that can be bought and sold in a market, vastly increasing its availability to the biorefinery and enabling large-scale facilities to operate with a continuous, consistent and economic feedstock supply. The commodity-scale system also removes the obligation for local farmers to contract directly with the biorefineries for biomass feedstocks.

Biomass commodities are storable and transportable and have many end uses. Implementing a commodity-based feedstock supply system promotes cropping options beyond local markets, which in turn promotes crop diversity and enhances crop rotation practices. Figure 4.4 provides a diagram of the end-state commodity supply system.

The supply system represented in Figure 4.4 incorporates many species and types of biomass that can be formatted at specialized biomass preprocessing depots. This provides communities with multiple options for participating in the bioenergy industry. The preprocessed biomass can be converted locally as appropriate to provide local energy needs, or it can be transported from the depots to central blending terminals, where it may be blended to end-use specifications to form a variety of consistent, uniformly formatted, and aerobically stable products. The biomass is then managed as a commodity to be distributed according to its highest value to biorefineries. The distribution system is analogous to the grain industry. As there are various grades of corn, different feedstocks could be blended to meet the needs of different conversion processes.

The Uniform-Format design overcomes the physical and equipment barriers inherent in working with biomass. This is accomplished by increasing the material dry matter bulk density through size reduction, reducing moisture content through drying, improving equipment performance to minimize dry matter losses, and taking advantage of biomass material properties to facilitate material deconstruction. The Uniform-Format system produces a commodity product, reduces plant handling costs, and is conducive to the long-term biomass supply sustainability required to meet the US annual biofuel production goals of 60 billion gallons by 2030.

This commodity system increases crop production options by providing access to diverse local and non-local markets. This allows producers to grow crops in rotation without being bound to supply contracts and limited local demand. Increasing cropping options promotes enhanced sustainable crop rotation practices (Kitchen *et al.*, 2005; Lerch *et al.*, 2005; USDA-NRCS, 2007; Williams *et al.*, 2008; Yan *et al.*, 2007).

The uniform-format solution: supply economics and accessing stranded resources

As discussed previously, available resources are not just those that can be sustainably grown, but also those that can be economically accessed, collected and transported to the conversion facility. Grower payments are the costs incurred to access the biomass and are in addition to the logistics costs for harvest and collection, moving the biomass to the field edge, and transport to the refinery. Grower payments are difficult to assess because there are no major markets for crop residues or related biomass feedstocks, such as energy crops, from which to impute a value (Hess *et al.*, 2009b). These estimated grower payments will, for the most part, reflect a minimum selling price and may be affected by residue density and availability where sold, competition for the feedstock in other uses (such as animal bedding), and the presence of alternative or substitute biofuel feedstocks. For low grower payments, supply will be limited to areas that can produce the biomass at the least cost. In the United States, this would confine corn stover to the midwestern Corn Belt states. However, as the grower payment increases, the amount of biomass entering the system would increase and the draw area (and therefore transport cost) would expand, but sustainability concerns will also need to come into play.

In the United States, many models analysing feedstock supply

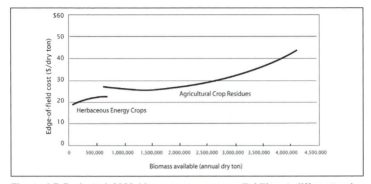

Figure 4.5 Projected 2008 biomass resource availability at different price levels without a grower payment

systems simplify the grower payment by assuming that a $10/ton biomass resource is the only feedstock that will be passing through the feedstock supply system (Aden *et al.*, 2002; Perlack *et al.*, 2005; Hess *et al.*, 2009a), and that the necessary amount of feedstock would be supplied at this cost. However, with increased demand for biomass and an increasing drive to understand total biofuels production cost, a more rigorous method of determining feedstock cost is needed. In addition, all categories of feedstock – from excess biomass, to residue co-products, to dedicated energy crops – will feed the supply system. Access to these resources is often constrained by agronomic, environmental, market, policy, and other limiting factors.

Kansas State University (KSU) participated in a study that shows an example of the effort to move beyond this $10/ton assumption and get a more realistic assessment of biomass resource availability. KSU developed a methodology for determining a better estimate of biomass supply, both in terms of type and quantity, which would enter the supply system as a function of grower payment and regional parameters. The study evaluated seven counties within the Tennessee Valley Authority power generation service region. The model of energy crop price and supply used in this analysis was based on the assumption that farmer/producers will convert their agricultural land to biomass production when the profit received from producing biomass meets or exceeds their profit margins from conventional agricultural crops or using their land for pasture. The study was able to roughly quantify the leverage points where farmers were willing to convert their crops to meet the needs of biorefineries. The data were then used to determine how much biomass will be available as the grower payment increases. Figure 4.5 shows the biomass supply available in the United States compiled using data from survey and modelling work performed under contract with Oak Ridge National Laboratory.

Figure 4.5 shows an example of the variation in biomass availability as a function of price, based on average annual biomass availability in Kansas and not including payment to the grower. The analysis included considerations of soil type, crop yields and land slope, and marginal lands were used for energy crop production. Figure 4.5 shows that as the purchase price increases, more biomass becomes available. This is intuitive; for example, more expensive recovery methods can be used at a higher purchase price. As well, at a very low purchase cost, only energy crops are available as it is assumed they are grown on marginal lands. The higher-value grain crops which yield the agricultural residues are grown on higher-quality lands, and therefore have a higher cost. As well, at a very low purchase cost, only energy crops are available as it is assumed they are grown on marginal lands. The higher-value grain crops which yield the agricultural residues are grown on higher-quality lands, and therefore have a higher cost.

Without the Uniform-Format solution and restricted 50-mile (80 km) radius transportation distance, there is potential for stranded resources. The variation in wheat straw residue availability from year to year supports the need for a Uniform-Format solution. Dry-land farming depends on precipitation that varies greatly from one year to the next. When rainfall is good, yields are good; however, in good rainfall years, too good for all the biomass to be utilized within the 50-mile radius, thus stranding resources. When rainfall is below average or insufficient for good cereal yields, there is too little biomass within the 50-mile radius to supply a refinery dependent on straw. In addition, the biorefinery competes for residue needed to sustain and maintain soil quality. To maintain sustainable production, cereal residue ranging from 3.4 to 5.6 tonnes/ha must remain in place in the field (Banowetz *et al.*, 2008). The wide range in these values depends on field location, soil type, soil slope and rainfall.

Conclusion

A variety of issues has been raised with respect to agriculture and bio-fuel production, and a number of conclusions can be drawn from the discussions in this chapter. First, there is abundant land available world-wide for agricultural production including crops for biofuel. Several dynamic issues, such as changing diets, growing populations and sustainability considerations will all place constraints on how this land will be used. The critical issue is to maximize aggregate productive capacity of all agricultural products while meeting these constraints and determining the best productive use of each landscape feature, as previously described.

Second, new commodity biomass feedstock supply system concepts will need to emerge that create accessible markets and provide economic viability while maximizing the quantity of resource that enters the system. The Uniform-Format concept will provide a gradual transi-tion from existing biomass supply systems to an economic and reliable commodity-scale supply system that provides uniform, aerobically stable, quality-controlled feedstocks to biorefineries. Furthermore, critical markets and economic drivers will be facilitated to support next-generation production systems.

The coupling of the sustainable landscape vision with the Uniform-Format supply system design provides a promising platform for what Tilman *et al.* (2009) describe as 'biofuels done right', the necessary condition for sustainable and integrated food, feed, fuel, and fibre pro-duction. Establishing criteria, and mechanisms, for guiding sustainable agricultural management practices is critical for implementing the landscape vision. Creating accessible markets that facilitate highly inte-grated production management strategies through Uniform-Format supply system design concepts is equally critical, as a sustainable land-scape vision will struggle to emerge without these markets.

References

Aden, A., M. Ruth, K. Ibsen, J. Jechura, K. Neeves, J. Sheehan, B. Wallace, L. Montague, A. Slayton and J. Lukas (2002) 'Lignocellulosic biomass to ethanol process design and economics utilizing co-current dilute acid prehydrolysis and enzymatic hydrolysis for corn stover', report, National Renewable Energy Laboratory, Golden CO, NREL/TP-510-32438.

Ali, Mir B. (2004) 'Characteristics and production costs of US sugarbeet farms', Statistical Bulletin No. 974-8, Economic Research Service (ERS), US Department of Agriculture (USDA), October, <http://www.ers.usda.gov/publications/sb974-8/sb974-8.pdf>.

Baldwin, B. (2009) Personal communication.

Banowetz, G. M., A. Boateng, J. J. Steiner, S. M. Griffith, V. Sethi and H. El-Nashaar (2008) 'Assessment of straw biomass feedstock resources in the Pacific Northwest', *Biomass and Bioenergy* 32 (7): 629–34.

Brown, L. R. (1995) *Who Will Feed China? Wake-up Call for a Small Planet*, Norton, New York, NY.

Doornbosch, R. and R. Steenblik (2007) 'Biofuels: is the cure worse than the disease?', draft report, SG/SD/RT (2007) 3, OECD, Paris.

Ernsting, A. and A. Boswell (2007) 'Agrofuels: towards a reality check in nine key areas', iofuelwatch, <www.biofuelwatch.org.uk> (accessed 29 April 2009).

FACTA (1990) Public Law 101-624, Title XVI, Subtitle A, Section 1603, Government Printing Office, Washington DC, <http://frwebgate.access. gpo.gov/cgi-bin/getdoc.cgi?dbname=browse_usc&docid=Cite:+7US C3103>.

Fales, S. L., W. W. Wilhelm and J. R. Hess (2007) 'Convergence of agriculture and energy II: producing cellulosic biomass for biofuels', research publication, Council for Agricultural Science and Technology, Ames IA, 2007.

Fargione, J., J. Hill, D. Tillman, S. Polasky and P. Hawthorne (2008) 'Land clearing and the biofuel carbon debt', *Science* 319 (5867): 1235–8.

Fischer, B. (2008) 'Implications for land use change', paper presented at the Expert Meeting on Global Perspectives on Ruel and Food Security, FAO, 18–20 February 2008.

Gerbens-Leenes, P. W. and S. Nonhebel (2002) 'Consumption patterns and their effects on land required for food', *Ecological Economics* 42 (1–2): 185–99.

Grigg, D. (1994) 'Income, industrialization and food consumption', *Tijdschrift voor Economische en Sociale Geografie* 85: 3–14.

Heaton, E. (2009) Personal communication.

Helms, D. (1992) 'The development of the land capability classification' in *Readings in the History of the Soil Conservation Service*, Soil Conservation Service, Washington DC, pp. 60–73.

Hess, J. R., T. D. Foust, L. Wright, S. Sokhansanj, J. H. Cushman, J. L. Easterly, D. C. Erbach, J. R. Hettenhaus, R. Hoskinson, J. J. Sheehan, S. Tagore, D. N. Thompson and A. Turhollow (2003) 'Roadmap for agriculture biomass feedstock supply in the United States', research publication, US

Department of Energy, DOE/NE-ID-11129.

Hess, J. R, K. Kenney, P. Laney, D. Muth, P. Pryfogle, C. Radtke and C. Wright (2006) 'Feasibility of a producer-owned ground-straw feedstock supply system for bioethanol and other products', research publication, INL/EXT-06-11815, 2006.

Hess, J. R., K. L. Kenney, L. P. Ovard, E. M. Searcy and C. T. Wright (2009a) 'Uniform-format solid feedstock supply system: a commodity-scale design to produce an infrastructure-compatible bulk solid from lignocellulosic biomass', research publication, INL/EXT-08-14752, <www.inl.gov/bioenergy/uniform-feedstock>.

Hess, J. R, K. L. Kenney, C. T. Wright, R. D. Perlack and A. Turhollow (2009b) 'Corn stover availability for biomass conversion: situation analysis', *Cellulose* 16 (4): 599–619.

Johnson, J. M. F., D. C. Reicosky, R. R. Allmaras, D. Archer and W.W. Wilhelm (2006) 'A matter of balance: conservation and renewable energy', *Journal of Soil and Water Conservation* 61: 120A–5A.

Keeney, D. R. (2008) 'Ethanol USA', *Environmental Science and Technology* 43 (1): 8–11.

Kitchen, N. R., K. A. Sudduth, D. B. Myers, R. E. Massey, E. J. Sadler and R. N. Lerch (2005) 'Development of a conservation-oriented precision agriculture system: crop production assessment and plan implementation', *Journal of Soil and Water Conservation* 60 (6): 421–30.

Lal, R. (2006) 'Managing soils to feed a global population of 10 billion', *Journal of Science, Food and Agriculture* 86: 2273–84.

Lerch, R. N., N. R. Kitchen, R. J. Kremer, W. W. Donald, E. E. Alberts, E. J. Sadler, K. A. Sudduth, D. B. Myers and F. Ghidey (2005) 'Development of a conservation-oriented precision agriculture system: water and soil quality assessment', *Journal of Soil and Water Conservation* 60 (6): 411–21.

Liebman, M. (2009) Iowa State University, personal communication.

Low, S. A. and A. M. Isserman (2009) 'Ethanol and the local economy: industry trends, location factors, economic impacts, and risks', *Economic Development Quarterly* 23 (1): 71–88.

NAS, NAE, NRC (2009) *Liquid Transportation Fuels from Coal and Biomass: Technological Status, Costs, and Environmental Impacts*, prepared for America's Energy Future Panel on Alternative Liquid Transportation Fuels, National Academies Press, Washington DC, <http://www.nap.edu/`catalog/12620.html> (accessed 30 June 2009).

Nelson, R. G. (2002) 'Resource assessment and removal analysis for corn stover and wheat straw in the eastern and midwestern United States: rainfall and wind erosion methodology', *Biomass Bioenergy* 22: 349–63.

Nelson, R. G, M. E. Walsh, J. J. Sheehan and R. L. Graham (2003) 'Methodology to estimate removable quantities of agricultural residues for bioenergy and bioproduct use', *Applied Biochemistry and Biotechnology* 113: 0013–26.

Owen, V. (2009) Personal communication.

Pacala, S. and R. Socolow (2004) 'Stabilization wedges: solving the climate problem for the next 50 years with current technologies', *Science* 305: 968–72.

Patterson, P. E. (2003) 'Availability of straw in eastern Idaho', report, Idaho Wheat Commission, 26 September 2003.

Perlack, R. D., L. L. Wright, A. F. Turhollow, R. L. Graham, B. J. Stokes and D. C. Erbach (2005) 'Biomass as feedstock for a bioenergy and bioproducts industry: the technical feasibility of a billion-ton annual supply', research publiction, DOE/GO-102005-2135 and ORNL/TM-2005/66.

Rainbolt, C. and R. Gilbert (2008) 'Production of biofuel crops in Florida: sugarcane/energycane', research publication, University of Florida Extension, SSAGR 298.

Rooney, W. L., J. Blumenthal, B. Bean and J. E. Mullet (2007) 'Designing sorghum as a dedicated bioenergy feedstock', *Biofuels, Bioproducts and Biorefining* 1: 147–57.

Searchinger, T., R. Heimlich, R. A. Houghton, F. Dong, A. Elobeid, J. Fabiosa, S. Tokgoz, D. Hayes and T.-H. Yu (2008) 'Use of US croplands for biofuels increases greenhouse gases through emissions from land use change', *Science* 319 (5867): 1238–40.

Sheehan, J., A. Aden, K. Paustian, K. Killian, J. Brenner, M. Walsh and R. Nelson (2004) 'Energy and environmental aspects of using corn stover for fuel ethanol', *Journal of Industrial Ecology* 7 (3–4): 117–46.

Shinners, K. J. and B. N. Binversie (2007) 'Fractional yield and moisture of corn stover biomass produced in the northern US corn belt, 2007', *Biomass and Bioenergy* 31 (6): 576–84.

Shinners, K. J., G. C. Boettcher, J. T. Munk, M. F. Digman, R. F. Muck and P. J. Weimer (2007) 'Single-pass, split-stream of corn grain and stover: characteristic performance of three harvester configurations', *Transactions of the American Society of Agricultural and Biological Engineers (ASABE)* 50 (2): 355–63.

Smith, J. R., W. Richards, D. Acker, B. Flinchbaugh, R. Hahn, R. Heck, B. Horan, G. Keppy, A. Rider, D. Villwock, S. Wyant and E. Shea (2004) '25 x 25: Agriculture's role in ensuring US energy independence – a blueprint for action', <http://www.25x25.org/storage/25x25/documents/Blueprint.pdf> (6 June 2007).

Tilman, D., R. Socolow, J. A. Foley, J. Hill, E. Larson, L. Lynd, S. Pacala, J. Reilly, T. Searchinger, C. Somerville and R. Williams (2009) 'Beneficial biofuels – the food, energy, and environment trilemma', *Science* 325 (5938): 270–1.

Urbanchuk, J. M. (2007) 'Contribution of the ethanol industry to the economy of the United States', paper prepared for the Renewable Fuels Association, LECG LLC, 19 February.

USDA-NASS (US Department of Agriculture National Agricultural Statistics Service) (2008) 'Quick Stats', <http://www.nass.usda.gov/QuickStats/PullData_US.jsp>.

USDA-NRCS (US Department of Agriculture Natural Resources Conservation

Service) (2007) *National Soil Survey Handbook*, US Department of Agriculture Natural Resources Conservation Service, Washington DC.

UW/UM (University of Wisconsin/University of Minnesota) (2000) 'Alternative field crops manual', <http://www.hort.purdue.edu/newcrop/afcm/> (accessed 11 August 2009).

WHO/FAO (World Health Organization/Food and Agriculture Organization of the United Nations) (2002) 'Diet, nutrition, and the prevention of chronic diseases', WHO Technical Report Series 916, WHO.

Wilhelm, W. W., J. M. F. Johnson, J. L. Hatfield, W. B. Voorhees, and D. R. Linden (2004) 'Crop and soil productivity response to corn residue removal: a review of the literature', *Agronomy Journal* 96 (2004), pp. 1–17.

Williams, C. L., W. W. Hargrove, M. Liebman and D. E. James (2008) 'Agro-eco-regionalization of Iowa using multivariate geographical clustering', *Agriculture, Ecosystems and Environment* 123: 161–74.

Yan, L., S. Zhou, L. Feng and L. Hong-Yi (2007) 'Delineation of site-specific management zones using fuzzy clustering analysis in a coastal saline soil', *Computers, Electronics and Agriculture* 56: 174–86.

5 The Role of Biofuels in Promoting Rural Development

Rocio Diaz-Chavez

The use of biomass for energy is not new. It has long been and still is being used in the form of fuelwood, charcoal and animal dung, on which many rural areas in developing countries still depend heavily. Since the 'rediscovery' of the use of biomass for modern and more efficient applications in recent decades, the debate has highlighted the possible use of biomass for biofuels and its contribution to reducing global warming and dependency on fossil fuels (Haberl and Erb, 2006). Simultaneously, many issues related to the impact of bioenergy crop production have been raised. They include population growth; changes in human diet; the use of biomass for construction, feed, other uses (fibre, pharmaceutical); and the role of policy targets as a continuous and often controversial driving force in various countries.

Discussion of these various drivers in the debate has been impacted particularly sharply by the production and use of biofuels (also referred to as agrofuels) for transport. The debate on sustainability issues when promoting the use of biomass as a renewable energy source is not limited to the effect of biomass on land demand, the quality of land use, or greenhouse gases (GHG) savings. Undoubtedly, biomass resources play a major role in sustaining most activities in rural areas, particularly in the developing world. The use of biomass has been extensively studied, and much attention has been paid to its role in providing access to fuel in many poor rural communities (Pimentel et al., 1988; Rosillo-Calle and Hall, 1987). Nevertheless, the focus on the socio-economic impacts of traditional biomass use for fuel in rural areas remains distinct from the impact of the most recent developments brought about by the expansion of biofuels production.

Recently, the debate on the sustainability of production and use of biofuels has centred on the environmental benefits (contribution to the reduction of GHG emissions) as well as the negative impacts. Additional environmental concerns relate to water, soil, biodiversity, landscape impacts, conservation areas, and the use of genetically modified (GM) crops. The social and economic impacts commonly referred to are working conditions (wages, child and forced labour), land-use rights, health and safety. These sustainability aspects have been reviewed not only in scientific papers but also in declarations by NGOs (Bailey, 2008) and, more commonly, by different initiatives for establishing standards and certifications, such as the Roundtable for Sustainable Biofuels (RSB, 2009).

Among the main social benefits considered are the protection of existing employment, but also the generation of new jobs and the promotion of rural development with further incentives to reduce poverty. Nevertheless, to consider these benefits it is necessary to review the current local, regional and even global scale of agricultural production, cash crops, and rural and urban population. In terms of socio-economic impacts or benefits, bioenergy crops should not be treated differently to other crops that have an international or local market. Global or regional environmental benefits, such as GHG savings, have little relation to the livelihoods of small-scale producers or out-growers for larger-scale projects. This chapter looks instead at the implications for rural development of the growing but not yet fully developed market for bioenergy crops (and, particularly, biofuels) in the associated context of food production. The main benefits and negative impacts on job creation, food security, gender, infrastructure and the links to sustainability will be explored in this chapter.

Job creation and wages

Among the social benefits considered in biofuel production are the protection of existing employment and also the generation of new jobs. Both aspects can be considered not only at the agricultural stage but also at the processing or industrial stages (mill, production, and transport). Various economic opportunities exist along the extended biofuels supply chain.

Some attempts have been made to analyse the job-creation potential of biofuel production. There is an obvious difference between more intensive labour roles at the production stage and the range of employment that may be required at the processing stage. Nevertheless, this situation changes according to the type of crop considered. Many projects and country proposals overestimate the benefits of job creation; for example, one study noted that instead of 700 permanent jobs in the neighbourhood of an ethanol plant, a more realistic estimate was 130–150 (Earley and McKeown, 2009). In some cases the estimates do not consider job quality, fluctuation by season (harvest time, for example) or movement from one sector to other – for example, from livestock or dairy farms to corn production in the USA (Macedo, 2005; Earley and McKeown, 2009).

A Zambian example reviewed the case for sweet sorghum, considered to have strong potential as an energy crop due to its high yields of biomass and fermentable sugars. A recent study by the Zambian National Technical Committee on the Biofuels Development Framework (2007), basing its assessment on current employment ratios per hectare of sugarcane bioethanol production for use in petrol blends, estimated that employment in this sector would increase from 1,595 to 8,526 by 2015.

A report by Macedo (2005) explored the case of Brazil. During the 1990s sugarcane production generated 2,200 direct jobs for every million tons of sugarcane produced (1,600 in production and 600 in processing). Including indirect jobs, the whole industry employed 380,000 people in São Paulo State (responsible for more than 60 percent of ethanol production). From 2000 to 2002, the number of direct jobs in the sugarcane industry rose by about 18 percent (from 643,000 to 764,600). In 2002, 62 percent of all formal jobs in the industry were offered in Brazil's Centre-South region (which includes São Paulo), and the remainder in the North and North-East regions (Walter *et al.*, 2008).

According to this study, in 2002 the mean monthly salary for all industries in Brazil was R$483.24, while for the sugar industry it was R$501.64, and for the ethanol industry R$554.83. Salaries were higher in the Centre-South region compared to those in North and North-East regions (Macedo, 2005). At that time, workers employed in soybean and citrus cropping had higher incomes, while the lowest incomes were earned by workers engaged in corn and cassava cropping.

It has been estimated that creation of one job in the ethanol agro-industry requires on average US$11,000 of capital investment, while a job in the chemical and petrochemical industry costs 20 times more; in general the investment needed for job creation in the sugarcane/ethanol sector is much lower than in other industrial sectors (Goldemberg, 2000, cited in Walter *et al.*, 2008).

Other aspects that need to be considered are the quality of the jobs created, the potential for transfer of skills and introduction of new ones, and the educational opportunities and training provided. One example is the biofuel electrification programme designed by Winrock in Ranidehra, Kabirdham district, Chattisgarh, India. This project was initiated by Ministry of New and Renewable Energy, the British High Commission and the Swiss Agency for Development and Cooperation, and implemented by Winrock India. In Ranidehra village 110 households are benefiting from electrification using fuel from the oil of *Jatropha curcas* (L.) seeds. The project created three formal jobs in the village for the operators of the electrification system, in a process which included training and skills transfer (COMPETE, 2009).

The case of jatropha plantations tends to be more difficult to calculate as the collection of fruits is manual and varies from one case to another. Nevertheless, in general terms it can be said that one area of 4 hectares in full season (three months) will require one to two persons per day. The work is non-skilled and is normally combined with the other activities of the family when it is done on an out-grower basis. There is variation in the data as some producers count the number of bags of fruit or seeds collected and do not count the number of workers per area or per day. According to the Council of Scientific and Industrial Research (CSIR), India, the typical picking rates are 16 to 20 kg per day, but since we do not have data for high-yielding areas it is difficult to say what they might be if there was a 5 ton/ha yield. The data from the CSIR trials are for areas with a yield of no more than .2 ton/ha. If the seeds are removed from the fruit by hand, this requires almost as much labour as the picking itself.

There is evidence in some cases in developing countries that the cultivation of some feedstocks, notably sugarcane and palm oil, has been linked to poor working conditions, health and safety risks, and both child and forced labour (Dufey, 2006). In the rural areas (particularly in Africa) labour is mostly provided by women and children. According to Walter *et al.* (2008), the nature of the labour force depends also on the technology in use during the different cycles of the crop (such as harvest and the growing periods between harvests). Normally, low-technology options imply more temporary labour and low salaries, while advances in technology – as in sugarcane mechanization – can reduce significantly the number of jobs in the agriculture sector, often replaced by fewer jobs which are more permanent and more qualified.

The benefits of job creation also apply to developed countries, as in the case of Europe. For instance, research carried out by the East of England Development Agency has estimated that around 900 jobs could be created or sustained for each 1,000 tons of biofuel produced (EEDA, 2006). Job creation and greater community cohesion are among the overall benefits projected for biofuels production in Europe.

Another programme trying to combine social inclusion and regional development was developed in Brazil to contribute to the targets imposed by the Biodiesel Law of 2005. This programme 'Social Fuel Seal' (Selo Combustível Social) was established to produce bioenergy crops (for biodiesel) in Brazil's least-developed regions, the North and North-East, by poor families organized in cooperatives. This programme also helps the buyer, who pays less federal income tax and obtains access to finance from the Brazilian Development Bank (FAO, 2008).

Health and gender

Although much of the global interest in the production of biofuels has centred on their use in the transport sector (mainly in developed countries), other significant alternative uses in developing countries relate to electricity generation and use of cooking stoves. The main health-related drawbacks in the traditional use of biomass include indoor air pollution, the heavy burden on women and children in rural areas of developing countries that need to collect firewood, and injuries caused by burns and carrying wood (Schirnding *et al.*, 2000). This topic has been extensively researched by international organizations such as the United Nations Development Programme and many non-governmental organizations. The benefits of cooking stoves using different sources of biomass such as waste agriculture briquettes or the use of some biofuels (ethanol) have been demonstrated in Asia and Africa.

Aspects of health and gender related to the production of biofuels, particularly on a large scale, have been less researched. Among the issues addressed has been the impact of HIV-AIDS on labour in some African countries, and how this affects key sectors such as agriculture. This is an important issue to consider not just in relation to biofuel production but also in the wider context of wages and workforce composition in developing countries.

A report by Rossi and Lambrou (2008), for instance, points to the benefits of bioenergy crops in terms of social and economic issues such as the increased availability and affordability of energy for household and commercial uses, and new markets and incomes for rural farmers supplying the raw materials for bioenergy industries. Nevertheless, they consider that for real benefits to be realized it is necessary to consider the gains for both men and women – which means addressing the social constraints and cultural biases that limit women's access to education, training, and decision-making processes, and restrict their rights to own land, borrow money, engage in business, and benefit from government programmes such as agricultural extension services. The authors propose that integrating energy projects into other types of development programmes can help shift the focus from technology-driven energy interventions – looking instead at initiatives that include the community's social and economic development needs, and thus allowing women's interests to be better incorporated (Rossi and Lambrou, 2008).

Impacts on food production

The agricultural commodity base of first-generation biofuels has ramifications for the sustainability of the food and animal-feed supply system, and many countries are looking to other biomass resources and second-generation biofuels for sustained growth. Overend (2007) considers that the existing large-scale use of forest resources for bioenergy implies that future expansion of biomass supplies will be obtained from two sources: the residues associated with current agricultural commodity production and processing, and the cultivation of energy crops on available land. Energy crops pose some challenges, now widely debated, to sustainability. Significant land requirements create concern over land availability in comparatively small, highly populated countries such as the UK and the Netherlands. Nevertheless, in countries with lower population density and land availability – such as Argentina, Brazil, Canada, the USA, Russia and other countries in eastern Europe – increased land utilization is quite feasible (Overend, 2007). Several countries in Africa, Asia and Latin America are also part of this picture, but environmental, economic and social issues need to be addressed.

According to Connor and Hernandez (2009), it is often viable to grow both food and fuel. Some examples already exist, although reported only with regard to small-scale production. One is the Small-Scale Jatropha Plantation for Rural Electrification project supported by the Mali Folk Centre in Garalo Commune, Mali, West Africa. Here farmers are growing jatropha and intercropping it with a cash crop such as peanuts (COMPETE, 2009). This can be compared with the Winrock electrification project in Ranidehra, India, discussed above. There, jatropha is planted for electrification purposes as live fences or hedges, without using additional land.

While noting positive cases such as these, Connor and Hernandez (2009) argue that the use of food crop species to produce biofuels will remain problematic because of the debate at the heart of this book, food versus fuel. They consider that dedicated energy crops will not avoid competition with food production because there is still a resulting pressure on inputs such as land, water and nutrients. They acknowledge, however, that research and development could improve the potential for producing both food and biofuels, while also changing some of the parameters of the debate by bringing forward new crops for biofuels.

Agricultural commodities that can be marketed as cash crops by poor farmers in developing countries can reduce long-term poverty by allowing subsistence farmers to invest in favour of productivity gains. In terms of competition for food production, unless there is land-use change, diversion of present food-source crops, or new constraints on land availability, many developing countries may be able to produce biofuels without affecting their food production – if environmental and social conditions are favourable.

Among the key determinants in terms of sustainability, as Vanner and Ekins (2009) point out, are (1) the ways in which these commodities are produced and sold; and (2) the competition between producers from developed and developing countries. Such competition, particularly, is a key factor, as developed countries will try to protect domestic production while importing low-cost products. We should note that protectionism in the production of food and other products is a live issue, but not one that I explore further in this chapter.

Contributions to poverty reduction and livelihoods

Biofuels, some have argued, help improve livelihoods, especially in rural areas, as well as contributing to rural development and poverty reduction. Empirical evidence in support of this argument is available at the local level for small scales of production. A number of research networks have synthesized and analysed such evidence, among them COMPETE (2009) and the Policy Innovation Systems for Clean Energy Security (PISCES) Energy Consortium (see Practical Action Consulting, 2009).

About three quarters of the world's population depend directly on agriculture (UNDP, 2007). At the same time, there are roughly 2.7 billion people living on a budget of less than US$2 per day who are considered as 'poor' by international agencies such as the World Bank, UNDP, UNEP and OECD (GNESD, 2004). Lacking adequate access to cleaner energy and services, they rely on traditional biomass to meet their energy needs. Most of them (nearly half of the world's population) live in rural areas, mainly in developing countries (Table 5.1). The vast majority lack access to electricity and modern fuels. They rely primarily on human and animal power for mechanical tasks, such as agricultural activities and transport, and on the direct combustion of biomass for activities that require heat or lighting. The lack of adequate energy services in the rural areas of developing countries has social

Table 5.1 Population and access[a] to electricity

Region	1970	1980	1990	2000	2007
World population (thousands)	3,600	4,400	5,300	6,124	6,515
Urban population	1,000	1,400	2,100	2,854	3,293
Rural population	2,600	3,000	3,200	3,270	3, 377
With access to electricity	610	1,000	1,400	b	b
Without access to electricity	2,000	2,000	1,800	b	b
Percentage of rural population with access	23%	33%	44%	b	b

a) Access: includes people living in villages connected to power lines.
b) No equivalent data.
Sources: Goldemberg, 2000; UN, 2007.

dimensions as well as serious environmental and health effects (Goldemberg, 2000). Furthermore, over the next 50 years, the world population is projected to increase by some 3 billion, primarily in developing countries (UN, 2007).

Poverty is a complex social and economic phenomenon, the dimensions and determinants of which are manifold. Whenever poverty is defined as some aggregate of income shortfalls, the authors of such studies will tend to consider that its reduction requires some combination of economic growth and narrowing of inequality (Ocampo *et al.*, 2002). Nevertheless, defining poverty may go beyond the 'poverty line' of economic income. Poverty can also be considered as deprivation of capacities, lack of opportunities, and social exclusion (Atria and Siles, 2003).

The Millennium Development Goals (MDGs) adopted at the Millennium Summit in 2000 proposed highly ambitious objectives. These goals were adopted as targets for reducing poverty, increasing primary education, promoting gender equality and empowering women, improving health conditions, and ensuring environmental sustainability. Although there was no specific MDG relating to energy, it was assumed that the other goals would be impossible to achieve without improving the quality and quantity of energy services in the developing world. In fact, access to energy services affects practically all aspects of sustainable development, including the availability of water, agricultural productivity, population levels, health care, education, job creation, gender equality and climate change impacts (UNDP, 2004; Johansson and Goldemberg, 2002). Later, in 2002, the World Summit for Sustainable Development brought energy to the centre of a global debate. The resulting Johannesburg 'Plan of Implementation' stressed that access to reliable and affordable energy services facilitates the eradication of poverty (UN, 2005).

There is as yet little evidence that biofuel production can reduce poverty directly. There is, however, a link to its role in creating local markets and local jobs. For instance, 'Energizing Poverty Reduction', the UNDP assessment report on Poverty Reduction Strategy Papers (PRSP) (Takada and Akong, 2007), showed that, compared to electrification, energy strategies relating to the provision of commercial fuels receive much less attention, and strategies concerning fuels for transportation are rare. The PISCES project has already reported on some of these possibilities for small-scale producers and bioenergy initiatives with a positive impact on livelihoods. Thus the positive impacts relate not only to economic benefits but also to sustainable livelihoods (including human, social, natural and physical capital). Seven PISCES case studies out of a total of fifteen relate to biofuels production at the local level – for different uses such as electricity production (Mali with jatropha, outlined above); cooking stoves (ethanol from sugarcane in Ethiopia); fuel for transport (palm oil in Tanzania and microdistilleries in Brazil); and seed/oil production for biodiesel (Guatemala and Thailand, using jatropha) (Practical Action Consulting, 2009). Although the project has reported only on the first year of a five-year programme, the results are encouraging.

Infrastructure, investment, and capacity development

Energy has become a basic human need in the modern economy, since it is critical to the alleviation of hunger. It is also essential for adequate warmth, lighting, refrigeration and productive activities (especially agriculture). According to Goldemberg (2000), energy initiatives along with new institutional measures will be most successful when integrated with other policies that promote development, including financing to cover the initial capital costs of devices and equipment. Rural energy must integrate with other measures dealing with agriculture, education and infrastructure, and with social and political factors.

In terms of sustainability, the UNDP has reviewed the energy theme in relation to infrastructure, investment and capacity development, without linking its structural vision of the role of energy to energy sources and particularly to the production of biofuels. In their PRSP assessment mentioned above, Takada and Akong (2007) found that there is no link between the level of energy discussions found in the PRSPs and the presence of actual budgetary provisions for energy. The authors found that the average *per capita* budgetary allocation for Medium Term Expenditure Frameworks in Energy across all regions assessed was US$9.90 – when the UN Millennium Project estimates that a $10–$20 *per capita* investment in energy is required to meet the goals described in the MDGs (Takada and Akong, 2007). The focus of most of the PRSPs reviewed was on biomass use for energy provision, but there were few related to biofuel production.

Yet while the drivers in terms of targets are mainly in the European Union and the United States of America, the greatest estimated potential for biofuel production lies in developing countries. In spite of the infrastructural weaknesses in countries in Africa and some parts of Asia, there is a clear, built-in tendency for energy production to spread as the major agricultural powers in the developed world reach the limits of their output of energy crops and are forced to turn especially to Africa – where they may be willing to invest in building necessary infrastructure (GNESD, 2007).

Education and training capacity has also been recognized among policy makers as a primary need in developing countries. Training and technical assistance are needed to transfer knowledge to farmers on growing biofuel crops and the use of associated by-products. In Africa, for instance, the COMPETE project has organized a number of conferences with high-level policy makers addressing this point, and giving consideration to the financial mechanisms necessary to develop a biofuel industry in different countries in Africa (COMPETE, 2009).

In terms of investment and financial mechanisms, the project has also identified the barriers to these services. There is a clear tendency for private capital to invest in large-scale plantations (see the cases of Tanzania and Mozambique) or in medium-scale schemes using out-growers in other cases that require less investment (Marli Investment in Zambia and FELISA in Tanzania are examples); international aid, mean-while, invests in specific exploratory cases such as the electrification platforms in Tanzania (Tatedo) or the Mali Folk Centre in Mali (discussed above). Overall, the very uneven pattern of these initiatives demonstrates that a global market has not yet developed.

Trade and globalization

The EU Commission for Agriculture (DG Agri, 2007) observed that it would require 18 Mha of agricultural land, using first-generation biofuels, to meet the transport sector's energy demand. Given internal land constraints, in order to achieve the new Renewable Energy Direc-tive (RED) targets (EC, 2009) it would thus be necessary to rely on a mixture of imported and locally derived biofuels. This imported incre-ment is expected to come mainly from sugarcane, soy bean/oil, palm oil, rape seed/oil, wood products and even some cereals.

One of the key (and contentious) issues in the debate over the socio-economic benefits of biofuels is the potential for trading this twenty-first-century commodity. The challenges such trading poses in terms of sus-tainability represent a shift from 'sustainable development' to 'develop-ment and fairness' through equitable arrangements (Ekins and Voituriez, 2008).

For instance, over the last twenty years – at local, national and international levels – commodity markets have responded not only to changing prices but also to changes in the structure of demand.

Figures 5.1 and 5.2 show the commodities ranked by value (in US$1000) from left to right. We can see how production of sugarcane, maize and soybeans increased from 1997 to 2007, with sugarcane retaining the same rank, and maize and soybeans both moving higher up the list in economic value. Other products such as cassava appeared for the first time in the top 20 ranking in 2007. The figures refer mainly

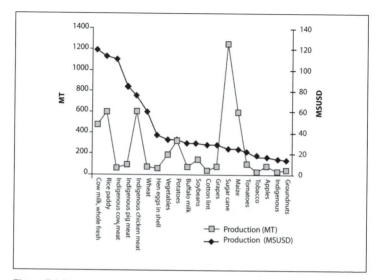

Figure 5.1 Twenty main commodities in 1997   *Source:* FAOSTAT, 2009

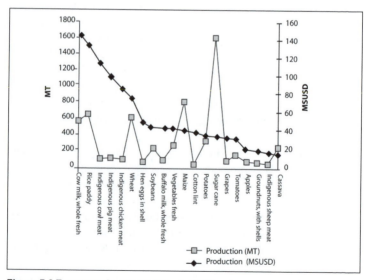

Figure 5.2 Twenty main commodities in 2007   *Source:* FAOSTAT, 2009

to food products (including staple crops), while other cash crops (such as cotton, tobacco, coffee or tea) are not considered.

The issue of commodities and trade is important because research has shown that after years of negotiations and a debate on the link between growth in trading and reduction of poverty and inequality, the evidence remains really weak (see Ekins and Voituriez, 2008). Regarding inequality in particular, the main problem is that trade liberalization is linked to a demand for skilled labour which cannot always be found, at least in developing countries. And while trade liberalization can help to reduce poverty in the long term, for some countries – depending on the products and distributional trends – the negative effects could worsen. Currently, there is a lack of information regarding the effect that bioenergy crops can have in terms of inequality and poverty alleviation in a liberalized market, because the market for biofuels is still quite new. The exception is Brazil, where the ethanol market impacts have been studied for many years (Walter *et al.*, 2008).

Policies and verification systems to promote sustainability

The new Renewable Energy Directive (EC, 2009) set a 20 percent share for renewable energy, of which 10 percent is for renewables in transport by 2020 (Diaz-Chavez and Rosillo-Calle, 2008). The RED also includes reporting obligations for the Commission on the sustainability of biofuels production. In addition, the EU biofuel policy also established the need for assessment of impacts on the availability of food at affordable prices, in particular for people living in developing countries. Based on the results of these new reporting obligations on social sustainability, a revision of the RED is foreseen – possibly to include additional criteria ensuring the socio-economic sustainability of biomass and biofuels.

In order to demonstrate that biofuels have been produced in a sustainable form and contribute to GHG reduction, a verification or certification system is needed. This is to ensure that biofuels have been produced from raw materials whose cultivation meets minimum environmental and social standards, and do not contribute to GHG emissions but, preferably, reduce them.

Various studies, including one by the Renewable Fuels Agency (RFA), have compared different international certification systems covering relevant areas such as the environment and the supply chain, forest production, agriculture, and general management standards. These studies identify where certification systems might be of relevance to biofuel production and supply the assurances required by policy instruments such as the RED (see RFA, 2008; Junginger, 2006; Lewandowski and Faaij, 2006).

Some of the currently available standards and certification systems are mainly focused on environmental and social issues for cash crops, food, and forest products. Standards may be set by governments, industry, or non-governmental organizations. Some systems are voluntary while others are mandatory; most of them have significant socio-economic implications, especially for trading.

Groups currently attempting to develop certification systems specifically dedicated to biofuels include the Roundtable on Sustainable Biofuels (RSB, 2009), the UK's Renewable Fuels Agency (RFA, 2008), and the Cramer Report from the Netherlands (ETSF, 2006). Other systems are related to vegetable oils or crops that may or may not be used for biofuels, such as the Roundtable for Sustainable Palm Oil system (RSPO, 2005). The European Commission is working on a proposal for the sustainability standards referred to in the RED. The Global Bioenergy Energy Partnership is also developing a series of indicators to be used at policy level (GBEP, 2009). There are additional efforts from private companies such as Sekab (2008) in Sweden and Greenergy (2008) in the UK. More recently the International Standards Organization (ISO) has lent its support to efforts by the European Standards Organization to develop biofuels standards (Diaz-Chavez and Rosillo-Calle, 2008).

Thus there are several initiatives at global, national and local levels to develop sustainability criteria for the so-called first-generation biofuels. The main object of these criteria is to ensure that biofuels are produced in an environmentally and socially sustainable manner. Nevertheless, sustainability does not depend only on social and environmental factors. Economic and policy issues need to be considered as well. A certification scheme cannot in itself aim to influence national policy goals and programmes regarding sustainability. Instead its approach must be flexible enough to put forward its essential criteria without compromising global trade and without being too prescriptive. There is an urgent need to harmonize different systems and to consider issues arising from wider implementation in developing countries according to different national interpretations. The next step is to focus on the implementation and monitoring of a sustainability scheme with these diverse national interpretations in mind.

Some aspects of these criteria may be of greater relevance in developing countries (such as Brazil and a number of African countries). Nevertheless, some of them also apply to EU member states, particularly those in eastern Europe. These concerns mainly relate to workers' rights and working conditions (including child labour), which need to be examined more closely in the light of prevailing conditions in each country (see Smeets *et al.*, 2006). Discussion of the socio-economic impacts of biofuel production must balance the negative side – the very real danger of environmental degradation and social challenges associated with food security, access to land and conflict over resources such as water – with the significant potential for rural development and value-added product generation, both in developed and developing economies.

It is fundamentally important to acknowledge that an unprecedented emphasis on certification schemes has resulted in a less than fair playing field for biofuels. The stringent sustainability and certification criteria proposed for biofuels result in market disadvantage, since the negative impacts of fossil fuels and agriculture practices in general are not being addressed in a similar manner – though the current debate on sustainability criteria and GHG accountability is moving towards this wider (and fairer) applicability (Diaz-Chavez and Rosillo-Calle, 2008).

While policies regarding energy or biofuel production (mainly the setting of targets) tend to be spreading worldwide, the links between energy concerns and other policy areas are less frequently emphasized. But the boom in biofuels has created a new opportunity – and necessity – for linkage between hitherto discrete policy agendas in agriculture, industry, environment, transport, and energy. In the EU this process is articulated through the specific directorates of energy, environment, transport and agriculture, whereas in many developing countries the participation of ministries such as industry needs to be enabled. There have also been concerns that the link with social policies and a gender-dedicated policy for energy should be taken into account (see the Zambian case in COMPETE, 2009).

It is not clear yet whether the EU's RED, with its new renewable fuels targets, will contribute to a rapid development of first-generation biofuels in developed and developing countries. It is clear, though, that the debate on the sustainable production of biofuels has ignited a review of sustainability issues in other sectors such as agriculture; the same analysis should be done for the fossil fuel industry, so that energy comparisons become fair and appropriate. Although there is no single policy or measure which can address all shortcomings, we need immediate action to improve the system of comparison. Countries and regions willing to engage in the 'bioenergy sector', and replace traditional use of biomass with more modern forms, need to ensure that they fulfil their own energy needs and that sustainability issues (environmental, social and economic) are incorporated into local policy and governance.

Two of the main – and, as we shall see briefly below, deeply inter-woven – concerns in developing countries regarding production of bio-fuel crops (and probably other crops as well) are land availability and property rights. Land availability in most large African and Latin American countries is not considered a major issue *in itself* (see Biofuels Declaration in Arusha: COMPETE, 2009). The limiting issues regarding bioenergy crops in most developing countries are related to water availability and competition with food crops or cash crops. Nevertheless, considering that farmers 'know' what to grow in the various niches afforded by available land, there will generally be little competition at the local level in small-scale production. The case of the Mali Folk Centre project, producing jatropha oil for electricity generation, demonstrates this by limiting to 6 hectares the land used by local farmers who wish to grow jatropha (COMPETE, 2009).

Direct and indirect land-use change is still a debatable topic in terms of the methodological frameworks used to assess it. Cotula *et al.* (2008) reviewed some of these impacts (displacement effects or increase in land value, for instance) and focused also on the social impacts for the small-scale producer. These impacts include the effects on pastoralism (disruption of customary arrangements, including transhumant[1] access to land), the change in land value, and the displacement of women and minority groups. Land tenure is central to all these concerns. In Africa, for instance, various types of property rights in different countries can be either advantageous or disadvantageous to biofuels production. Land is a significant source of security for those with ownership or other types of access or rights to land. If investment in land is foreign-based, it is likely to be seen as problematic by local people. Cotula *et al.* (2008) stress that land access for rural people requires policy attention – not only in terms of land tenure but also in the light of broader social circumstances that determine land use and agricultural economics.

Conclusions

Sustainability concerns regarding the production of biofuels vary in different parts of the world. Ongoing projects (such as electrification in villages in India and Mali) have already demonstrated some of the benefits of biofuels in small-scale applications. The implications for food production differ by region, especially concerning land availability and food security, whether based on subsistence, cash crops, or (frequently) a mixture of both. A certification and standardization system may help reduce uncertainties about some aspects of the biofuels impact, but will not eliminate them completely. Some aspects will have further implications as a global market starts to develop, but there seems little doubt that sustainable biofuels markets could present opportunities for development in the South, for those countries willing to participate in such markets.

I close this chapter with five broad observations, all of which testify to the complex and rapidly changing role of biofuel production in rural development.

1 The global market for biofuels is still developing, as are several mechanisms necessary to support it (subsidies, incentives and regulations, among others).
2 The social and economic impacts of biofuels, both positive and

negative, require broad and comprehensive research. There is a distinct lack of hard data to sustain many current assumptions – particularly as some crops are still new in the market and differences in the scale of production can significantly influence the outcome. There is no question that biofuels generate employment in rural areas, but data are still weak and depend on local conditions.

3 There is some convergence towards a global standard or certification scheme, but it will be difficult to implement for the following reasons: the lack of national-level interpretation for many of the principles; the lack of local/national policies linking renewable energy and agricultural production, especially in developing countries; inadequate articulation within the international trading systems and WTO regulations; the vast number of stakeholders involved in this 'new market' at all levels, and the dominance and experience of just a few countries in the present emerging market.

4 Consideration of wider sustainability in agriculture production, and of what is important at (diverse) national levels may substantially reduce fears of competition between food production and bioenergy crops.

5 Whatever global scheme is defined should not jeopardize the growth of this new market, and should not be an obstacle to emergent trading relationships.

Note

1   Transhumant: relating to the seasonal and/or alternating movement of livestock, together with the persons who tend the animals.

References

Atria, R. and M. Siles (eds) (2003) *Capital Social y Reduccion de la Pobreza en America Latina y el Caribe: en Busca de un Nuevo Paradigma*, CEPAL and Economic Commission for Latin America and the Caribbean (ECLAC), Santiago.

Bailey, R. (2008) *Another Inconvenient Truth: How Biofuel Policies are Deepening Poverty and Accelerating Climate Change*, Oxfam, Oxford.

COMPETE (2009) 'Competence Platform on Energy Crop and Agroforestry Systems for Arid and Semi-arid Ecosystems – Africa', <http://compete-bioafrica.net/>.

Connor, D. J. and C. G. Hernandez (2009) 'Crops for biofuels: current status and prospects for the future', in R. W. Howarth and S. Bringezu (eds), *Biofuels: Environmental Consequences and Interactions with Changing Land Use*, Cornell University Press, Ithaca NY, <http://cip.cornell.edu/biofuels/>.

Cotula, L., N. Dyer and S. Vermeulen (2008) *Fuelling Exclusion? The Biofuels Boom and Poor People's Access to Land*, International Institute for Environment and Development, London.

DG Agri (2007) 'The role of the European Commission in the development of sustainable biofuels', paper presented at the Waterfront Conference, 'Developing Biofuels Sustainably: Can It be Done?', London, 17 April 2007.

Diaz-Chavez, R. and F. Rosillo-Calle (2008) 'Biofuels for transport – sustainability and certification: where we are now and where are we going. A short review', report for the Department for Transport, UK.

Dufey, A. (2006) 'Biofuels production, trade and sustainable development: emerging issues', Sustainable Markets Discussion Paper No. 2, International Insitute for Environment and Development, London.

Earley, J. and A. McKeown (2009) 'Smart choices for biofuels', report, Worldwatch Institute and the Sierra Club, USA.

EC (2009) 'Directive 2009/28/EC on the promotion of the use of energy from renewable sources and amending and subsequently repealing Directives 2001/77/EC and 2003/30/EC', European Commission.

EEDA (2006) 'Smart productivity securing sustainable development in the English regions', research report, East of England Development Agency, <http://www.eeda.org.uk/files/Smart_Productivity.pdf>.

Ekins, P. and T. Voituriez (eds) (2008) *Trade, Globalization and Sustainability Impact Assessment: A Critical Look at Methods and Outcomes*, Earthscan, London.

ETSF (2006) 'Criteria for sustainable biomass production', final report of the project group on 'Sustainable production of biomass', Energy Transition Task Force, The Netherlands.

FAO (2008) *The State of Food and Agriculture. Biofuels: Prospects, Risks and Opportunities*, Food and Agriculture Organization, Rome.

FAOSTAT (2009) Commodities, <http://faostat.fao.org/site/339/default.aspx>.

GBEP (2009) Task Force on Sustainability, <http://www.globalbioenergy.org/fileadmin/user_upload/gbep/docs/2008_events/6th_Steering_Comittee/TF_Sustainability-Report_to_6th_SC1.pdf>.

GNESD (2004) *Energy for Sustainable Development* 8 (4) (Global Network on Energy for Sustainable Development).

—— (2007) 'Renewable energy technologies and poverty alleviation: overcoming barriers and unlocking potentials', research paper, Global Network on Energy for Sustainable Development.

Goldemberg, J. (2000) 'Rural energy in developing countries', in J. Goldemberg (ed.), *World Energy Assessment: Energy and the Challenge of Sustainability*, United Nations Development Programme, New York, NY, pp. 367–89.

Greenergy (2008) 'Greenergy and sustainable bioethanol production: working in partnership with Brazilian suppliers', Carlos Lyra case study, <http://www.greenergy.com/feedstock_sourcing/case_study/Carlos-Lyra_eng.pdf>.

Haberl, H. and K. Erb (2006) 'Assessment of sustainable land use in producing biomass', in J. Dewulf and H. Langenhove (eds), *Renewables – Base Technology*, John Wiley and Sons, New York, NY.

Johansson, T. B. and J. Goldemberg (eds) (2002) *Energy for Sustainable Development: A Policy Agenda*, UNDP, IIIEE and IEI, Lund, Sweden.

Junginger, M. (2006) 'Overview of biomass-related sustainability certification efforts and policy', study for International Energy Agency (IEA) Bioenergy, Task 40, Projectgroep duurzame import biomasss.

Lewandowski, I. and A. Faaij (2006) 'Steps towards the development of a certification system for sustainable bio-energy trade', *Biomass and Bioenergy* 30: 83–104.

Macedo, I. C. (2005) *Sugar Cane's Energy: Twelve Studies on Brazilian Sugar Cane Agribusiness and Its Sustainability*, UNICA.

Ocampo, J., E. Martinez, and R. Borges Martins (2002) 'Meeting the Millennium Poverty Reduction Targets in Latin America and the Caribbean', report, United Nations Development Programme, New York, NY.

Overend, R. P. (2007) 'Bioenergy', in *Survey of Energy Resources*, World Energy Council, London.

Pimentel, D., A. F. Warneke, W. S. Teel, K. A. Schwab, N. J. Simcox, D. M. Ebert, K. D. Baenisch and M. R. Aaron (1988) 'Food versus biomass fuel: socioeconomic and environmental impacts in the United States, Brazil, India, and Kenya', *Advances in Food Research* 5 (32): 185–238.

Practical Action Consulting (2009) 'Small-scale bioenergy initiatives: brief description and preliminary lessons on livelihood impacts from case studies in Asia, Latin America and Africa', report prepared for PISCES and FAO, January.

RFA (2008) 'The Renewable Transport Fuel Obligations (Amendment) Order 2009', report by the Renewable Fuels Agency, St Leonards-on-Sea.

Rosillo-Calle, F. and D. Hall (1987) 'Brazilian alcohol: fuel versus food?', *Biomass* 12: 97–128.

Rossi, A. and L. Lambrou (2008) 'Gender and equity issues in liquid biofuels production: minimizing the risks to maximize the opportunities', report, FAO, Rome.

RSB (2009) 'Version One principles and criteria', Roundtable on Sustainable Biofuels, <http://cgse.epfl.ch/page84341.html>.

RSPO (2005) 'RSPO principles and criteria for sustainable palm oil production', Round Table on Sustainable Palm Oil, public release version, 17 October.

Schirnding, Y., N. Bruce, K. Smith, G. Ballard-Tremeer and M. Ezzati (2000) 'Addressing the impact of household energy and indoor air pollution on the health of the poor: implications for policy action and intervention measures', report, Energia and UNDP.

Sekab (2008) 'Verified sustainable ethanol initiative', <http://www.sustainable ethanolinitiative.com/default.asp?id=1062>.

Smeets, E., M. Junginger, A. Faaij, A. Walter and P. Dolzan (2006) 'Sustainability of Brazilian bio-ethanol', research paper, Copernicus Institute Department of Science,Technology and Society, University of Utrecht, Netherlands.

Takada, M. and N. Akong (2007) 'Energizing poverty reduction: a review of the energy–poverty nexus in Poverty Reduction Strategy Papers', United Nations Development Programme, New York, NY.

UN (2005) *Investing in Development: A Practical Plan to Achieve the Millennium Development Goals*, overview and full report of the UN Millennium Project, UNDP, New York, NY.

—— (2007) 'Urban and rural areas 2007', United Nations Department of Economic and Social Affairs, Population Division, <www.unpopulation.org>.

UNDP (2004) 'Energy for sustainable development', report, Bureau for Development Policy, Energy and Environment Group, United Nations Development Programme, New York, NY.

—— (2007) *Fighting Climate Change: Human Solidarity in a Divided World*, Human Development Report 2007/2008, United Nations Development Programme, New York, NY.

Vanner, R. and P. Ekins (2009) 'The impacts of liberalising trade in commodities', in P. Ekins and T. Voituriez (eds), *Trade, Globalization and Sustainability Impact Assessment: A Critical Look at Methods and Outcomes*, Earthscan, London.

Walter, A., P. Dolzan, O. Quilodrán, J. Garcia, C. da Silva and P. Piacente (2008) 'Analysis of environmental and social impacts of bio-ethanol production in Brazil', report sponsored by UK Embassy, Brasilia, UK Department for Environment, Food and Rural Affairs (Defra) and University of Campinas, Brazil.

Zambian National Technical Committee on the Biofuels Development Framework (2007) 'Productising the biofuels development', report, Government of the National Republic of Zambia, Lusaka.

6 Biofuels and Climate Change

N. H. Ravindranath, Ritumbara Manuvie, and
C. Sita Lakshmi

The use of biofuels as a strategy for the mitigation of climate change has attracted worldwide attention from policy makers at the highest levels, particularly because of its implications for food crises and greenhouse gas (GHG) benefits. Biofuels are under consideration in the pursuit of many different objectives: as a substitute for fossil fuels in the transportation sector, also offering a (debated) climate change mitigation advantage; in the promotion of energy security, by reducing dependence on imported petroleum fuels; and, finally, as a means of advancing rural development by creating rural jobs and incomes. Biofuels are of particular interest to developing countries from the perspective of enhancing energy security in petroleum-importing countries, and promoting rural development.

In recent years a number of countries, both industrialized and developing, have set targets for substituting diesel and gasoline by biofuels, with proportions ranging from 5 to 20 percent to be met at various times within the period 2010–30. The increasing interest in biofuels at the policy level has also generated enormous interest in the scientific community, leading to a flood of literature highlighting the technological, environmental, economic and social implications of biofuels. In the climate change context biofuels have become controversial because of uncertainty regarding the net GHG benefits as well as implications for biodiversity. Furthermore, predicted climate change will have an impact on agricultural productivity in many regions, and thus is likely to influence biofuel production as well.

This chapter aims at assessing, first, the CO_2 emissions from biofuel production in the context of climate change mitigation; second, the implications of biofuel production for biodiversity; and, finally, the potential impacts of climate change on sustainable biofuel production –

together with possible adaptation options. The focus of the chapter is on biofuel production in developing countries, though the demand for biofuels from industrialized countries, and their biofuel policies, also influence production in developing countries. Although in this chapter our main focus will be on issues related to biofuel use in the transport sector, there are of course a number of technological options for using biofuel in other areas such as the power sector or domestic and industrial heating. Transportation fuels contribute about 13 percent of the global CO_2 emissions (IPCC, 2007). The biofuels considered in this chapter include bioethanol and biodiesel as transportation fuels for substituting gasoline and diesel respectively; our focus is thus mainly on the contentious first-generation, agro-based biofuel crops.

Biofuel crops and technologies

There are many sources of biomass feedstock for biofuel production, which include sugar crops, starchy crops, cellulosic material and oil crops: see Figure 6.1 (FAO, 2008). However, in recent years the expansion of biofuel crops for the production of liquid biofuels for transport has been based mainly on agricultural crops – such as sugarcane and maize as the feedstock in ethanol production, or oil palm, soybean and rapeseed in biodiesel production. For example 85 percent of global production of biofuels is in the form of ethanol from sugarcane and maize, with Brazil and the USA accounting for 87 percent of global ethanol production (FAO, 2008).

Theoretically, biofuels can be produced from any organic material (Ruth, 2008), but – depending on the types of crop, cultivation practices and processes involved – biofuel crops are classified as belonging to the first or second (next) generation. Examples of these crops are as follows:
- First-generation crop/feedstock: jatropha, palm oil, soybean (for biodiesel); maize, sugarcane, sweet sorghum, wheat, cassava (for ethanol);
- Second/next generation: woody biomass, tall grasses, agricultural and plantation residues – largely for ethanol.

First-generation biofuels
Currently, all biofuel production uses first-generation food crops as feedstock, except when biodiesel is derived from jatropha. First-generation

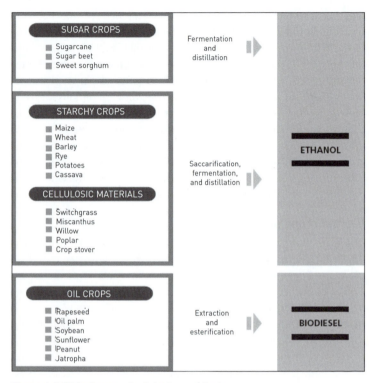

Figure 6.1 Biofuel crops, feedstocks, and fuels
Source: FAO, 2008.

biofuel production depends largely on sugar grains and vegetable crops. These are harvested for their sugar, starch, or oil content, which is converted to biofuels using different processes. The focus of the current debate is largely on the environmental and socio-economic implications of first-generation biofuel crops, since they compete for land with food and livestock production.

There are technologies with the potential to increase the yields of first-generation biofuel crops (IEA, 2006; FAO, 2008; Staley and Bradley, 2008). The yield depends upon crop variety, soil quality, rainfall and irrigation, nutrient supplement and cultural practices. Biofuel conversion technologies such as fermentation and distillation for ethanol production and extraction and esterification for biodiesel are commercially established and viable. First-generation crops are likely to dominate biofuel production for many years to come, since these existing technologies have already enabled a large production programme.

Ethanol: Sugarcane dominates ethanol production in developing countries. Maize, sweet sorghum, sugar beet, cassava, rice and wheat are also used as feedstock for ethanol production. Among the first-generation biofuel crops, sugarcane provides the highest ethanol yields at 6,000 l/ha/yr in Brazil (see also Table 3.7 on page 76), with a global average of 5,005 l/ha/yr. The maize yield is 3,651 l/ha/yr in the USA, whereas the global average is around 2,372 l/ha/yr (Sims *et al.*, 2008; Mielke, 2007; Jongschaap *et al.*, 2007; Fresco, 2007; Thow and Warhurst, 2007).

Biodiesel: The dominant biodiesel crops are rapeseed oil in Europe and soybean in Brazil and USA. In some developing countries such as Indonesia and Malaysia palm oil is the dominant crop (Stone, 2007) and increasingly jatropha is being grown for biofuel in many countries, including India and China. In addition many oil-producing trees such as *pongamia pinnata* are also used as a source of feedstock for biodiesel. Oil palm provides the highest biodiesel yield (4,594 l/ha/yr) (Sims *et al.*, 2008; Mielke, 2007; Jongschaap *et al.*, 2007; Fresco, 2007; Thow and Warhurst, 2007).

Next/second-generation biofuels
The next-generation biofuel crops are a source of feedstock comprising lignocellulosic material, which is harvested for its total biomass. The feedstocks from these biofuel crops – woody biomass, tall grasses, agricultural residues (bagasse, shells, straw, stocks, leaves and reproductive parts) and plantation residues (leaves, sawdust, nutshells, reproductive parts) – are available in abundance and can be harvested at a much lower cost (Sims *et al.*, 2008). Some of the crops that can be grown for next-generation biofuel production include perennial grasses (such as switchgrass and *Miscanthus*), short-rotation willows, hybrid poplar and eucalyptus (Worldwatch Institute, 2006).

Biofuel production, programmes, and targets

Biofuel production, in particular ethanol production, has more than doubled during the period 2000–05, and global biofuel production during 2007 was reported to be 52 billion litres of ethanol and 10 billion litres of biodiesel (FAO, 2008). In tons of oil equivalent (toe) terms, global production has climbed from 15.5 Mtoe in 2004 (IEA, 2006) to 34.72 Mtoe during 2007 (RFA, 2008; FAO, 2008; FAPRI, 2008). In 2007 the USA dominated this rise in production, accounting for about 43 percent, followed by Brazil with 32 percent and the EU with 15 percent, while all other countries together accounted for about 10 percent.

Bioethanol

Global production of bioethanol increased from 17.25 billion litres in 2000 to over 46 billion litres in 2007 (Balat and Balat, 2009). USA and Brazil are the key ethanol producers, from corn and sugarcane respectively.

Biodiesel

The European Union remains the source of most of the world's biodiesel (about 85 percent), with about half of this coming from Germany. The USA accounts for nearly all of the remaining 15 percent.

Projected future demand

Developing countries such as China, India, Malaysia, Indonesia, and South Africa have also initiated significant biofuel programmes. Various projections are available for the future demand or consumption of biofuels globally, as well as for key countries and regions. For example an OECD-FAO report (2008) projects an annual growth in consumption of 6.6 percent for biodiesel and 5.12 percent for ethanol during the period 2008–17, based on current trends: ethanol production is projected to reach 127 billion litres, and biodiesel 24 billion litres by 2017. The International Energy Agency's *World Energy Outlook* (IEA, 2006) projects that biofuel consumption will increase from 20 Mtoe in 2005 to 92 Mtoe in 2030 under its Reference Scenario, while under its enhanced Alternative Policy Scenario it will reach 147 Mtoe. A projection made by Ravindranath *et al.* (2009) for 2030, assuming a 10 percent petroleum

Table 6.1 Projections for biofuel production (2017) and petroleum/biofuel demand in transport sector (2030)

	OECD (Mt)	Non-OECD (Mt)	World(Mt)
Total Biofuel Production, 2017 (Mt)[a]	−	−	153
Bioethanol	−	−	127
Biodiesel	−	−	24
Total projected petroleum demand for transportation, 2030 (Mt)[b]	1,725	1,665	3,390
Gasoline	940	907	1,848
Diesel	785	758	1,542
Total projected demand for biofuels in 2030 considering 10% petroleum fuel substitution (Mt)[c]	238	230	468
Bioethanol	147	142	289
Biodiesel	91	88	179

Sources: [a] OECD/FAO, 2008; [b] EIA, 2008; [c] Ravindranath *et al.*, 2009.

fuel substitution by biofuels (Table 6.1), estimates a total demand of 468 Mt (289 Mt of ethanol and 179 Mt of biodiesel).

Land area for biofuel production

Land area required and the land category for growing biofuels are at the heart of the debate on the environmental and economic impacts of biofuel production. Land used for biofuel production was estimated to be around 13.8 Mha in 2004, accounting for about 1 percent of the current cropped area (IEA, 2006). The area estimate reported in Ravindranath *et al.* (2009) is 26.6 Mha in 2007, almost double the 2004 figure. Several estimates are available for the land area required for meeting different future targets in different years. But estimates of future demand for land for biofuel production seem to be highly uncertain (RFA 2008).

Land area under biofuel production currently or in the future depends on a number of variable factors: the year for which the projection is made; targets assumed for petroleum fuel substitution; biofuel crops selected; soil fertility and moisture status; production practices; projected feedstock yields; market and policy incentives; and conversion technologies.

Projections

Some important projections compare the land areas required for producing biofuels and for meeting the food and livestock feed requirement in the years 2020 and 2030.

1 Bates: Estimates by Bates *et al.* (2008), assuming a 7 percent GHG reduction target for 2020, show that the land area required for first-generation biofuel crops would be 196–276 Mha with no co-products, and 167–247 Mha with co-products, under different scenarios of yield.

2 Gallagher: The Gallagher Review (2008) estimates that 56–166 Mha of land area will be required to substitute 10 percent of petroleum fuel demand by 2020. The lower figure (56 Mha) takes into account the benefits of co-products in terms of avoided land conversion, next-generation technologies from wastes and residues, and significant improvements in yield. The higher estimate (166 Mha) is a gross figure for the low-yield scenario, not taking into account the anticipated benefits of co-products and without a positive contribution from next-generation technologies (RFA 2008).

3 International Energy Agency: The IEA's *World Energy Outlook* (2006) projects the total areas and percentages of arable land under biofuel crops in different scenarios in 2030 as follows –

Reference scenario: 34.5 Mha (2.5 percent of arable land)
Alternative policy scenario: 52.8 Mha (3.8 percent of arable land)
Next-generation biofuel scenario: 58.5 Mha (4.2 percent of arable land).

4 FAO: A hypothetical estimate by the FAO (2008) shows that 600 Mha of land area dedicated to ethanol production, including several crops, have a maximum production potential of 940 billion litres, equivalent to 630 billion litres (555 Mt) of gasoline, which is 16 percent of projected total petroleum consumption for transportation in 2030.

5 Ravindranath: Ravindranath *et al.* (2009) have made an estimate of the land required for biofuel production if biofuels were to substitute 10 percent of projected petroleum fuel demand for transportation in 2030

Table 6.2 Total land area required (in Mha) for meeting total projected biofuel demand, where each biofuel crop is assumed to meet 10 percent of the biodiesel or ethanol demand, for 2030[a]

Region	Land required to meet 10% of biodiesel demand under single crop scenario			Land required to meet 10% of ethanol demand under single crop scenario		
	Jatropha	Palm oil	Soybean	Maize	Sugar-cane	Sweet sorghum
OECD	73	20	152	62	29	49
Non-OECD	70	20	147	60	28	47
World	143	40	299	122	58	96

a) Area required for meeting the biofuel demand is calculated by dividing the total biodiesel or ethanol demand by the mean yield of the respective biofuel crop assuming 10% of the demand of biodiesel or ethanol is met by a single selected biofuel crop, for each of the four scenarios. Biofuel yields assumed in kg/ha/year are: jatropha (biodiesel) 1,250 l/ha/yr; oil palm (biodiesel) 4,594 t/ha/yr; soybean (biodiesel) 601 l/ha/yr; maize (ethanol) 2,372 l/ha/yr; sugarcane (ethanol) 5,005 l/ha/yr; sweet sorghum (ethanol) 3,000 l/ha/yr.

Source: Mielke, 2007; Jongschaap et al., 2007; Fresco, 2007; Thow and Warhurst, 2007; Sims et al., 2008.

(see Table 6.2). Different first-generation biofuel crops and global average yields are considered for estimating the land area required. Each biofuel crop is considered to meet the total projected diesel or gasoline requirement. Under each biofuel crop scenario either jatropha, palm oil or soybean will meet the total projected demand for biodiesel, while maize, sugarcane or sweet sorghum will meet the total projected demand for ethanol, though several combinations of these and other crops are feasible. Globally the total land required to meet the biodiesel demand is estimated to be:

143 Mha for jatropha

40 Mha for palm oil

299 Mha for soybean.

Similarly, the land required for meeting the ethanol demand using different biofuel crops is estimated to be:

122 Mha for maize

58 Mha for sugarcane

96 Mha for sweet sorghum.

The total land required for substituting 10 percent of petroleum fuel depends on the biodiesel and ethanol crops selected and the crop yields. For example, on the basis of current assumed yields, if a combination of jatropha and sugarcane is considered, the total land required will be 201 Mha.

Projections of the area likely to be under biofuel crops by 2030 range from 201 Mha to 421 Mha, accounting for 14.4 percent and 30.2 percent of arable land in 2030, depending upon various factors like targets assumed for petroleum fuel substitution, biofuel crops selected, soil fertility and moisture status, production practices, projected feedstock yields, or market and policy incentives (IEA, 2006).

Implications for food production

Biofuel crops compete for land, water, nutrients and other resources with food crops. Biofuel production is likely to have direct as well as indirect effects on food security (as discussed in other chapters of this book). Currently only 1 percent of crop land is under biofuel crops (IEA, 2006); by 2030 this is projected to vary in the range of 3.8–4.2 percent of total arable land under the Advanced Policy Scenario, depending upon whether next-generation (the lower range) or first-generation feedstock (the higher range) is used. The current land area under crop production is around 1,500 Mha and it is projected to increase by 200–500 Mha by 2020. Since the land area required to substitute 10 percent of petroleum fuel by 2030 may be in the range of 201 to 421 Mha, this new demand is likely to lead to competition for land. Thus, even a modest projection of substitution of petroleum by biofuels is likely to lead to competition for land between food and biofuel crops.

Currently, food production in many tropical countries is under water stress due to disturbed monsoon patterns, less annual rainfall, increasing demand for water due to rising population, and declining groundwater levels. Food scarcity is directly linked to water scarcity in most parts of the developing world. According to the FAO (2008) water scarcity, rather than land scarcity, may prove to be a key limiting factor for biofuel production in many regions. Many of the crops used for biofuel production currently – such as sugarcane, oil palm and maize – have a relatively high requirement for water. Thus, moderate to high yields can only be obtained under irrigated conditions or in tropical regions with high rainfall. Extensive cultivation of biofuel crops for commercial purposes may lead to competition for water between biofuel production and subsistence food production (Royal Society, 2008; Peña, 2008).

Biofuel production and GHG emissions

Sources of GHG emissions in biofuel production
Globally biofuels are considered as an important option to mitigate GHG emissions, by substitution of petroleum fuels in the transport sector. GHG emissions occur due to various processes and at various stages – such as land conversion, biofuel production (cultivation practices), processing, conversion technology and transportation (Righelato and Spracklen, 2007). The GHGs emitted include carbon dioxide (CO_2), methane (CH_4) and nitrous oxide (N_2O) (Scharlemann and Laurance, 2008). Estimation of GHG emissions from biofuel crops is one of the most contentious issues in using biofuels for mitigation of climate change. Significant new scientific literature during recent years has changed thinking on biofuels use for GHG emission reduction. Currently available literature is largely focused on potential emissions from biofuels in developed countries, and very few studies are available from developing countries.

Estimation of net GHG benefits from biofuels substituting petroleum fuel requires life cycle analysis of GHG emissions. The following factors determine GHG emissions from the biofuel sector, including both direct and indirect effects:

- Land category or land type used for biofuel production;
- Conversion of native lands or currently cropped lands;
- Biofuel crop used, such as first-generation food crops or grasses or forest residue;
- Indirect effects of the conversion of area under food crops or livestock feed to biofuels, leading to compensatory conversion of lands elsewhere;
- Production practices such as fertilizer application, use of machinery, and soil disturbance;
- Processing of biofuels into transportation fuel;
- Transportation of feedstock as well as biofuels.

GHG emissions from land conversions

A review carried out by OECD (2008) and Menichetti and Otto (2009), from a life cycle analysis (LCA) perspective and covering nearly 60 studies, concluded that first-generation biofuel production could result in a net GHG emission reduction in the range of 20–60 percent compared to fossil fuels, excluding GHG emissions from land-use conversion (it is important to note that the majority of studies covered in reviews do not include this last source of GHG, especially since several studies have emphasized that the direct and indirect land-conversion process dominates the GHG implications of biofuel production) (OECD, 2008; FAO, 2008). Several studies have estimated GHG emissions resulting from land conversion to biofuel crops (Gibbs *et al.*, 2008; Fargione *et al.*, 2008; Searchinger *et al.*, 2008).

Table 6.3 Biofuel carbon debt, and the number of years required to repay it in nine scenarios of biofuel production

Land conversion	GHG emissions (tCO_2/ha)	Time to repay carbon debt (years)
Tropical rainforest to palm oil	702	86
Peat land rainforest to palm oil	3,452	423
Tropical rainforest to soybean	737	319
Cerrado woodland to sugarcane	165	17
Cerrado grassland to soybean	85	37
Central grassland to maize	134	93
Abandoned cropland to maize	69	48
Abandoned cropland to prairie biomass	6	1
Marginal cropland to prairie biomass	0	0
Conversion of forest to palm oil[*]		75–93
Conversion of peat land to palm oil[*]		→ 600
Conversion of degraded grassland to palm oil[*]		← 10

Sources: Fargione *et al.*, 2008; [*]Danielsen *et al.*, 2009.

GHG emissions from direct land conversion: Growing demand for biofuels in industrialized countries as well as developing countries will require bringing new land into biofuel feedstock production. Even if current grain cropland is used to produce biofuel feedstock, new land may be required to offset the grain loss. Three recent publications that have made a significant impact on the debate on net CO_2 benefit are those of Fargione *et al.* (2008), Searchinger *et al.* (2008) and Gibbs *et al.* (2008). Fargione *et al.* introduced the concept of 'carbon debt' from biofuel production, which indicates tons of CO_2 resulting from land conversion to be offset by biofuel substituting fossil fuels. Carbon debt can also be presented as the number of years in which biofuel production can offset total CO_2 emission resulting from land conversion. The carbon debt values for various land conversions are given in Table 6.3. Native or pre-conversion land use and the carbon (soil and biomass) density of the land influences the net CO_2 benefit. Among the first-generation crops, carbon debt is highest for conversion of peat land to biodiesel (3,452 tCO_2/ha) followed by conversion of tropical rainforest to soybean (737 tCO_2/ha) and oil palm for biodiesel production (702 tCO_2/ha). Conversion of grassland to maize and cerrado woodland to sugarcane leads to net carbon debts of 139 and 165 tCO_2/ha respectively. The carbon debt is very low for abandoned croplands, which have low carbon density. The study also concludes that conversion of marginal cropland could have no net CO_2 debt. Similar results are also reported by Danielsen *et al.* (2009). The estimates by Fargione *et al.* (2008) given above do not include CO_2 emissions from biofuel production and conversion processes.

Searchinger *et al.* (2008) have further analysed incorporating production, refining and distribution as well as CO_2 uptake in lands and CO_2 emissions from land conversion. The study has concluded that emissions from land conversion and loss of carbon uptake could lead to 93 percent higher CO_2 emissions from corn production for ethanol compared to gasoline used. Exclusion of CO_2 emissions from land conversion and inclusion of carbon uptake in lands could lead to net CO_2 reduction from corn production for ethanol.

GHG emissions from indirect land conversion: Assessment of indirect land conversion for biofuel production and the resulting emissions is very complex and requires modelling, since it is difficult to directly link the two. Indirect land conversions can be a function of multiple, complex and interrelated drivers, particularly deforestation. For example, conversion of pasture land to soybean cultivation could shift cattle grazing to other areas, potentially leading to deforestation (Bates *et al.*, 2008). Searchinger *et al.* (2008) analysed the impacts of displacing, for example, maize production in the US to uncultivated land in the US, Brazil, India and China. The study showed that ethanol production of 56 billion litres diverting maize from 12.8 Mha of the US could in turn bring 10.8 Mha of additional land into cultivation; potential locations could include Brazil, China, India and the US. The rising price of soybean in the US due to conversion of soybean land to biofuel maize is estimated to have led to conversion of Amazon forest to soybean production (Laurance 2007). Indirect land conversion, due to biofuel demand in industrialized countries, driving the conversion of forest, peats, wetlands and native grasslands in developing countries is a critical issue, potentially leading to large GHG emissions which are too complex to link and estimate (Peña, 2008).

Gallagher (2008) and RFA (2008) assessed the impacts of indirect land conversion by considering the *potential* release of GHG from land conversion caused by displacement. These are derived using a function of the land used to produce agricultural products for export purposes on the basis that only trade flows will be affected by displacement. The 'indirect land conversion factor' approach suggests no net savings for biodiesel from rapeseed oil, and only small savings for ethanol from maize and wheat, for the 'minimum' indirect land conversion factor. With a medium level of 50 percent risk to induce indirect land conversion, rapeseed, wheat and maize will not be reducing GHG emissions. For a high level of indirect land conversion factor, only ethanol from sugarcane will lead to GHG reduction. It is also important to consider the extent to which biofuels drive higher commodity prices that potentially stimulate indirect land-use changes elsewhere.

Implication of co-products: Production of many biofuels crops lead to several co-products (agricultural residue, straw, bagasse, corn stover, et cetera) and processed co-products (soy meal, oilseed cake, rape meal, glycerin, distillers dark grains with solubles, sugar-beet pulp, et cetera). These co-products have potential applications for livestock feed, feedstock for power generation, and other uses. Incorporation of the co-products and their use for livestock feedstock production and energy generation will have implications for net GHG emissions, in most cases positive implications. Analysis by Croezen *et al.* (2008) indicates that co-products have a significant positive impact on land-use requirements for biofuels and net GHG benefits; the scale of the effects will depend upon the substitution adopted in the co-product analysis. The Gallagher Review (RFA, 2008) concludes that most first-generation crops out-perform the next-generation energy crops if co-products and straw utilization are considered.

GHG emissions from land conversion to biofuel production: global assessment
The study by Ravindranath *et al.* (2009) makes an attempt to estimate CO_2 emissions associated with land conversion at the global level in the case of first-generation biofuel crops. CO_2 emissions are estimated by considering a scenario of biofuels substituting 10 percent of the petro-leum fuel used for transportation in 2030. The following method is used:

- Demand for diesel and gasoline for the transportation sector is estimated based on the *International Energy Outlook* (EIA, 2008) for 2030.
- The land required for production of biofuels assumes that 10 percent of the projected diesel and gasoline demand of the transportation sector in 2030 will be met by biodiesel and ethanol, respectively (Table 6.3).
- The potential CO_2 emissions from land conversion are estimated for different land category conversions for different biodiesel and ethanol crops, and mean annual CO_2 emissions per hectare due to land conversions, based on the study by Fargione *et al.* (2008).

CO_2 emissions from land conversion are estimated by considering six scenarios of land conversion and the total area required for each biofuel crop (Table 6.4). The mean annual CO_2 emission estimates for meeting the biodiesel demand for substituting 10 percent of diesel demand in 2030 ranges from 537 Mt CO_2 for jatropha to 1,119 Mt CO_2 for soybean.
Similarly, the mean annual CO_2 estimation from land conversion for

Table 6.4 Mean annual CO_2 emission (Mt CO_2/yr) averaged over a 30-year period from land conversion, under different scenarios where each biofuel crop is assumed to meet 10 percent of the biodiesel or ethanol demand in 2030

Region	Emissions required from land-use conversion when 10% biodiesel demand is met by single crop in 2030 crop scenario			Emissions from land-use conversion when 10% of ethanol demand is met by single crop in 2030		
	Jatropha	Palm oil	Soybean	Maize	Sugar-cane	Sweet sorghum
OECD	273	436	569	359	110	183
Non-OECD	264	421	550	347	106	177
World	537	857	1,119	706	216	360

Mean annual CO_2 emissions = (area of native/original land use converted to the selected biofuel crop under each scenario) X (CO_2 emission factor associated with the conversion from native/original land use to the selected biofuel crop).

Emission factors considered for the 30-year period as well as on a mean annual basis are: grassland to jatropha (93 tCO_2/ ha over 30-year period) = 3.1 tCO_2/ha/yr; tropical forest to oil palm (535 tCO_2/ ha over 30-year period) = 17.4 tCO_2/ha/yr; grassland to soybean (93 tCO_2/ ha over 30-year period) = 3.1 $tCO_2$2/ha/yr; abandoned crop land to maize (145 tCO_2/ ha over 30-year period) = 4.1 tCO_2/ha/yr; grass-land to sugarcane (93 tCO_2/ ha over 30-year period) = 3.1 $tCO_2$2/ha/yr; grassland to sweet sorghum (93 tCO_2/ ha over 30-year period) = 3.1 $tCO_2$2/ha/yr.

Source: Ravindranath *et al.*, 2009.

producing ethanol to replace 10 percent of gasoline in 2030 ranges from 216 Mt CO_2 for sugarcane to 706 Mt CO_2 for maize.

Thus, to meet 10 percent petroleum fuel substitution, the CO_2 emissions from land conversion alone can range from 753 Mt CO_2 (grassland to jatropha and sugarcane) to 1825 Mt CO_2 (grassland to soybean).

The total CO_2 emission from 10 percent of the diesel and gasoline consumption during 2030, which is to be substituted by biofuels, is estimated to be 0.84 Gt CO_2 annually, whereas the annual CO_2 emission from land conversion alone is estimated to be in the range of 0.75 to 1.83 Gt CO_2. This does not take into account the emissions released in cultivation, indirect land conversions, transportation, and processing of the biofuels, which would reduce the amount of CO_2 substitution by 20–90 percent (Thow and Warhurst, 2007) – that is, from 0.84 to between 0.17 and 0.76. Thus, the potential CO_2 emission from land conversion to biofuel crops by growing first-generation biofuel crops is likely to be greater than the savings expected from the first thirty years of growing biofuel crops (Ravindranath *et al.*, 2009).

Nitrous oxide emission

N_2O is produced in the soil from nitrogenous fertilizers and from natural mineralization of nitrogen through nitrification and de-nitrification processes. Application of nitrogen-based fertilizers for biofuel production, particularly in marginal lands, could potentially lead to increased N_2O emissions. N_2O is a GHG with a global-warming potential higher than that of CO_2 (Prather *et al.*, 2001). Thus, cultivation of biofuels with nitrogenous fertilizer application may reduce the net GHG benefit of biofuels. Bates *et al.* (2008) have concluded that N_2O emission by soil is a significant source of GHG emissions for first-generation biodiesel crops. Further, inclusion of N_2O emissions in the estimates of CO_2 emissions, especially for crops with lower net CO_2 benefit, may lead to no net savings: thus, net CO_2 benefit from many biofuel crops will be sensitive to inclusion of N_2O emissions.

Biodiversity

The impact of biofuel production on biodiversity is one of the important contentious issues. Large-scale biofuel production could have negative as well as positive implications for biodiversity. The variable factors to be considered here include the land category to be converted (direct and indirect conversion) for biofuel production; the biodiversity status of the land before conversion; the biofuel crop; and the cultivation practices. The Convention on Biodiversity (CBD) has acknowledged concerns about biofuel production on biodiversity and recommends scientific research to assess the positive as well as negative impacts.

Increased biofuel production is likely to have large implications for biodiversity, where biodiversity is defined as species richness and estimated as the number of species of plants, animals and microorganisms per unit area. According to Sala *et al.* (2009) and FAO (2008), increased biofuel production will have negative implications on biodiversity due to habitat conversion and loss, agricultural intensification, invasive species, and pollution.

Habitat conversion and loss

Biofuel production requires the expansion of the area presently under food crops, most often into natural forests, peat lands, grasslands, wetlands and marginal or abandoned lands. As the CBD (2008) notes, many current biofuel crops are well suited to tropical areas. De Vries *et al.* (2007) suggest that grassland could be the primary target for biofuel expansion in many regions. In Brazil expansion of sugarcane area during 2007 was largely based on the conversion of pasture land (65 percent), followed by conversion from soybean, maize and other crops (CONAB, 2008). Thus, increasing demand for biofuels may create economic incentives leading to the conversion of natural ecosystems to biofuel crops – for example, the conversion of forests to oil palm plantations in South-East Asia (Danielsen *et al.*, 2009) and soybean production in Brazil (Cerri *et al.*, 2007). Such a habitat conversion will lead to significant biodiversity loss; in particular, the conversion of protected areas with a high species density will accentuate this negative impact. It is important to note that even the conversion of marginal or degraded lands could have adverse implications for biodiversity (Robertson *et al.*, 2008). Virtually any land converted to biofuels raises the difficulty of potential competition with either food production or conservation (Sala *et al.*, 2009).

Agricultural intensification

Commercial large-scale biofuel plantations are likely to be based on monoculture crops, often using a single species with low genetic diversity. This genetic uniformity may increase the susceptibility of biofuel crops to new pests and diseases. Studies have reported that plantations adversely impact biodiversity, compared to natural forests, since plantations host only a fraction of the fauna – birds, mammals, bats et cetera – that find a home in the latter. Plantations, it would seem, are basically incompatible with biodiversity (Stone, 2007).

Invasive species

Taxa that invade or are introduced into the areas outside their natural ranges often have large negative impacts on biodiversity. Non-native taxa (species and genotypes) have facilitated extinction of native species, altered the composition of ecological communities, and affected eco-system processes (Sala *et al.*, 2009). Many of the species identified for biofuel production are also potential invaders outside their native range (Barney and DiTomaso, 2008). Further, habitat changes associated with biofuel production are likely to increase the risk of invasion by non-native taxa. Whether these habitats are clear-cut in large patches or small patches, or selectively harvested for particular species, leading to disturbance, each case will bring its own invasion risks (Davis *et al.*, 2000).

Pollution

Large-scale commercial biofuel production will require the use of fertilizers and pesticides, which is likely to have an impact on terrestrial and aquatic biodiversity. Many of the biofuel crops such as sugarcane or maize are particularly fertilizer- and pesticide-intensive under com-mercial production. Eutrophication caused by nutrient pollution could lead to changes in the biogenic habitat and balanced functioning of aquatic ecosystems (Carpenter *et al.*, 1998).

The above-mentioned drivers, each of which has a distinct set of impacts on biodiversity, may also occur simultaneously and interact with one another. Multiple drivers can affect biodiversity in an additive, synergistic or antagonistic fashion; the implications of this interaction are not well known (Sala *et al.*, 2009).

Biofuel production under sustainable production practices involving high-diversity mixtures of native grassland perennials, which offer a range of ecosystem services along with reduced GHG emissions and with low agro-chemical pollution, could have positive implications for biodiversity. The implications of expanded biofuel production on bio-diversity would be heterogeneous, depending on the region under consideration, the biofuel crop, and the production practices (Sala *et al.*, 2009). Use of next-generation grasses for expanding biofuel production is likely to have less impact on biodiversity than oil palm or soybean or maize replacing tropical forests or grasslands. Currently, a comparative understanding of the biodiversity implications of first-generation as opposed to next-generation crops is beyond reach and requires research.

Projections of climate change

A report by the Intergovernmental Panel on Climate Change (IPCC, 2007) has shown that continued GHG emissions at or above current rates would cause further warming and induce many changes in the global climate system during the twenty-first century. For the two decades a warming of about 0.2°C is projected for a range of emission projection scenarios. The warming is projected to be in the range of 1.8–4°C by the end of the current century. Warming is projected to be higher over land surface compared to the global mean. For example, the African continent is likely to experience warming at higher levels than

Table 6.5 Biofuel crops: rainfall and land/climate requirements, and cultivation practices

Biofuel crops	Rainfall (cm)	Land and climate	Cultivation practice
Sugarcane	150–250	Tropical and sub-tropical	Intensive irrigation and fertilization in semi-arid and sub-humid regions. Rain-fed crop in humid regions
Oil palm	180–500	Moderate to high-quality land; humid tropical	No irrigation in humid regions. Fertilize for high yields
Maize (grain)	70–150	Semi-arid, moderate to high-quality land	Rain-fed – with intensive practices, irrigation and fertilization for high yields
Jatropha (seeds)	60–120	Tropical, sub-tropical and semi-arid. Poor to moderate land. Not irrigated, drought-resistant	Not intensive. No irrigation and fertilizer application
Woody biomass (ligneous biomass)	50–500	Arid, semi-arid, humid tropical to temperate. Poor-quality land tolerated. Drought-resistant	No irrigation, moderate fertilizer application

the global mean, which could be in the range of 3–5°C by the end of this century. It is very likely that hot extremes, heat waves and heavy precipitation events will become more frequent. Tropical cyclones will become more intense. Regional changes in precipitation patterns are projected, with most sub-tropical regions likely to experience a decline in precipitation. Thus most tropical regions are likely to undergo significant warming – with many regions becoming drier, with changes in precipitation, and with many regions experiencing reduction in rainfall.

Changes in precipitation and temperature lead to changes in run-off and water availability. Many of the semi-arid areas will suffer decrease in water resources due to climate change. Drought-affected areas are projected to increase, with potential adverse impacts on natural and human systems. Climate change is expected to exacerbate current stresses on water resources from population growth and land-use change factors. Semi-arid and arid areas are likely to increase by 5–8 percent in Africa and Asia. All these projected changes in climate – rise in temperature, changes in rainfall pattern, increased recurrence of droughts and floods, water stress and expansion of dry areas – are likely to harm ecosystems, food production, water availability, and coastal areas.

Impacts of climate change on biofuel production

Rainfall, land, and climate requirements for biofuel crops
The broad land and climate requirements of biofuel crops, together with their irrigation practices, are given in Table 6.5. Oil palm requires humid conditions, while sugarcane is largely irrigated or grown under humid conditions. Other biofuel crops such as maize, sweet sorghum, and jatropha can be grown under rain-fed conditions, but maize requires irrigation and fertilization for high yields. Projected climate warming and droughts would lead to increased water stress and demand for irrigation.

Impacts of projected climate change on biofuel crops
There are no dedicated studies on the likely impacts of projected climate change on biofuel crops in different regions. There are annual (maize,

sorghum and sugarcane) as well as perennial (jatropha and oil palm) biofuel crops. The projected impacts of climate change on food and cash crops are likely to provide an indication of the climate impacts on biofuel crops. Some projected impacts, as presented in the IPCC report (2007) discussed above, can be extrapolated for the case of biofuel crops.

Impacts on crop production: Climate change is likely to have a major impact on crop productivity in lower latitudes, especially in seasonally dry and tropical regions. In some regions of Africa crop yields from rain-fed agriculture could be reduced by up to 50 percent. The projected climate change is likely to increase water stress as well as the demand for increased irrigation, leading to reduction in crop yields. Large parts of Africa, South Asia and semi-arid regions of Latin America are likely to experience decline in rainfall, land degradation and water stress, with a corresponding decline in crop yields.

Sugarcane: As an irrigated crop it is unlikely to suffer a direct adverse impact from climate change. However, reduction in the rainfall and increase in temperature contributes to water stress, leading to increased demand for irrigation. With warming and reduction in rainfall water, availability of irrigation would also decline. Increasing the area under sugarcane is likely to be limited by this factor.

Maize: Maize is largely a rain-fed crop and is likely to be hit hard by warming, reduction in rainfall and water stress. Maize yields could decline by 25 to 50 percent even in the short term.

Sweet sorghum: Sweet sorghum will experience impacts similar to maize, under rain-fed conditions. Under irrigated conditions the demand for water for irrigation may increase due to warming.

Jatropha: This is a perennial crop likely to be suited to semi-arid conditions. It is usually cultivated in marginal lands under rain-fed conditions, and thus likely to be subjected to reduction in yields due to water stress, unless irrigated.

Oil palm: Oil palm is a perennial crop grown under humid conditions. It is projected to enjoy initial increases in yield in the short term due to elevated CO_2, if no significant reduction in rainfall occurs. However, it could experience decline in yield beyond moderate warming.

The overall prognosis, then, is that annual as well as perennial biofuel crops are likely to be subjected to adverse impacts of climate change, particularly from warming, reduction in rainfall, water stress, droughts and increased occurrence of pests, leading to reduction in yield.

Potential adaptation strategy for sustainable biofuel production
In the context of projected climate change and the likely adverse impacts, it is necessary to develop and implement adaptation strategies for sustained biofuel production. Currently, there is limited research on potential adaptation practices and strategies, even for food crops. Thus, only potential win-win adaptation strategies could be considered. It is important to note that the majority of adaptation strategies designed to cope with current environmental stresses are also required to cope with climate change impacts. An illustrative list of potential adaptation strategies reads as follows:

- *Sugarcane*: Increase in area under irrigation, assured irrigation, increase in irrigation efficiency and efficient water management practices.
- *Maize and sweet sorghum*: Development and adoption of drought- and pest-resistant varieties and soil water conservation practices.
- *Jatropha*: Breeding for drought and pest resistance, and adoption of soil and water conservation practices.

Conclusion

The current global interest in biofuels, particularly in the industrialized countries, is driven by the need for mitigation of climate change through substitution of fossil fuels by biofuels. The area under biofuel production has increased significantly in the last few years, and continues to grow at a steady pace. A number of countries have announced steep targets ranging from 5 to 20 percent substitution of petroleum fuels in transportation within the period 2020–30. However, the new scientific literature, particularly since 2007, has highlighted the uncertainties involved in biofuel production and use, and the controversial nature of supposed GHG benefits – as well as implications for food security, biodiversity and environmental pollution.

Most of the recent scientific literature concludes that life cycle analysis shows a net GHG benefit (30–100 percent compared to petroleum fuels), when the analysis includes use of co-products and excludes GHG emissions from land conversion. However, incorporation of the GHG emissions from direct and indirect land conversions can cancel any GHG benefit for most first-generation biofuel crops, in some cases incurring instead a large carbon debt with repayment periods up to several hundred years. For conversion of abandoned cropland and/or marginal lands, little or no carbon debt will be incurred. Thus, first-generation biofuel crops are most likely to provide net GHG benefits only under certain conditions: when cultivated on abandoned or degraded lands (involving no direct or indirect land conversion), where there is considerable utilization of co-products, and/or when sustainable production practices are adopted (such as avoiding/minimizing the use of nitrogenous fertilizers). It should also be noted that GHG emissions from land conversion are not specific to biofuel production; the emissions would also occur when land is cleared or converted for production of feed, food, fibre, or other uses.

Biofuel production is likely to have direct as well as indirect effects on food security and water, particularly in developing countries where the bulk of the future biofuel production is likely to occur owing to lower costs of production. Cultivation of first-generation biofuel crops has also been shown to have adverse implications for biodiversity, through habitat conversion, agricultural intensification, the spread of invasive species, and pollution of soil and water.

Tropical countries are projected to experience climate change on a significant scale with a rise in temperature, decline in rainfall in many regions, and increased occurrence of drought and floods. The projected climate change is likely to lead to land degradation, water stress, increased pest occurrence and, ultimately, reduction in yields of annual as well as perennial crops. If biofuels are going to be cultivated on a large scale in the tropical regions to produce ethanol and biodiesel, they are likely to be adversely impacted by climate change. Sustainable biofuel production will thus require suitable adaptation practices and strategies, but there is limited research and knowledge on the impacts of climate change on biofuel crops and potential adaptation strategies at regional level. Thus, it is very important to recognize the importance of climate change and to initiate research on the assessment of climate change impacts on biofuels, and to developing adaptation strategies for different biofuel crops in different regions. As a recent article in *Science* concluded: 'Sustainable biofuel production systems could play a highly positive role in mitigating climate change, enhancing environmental quality and strengthening global economy but it will take sound, science based policy and additional research' (Robertson *et al.*, 2008).

References

Balat, M. and H. Balat (2009) 'Recent trends in global production and utilization of bio-ethanol fuel', *Applied Energy* 86: 2273–82.

Barney, J. N. and J. M. DiTomaso (2008) 'Non-native species and bioenergy: are we cultivating the next invader?' *Bioscience* 58: 64–70.

Bates, J., P. Howes, C. Dent, A. Brown and D. Rapson (2008) 'Review of indirect effects of biofuels', report, Renewable Fuels Agency, London.

Carpenter, S. R., N. F. Cararo, D. L. Correll, R. W. Howarth, A. N. Sharpley and V. H. Smith (1998) 'Nonpoint pollution of surface waters with phosphorus and nitrogen', *Ecological Applications* 8: 559–68.

Cerri, C. E. P., M. Easter, K. Pautian, K. Killian, K. Coleman, M. Bernoux, P. Falloon, D. S. Powlson, N. H. Batjes, M. Milne and C. C. Cerri (2007) 'Predicted soil organic carbon stocks and changes in Brazilian Amazon between 2000 and 2030', *Agriculture, Ecosystems and Environment* 122 (1): 58–72.

CONAB (Companhia Nacional de Abastecimento) (2008) 'Perfil do Setor do Açúcar e do Álcool no Brasil: situação observada em novembro de 2007', report, CONAB, Brasília.

Convention on Biological Diversity (CBD) (2008) *Biodiversity and Agriculture: Safeguarding Biodiversity and Securing Food for the World*, United Nations Environment Programme (UNEP), Montreal.

Croezen, H. and F. Brouwer (2008) 'Estimating indirect land use impacts from by-products utilization', report, CE Delft and AEA Technology, Delft.

Danielsen, F., H. Beukema, N. D. Burgess, F. Parish, C. A. Bruhl, P. F. Donald, D. Murdiyarso, B. Phalan, L. Reijnders, M. Struebig and E. B. Fitzherbert (2009) 'Biofuel plantations on forested lands: double jeopardy for biodiversity and climate', *Conservation Biology* 23: 348–58.

Davis, M. A., J. P. Grime and K. Thompson (2000) 'Fluctuating resources in plant communities: a general theory of invisibility', *Journal of Ecology* 88: 528–34.

de Vries, B., D. V. Vuuren and M. Hoogwijk (2007) 'Renewable energy sources: their global potential for the first half of the twenty-first century at a global level: an integrated approach', *Energy Policy* 35: 2590–610.

EIA (Energy Information Administration) (2008) *International Energy Outlook*, US Department of Energy/EIA, Washington DC.

FAO (2008) *The State of Food and Agriculture*, Food and Agriculture Organization, Rome.

FAPRI (2008) *US: Baseline Briefing Book*, Food and Agricultural Policy Research Institute, University of Missouri.

Fargione, J., J. Hill, D. Tilman, S. Polasky and P. Hawthorne (2008) 'Land clearing and the biofuel carbon debt', *Science* 319 (5867): 1236–8, <www.science express.org> (7 February).

Fresco, L. O. (2007) 'Biomass for food or fuel: is there a dilemma?' report (with Daan Dijk and Wouter de Ridder), Rabobank, Utrecht.

Gallagher, E. (2008) 'The Gallagher Review of the Indirect Effects of Biofuels Production', report, Renewable Fuels Agency, London.

Gibbs, H. K., M. Johnston, J. Foley, T. Holloway, C. Monfreda, N. Ramankutty and D. Zaks (2008) 'Carbon payback times for crop-based biofuel expansion in the tropics: the effects of changing yield and technology', *Environmental Research Letters* 3 (2008) (IOP Electronic Journals).

IEA (2006) *World Energy Outlook*, Organisation for Economic Co-operation and Development and the International Energy Agency.

IPCC (2007) 'Mitigation of climate change: technical summary', report, Intergovernmental Panel on Climate Change, Geneva.

Jongschaap, R. E. E., W. J. Corre, P. S. Bindraban and W. A. Bandenburg (2007) 'Claims and facts on *Jatropha curcas L.*: global jatropha curcas evaluation, breeding and propagation programme', report, Plant Research International, Wageningen.

Laurance, W. (2007) 'Switch to corn promotes amazon deforestation', letter in *Science* 318 (5857): 1721.

Menichetti, E. and M. Otto (2009) 'Energy balance and green house gas emission of biofuel from a product life-cycle perspective', in R. W. Howarth and S. Bringezu (eds), *Biofuels: Environmental Consequences and Interactions with Changing Land Use*, Proceedings of the Scientific Committee on Problems of the Environment (SCOPE) International Biofuels Project Rapid Assessment, 22–25 September 2008, Gummersbach, Germany, pp. 81–109.

Mielke, T. (ed.) (2007) *Oil World Annual 2007*, Hamburg.

OECD (2008) 'Economic assessment of biofuel support policies', report, Directorate for Trade and Agriculture, Organisation for Economic Co-operation and Development.

OECD-FAO (2008) *World Agricultural Outlook 2007–2017*, Organisation for Economic Co-operation and Development and Food and Agriculture Organisation, Rome.

Peña, N. (2008) 'Biofuels for transportation: a climate perspective', report, Pew Center on Global Climate Change, Arlington VA.

Prather, M., D. Ehhalt, *et al.* (2001) 'Atmospheric chemistry and greenhouse gases', in J. T. Houghton, Y. Ding, D. J. Griggs, M. Noguer, P. J. van der Linden, X. Dai, K. Maskell and C. A. Johnson (eds), *Climate Change 2001: The Scientific Basis*, Cambridge University Press, Cambridge, 2001.

Ravindranath, N. H., R. Manuvie, J. Fargione, J. G. Canadell, G. Berndes, J. Woods, H. Watson and J. Sathaye (2009) 'Green house gas implications of land use and land conversion to biofuel crops', report, Scientific Committee on Problems of the Environment (SCOPE).

Righelato, R. and D. V. Spracklen (2007) 'Carbon mitigation by biofuels or by saving and restoring forests?', *Science* 317 (5840): 902.

RFA (2008) *Changing the Climate: Ethanol Industry Outlook 2008*, Renewable Fuels Association, Washington DC.

Robertson, G. P., V. H. Dale, O. C. Doering, S. P. Hamburg, J. M. Melillo, M. M. Wander, W. J. Parton, P. R. Adler, J. N. Barney, R. M. Cruse, C. S. Duke, P. M. Fearnside, R. F. Follett, H. K. Gibbs, J. Goldemberg, D. J. Mladenoff, D. Ojima, M. W. Palmer, A. Sharpley, L. Wallace, K. C. Weathers, J. A. Wiens and W. W. Wilhelm (2008) 'Sustainable biofuels redux', *Science* 322 (5898): 49–50.

Royal Society (2008) 'Sustainable biofuels: prospects and challenges', report, Royal Society, London.

Ruth, L. (2008) 'Bio or bust? The economic and ecological cost of biofuels', *EMBO Journal* (European Molecular Biology Organization) 9 (2): 130–4.

Sala, O. E., D. Sax and H. Leslie (2009) 'Biodiversity consequences of increased biofuel production', report, Scientific Committee on Problems of the Environment (SCOPE).

Scharlemann, J. P. W. and W. F. Laurance (2008) 'How green are biofuels?', *Science* 319 (5859): 43–4.

Searchinger, T., R. Heimlich, R. A. Houghton, F. Dong, A. Elobeid, J. Fabiosa, S. Tokgoz, D. Hayes and T. Yu (2008) 'Use of US cropland increases greenhouse gases through emissions from land use change', *Science* 319 (5867): 1238–40, <www.scienceexpress.org> (7 February 2008).

Sims, R., M. Taylor, J. Saddler and W. Mabee (2008) 'From first to second generation biofuel technologies: an overview of current industry and RD & D activities', report, International Energy Agency (IEA).

Staley, B. C. and R. Bradley (2008) 'Plants at the pump: reviewing biofuels', report, World Resources Institute.

Stone, R. (2007) 'Can palm oil plantations come clean?', *Science* 317 (5844): 1491.

Thow, A. and A. Warhurst (2007) 'Biofuels and sustainable development', report, Maplecroft Company, Bath, UK.

Worldwatch Institute (2006) *Biofuels for Transportation: Global Potential and Implications for Sustainable Agriculture and Energy in the Twenty-First Century*, Earthscan, London.

7 Future Trends in Biomass Resources for Food and Fuel*

Francis X. Johnson and Ivar Virgin

The global biomass resource base will undergo a fundamental transformation in the coming decades as a result of the convergence of many driving forces. Agricultural and forest production systems must feed and shelter a growing world population and at the same time meet the demands for fuel, fibre, fertilizer and the many other types of goods and services that are derived from bio-based sources and conversion systems. The rapidly dwindling stock of non-renewable resources and the continued heavy dependence of developing countries on traditional biomass points to a unique role for biomass resources in the sustainability transition of the coming decades. Bioenergy is the only class of renewable energy that is continuously available across all energy carriers; unlike intermittent wind and solar used for electricity, bioenergy is available as heat, mechanical and electrical energy, as well as in liquid, solid and gaseous forms (Leach and Johnson, 1999).

The high efficiency of tropical and sub-tropical biomass means that the developing world has a comparative advantage over the temperate regions where most OECD countries are located. Brazil has exploited this advantage in its ethanol programme, offering the best example to date of a biofuel system that has been continuously improved and optimized over time in economic and environmental terms (see Chapter 3 in this volume). The growth of biofuel markets and international trade have also presented new opportunities for rural development and agricultural investment in many developing countries (see Chapter 5 in this volume). Nevertheless, constraints on availability of technology,

* Financial support from the Swedish International Development Cooperation Agency through the Climate for Development Programme of the Stockholm Environment Institute is gratefully acknowledged. Special thanks also to Richard Klein for support and encouragement for this book project in his role as director of that programme.

infrastructure and investment will continue to be an impediment in some world regions, particularly in sub-Saharan Africa. Conversely, in the more densely populated regions of Asia, land resources present a greater constraint to expansion for both food and fuel; higher yields and more advanced technologies will be needed. There is also tremendous room for improvement in the efficiency and quality of land use through methods such as optimizing multiple-product biomass logistics and adopting landscape ecology approaches (Chapter 4 in this volume).

The uncertainties of a changing climate add another set of factors that will require major adjustments to agricultural and energy systems, with a number of implications for how biomass resources are produced and managed. Even when bioenergy systems are managed well, the clearing of productive land for biofuel production will inevitably lead to net GHG emissions due to carbon sequestered in soils and root systems (Chapter 6 in this volume), so that preference should be given to degraded or marginal lands. Climate change will also affect the productivity of crops, induce changes in water availability and increase the probability of extreme events that could lead to severe strains on food security in some regions. Consequently, there are also ethical concerns when food crops are diverted for fuel production. Ethanol from corn in the USA appears to be a case where the costs outweigh the benefits, even in purely economic and environmental terms, with additional ethical and moral concerns as well (Chapter 2 in this volume).

This chapter considers the key driving forces in the ongoing transformation in global use of biomass resources for food, feed, fibre, fuel, fertilizer and many other uses. A more effective use of biomass resources is critical to the overall sustainability transition – a transition that is further strained by population growth, environmental pressures, and the aspirations of the developing world to a higher material standard of living. The potential competition between food and fuel will need to evolve towards better complementarities through multiple uses, products and applications if biomass resources are to play a fundamental role in the sustainability transition. This chapter considers the alternatives, in relation to the basic food/fuel equation, presented by future biomass and biofuel markets, technologies and policy actions – and offers some thoughts on the direction of future trends.

Future resource demands

According to analysis by the FAO, slightly over one billion persons were undernourished in 2009, a number which is greater in absolute terms than at any time since 1970, and represents an increase of more than 10 percent since 2008 (FAO, 2009). Indeed, the *percentage* of undernourished persons in the population has increased for the first time, attributed mainly to the impact of the global financial crisis as well as to some lingering effects of the high food prices experienced in 2007 and 2008. Reversing this trend in the future will require much greater investment in agriculture as well as improvements in distribution and transportation infrastructure, along with the non-agricultural investments that lead to new income-generating activities and the creation of more secure livelihoods.

The growing demand for food and feed
According to UN estimates the world population will reach 9.1 billion by 2050 (see Table 7.1), and is expected to peak before 2075 (FAO, 2006a). Most of the population increase is concentrated in Africa, South Asia and South-East Asia. A billion more persons are expected to live in sub-Saharan Africa in 2050 compared to 2000, and the same is true for South/South-East Asia. Given that these are already the regions where food security is a great concern, it becomes clear that these two regions represent the regional loci for potential food vs fuel conflicts. At the same time, such regional differences can be mitigated in an increasingly global economy through international trade, foreign investment and technology transfer.

On the basis of this demand, FAO predicts that agricultural production must increase by 70 percent in 2050 to cope with the increase in world population and the changing demands. This would translate into an additional billion tonnes of cereals and some 300 million tonnes of additional meat to be produced annually by 2050 (Table 7.2). Most experts would agree that the increase in production has to come from higher crop productivity rather than agricultural land expansion. According to FAO, some 90 percent of the growth in production would be the result of higher crop yields and increased cropping intensity, and only 10 percent would come from land

Table 7.1 Population development projections (millions)

Year	2000	2010	2020	2030	2040	2050	% change 2000–2050
North America	306	337	367	392	413	430	41%
Europe & Russia	752	762	766	761	748	729	-3%
Pacific OECD	150	153	152	148	142	135	-10%
Africa, sub-Saharan	655	842	1,056	1,281	1,509	1,723	163%
Latin America	505	574	638	689	725	744	47%
Middle East & North Africa	303	370	442	511	575	629	108%
Asia, East	1,402	1,500	1,584	1,633	1,630	1,596	14%
Asia, South/South-East	1,765	2,056	2,328	2,553	2,723	2,839	61%
Developed	1,141	1,177	1,202	1,211	1,210	1,198	5%
Developing	4,696	5,417	6,132	6,758	7,257	7,627	62%
Rest of World	210	233	249	262	272	280	33%
World	6,047	6,827	7,582	8,231	8,739	9,105	51%

Source: UN, 2009.

Table 7.2 Expected demand for cereals by region for all uses, food, and feed

	All uses			Food			Feed		
	2000	2050	%chg	2000	2050	%chg	2000	2050	%chg
Asia, South/South-East	250	427	71%	218	360	66%	3	12	266%
East Asia and Pacific	524	688	31%	347	376	8%	102	205	100%
Europe & Central Asia	235	267	13%	79	80	1%	108	124	14%
Latin America	180	287	60%	63	88	40%	50	112	122%
Middle East & North Africa	90	182	103%	56	102	83%	23	58	147%
Africa, sub-Saharan	84	243	190%	65	187	189%	7	18	155%
North America	619	853	38%	114	148	30%	324	401	24%
World	1,982	2,947	49%	942	1,341	42%	617	930	51%

Source: IFPRI IMPACT projections (Msangi and Rosengrant, 2009).

Note: 'All uses' includes other uses besides food and feed, such as bioenergy and industrial feedstocks.

expansion. The share due to intensification goes up to 95 percent in land-scarce regions in most parts of South Asia, and to over 100 percent in the Near East/North Africa. Arable land expansion will remain an important factor in crop production growth in many countries of sub-Saharan Africa and Latin America, although less so than in the past (Bruinsma, 2009).

To feed a growing population will be a formidable challenge in many parts of the world, but the problems are without doubt worst in sub-Saharan Africa, where there has been stagnation or decline in the agricultural productivity of small-scale farmers. African farmers are facing a host of challenges, including lack of infrastructure, management capacity, the degradation of their natural resource base, weak markets, poor credit facilities and other socio-economic constraints. The severe effects of HIV/AIDS and malaria also present dramatic challenges, negatively affecting the availability of agricultural labour and the productivity of rural communities. Farmers are also confronted with challenging biological and environmental constraints, such as frequent droughts and a large number of devastating plant pests and diseases. Poor soil fertility and inability to afford and use a sufficient amount of fertilizer is also one of the key factors for the low crop productivity in many African countries; indeed, fertilizer use in sub-Saharan Africa has been nearly flat since the 1960s, whereas all other regions have seen marked increases (Fischer *et al.*, 2009).

Changing diets and the impact of the livestock sector

The projections of future food and feed demands are uncertain for many reasons. Globalization is contributing to a tremendous increase and trade in livestock feed and products. This is underpinned by a transition in the developing world in favour of a diet of more meat and dairy products, which will require a dramatically higher feed production than today. Global production of meat is projected to double from 229 million tonnes in 1999/2001 to 465 million tonnes in 2050, and that of milk to grow from 580 to 1,043 million tonnes (FAO, 2006b). At the same time the livestock sector is undergoing a technical and geographical change, which is also shifting the balance of problems caused by the sector. Livestock production is relocating to urban and peri-urban areas to move closer to consumers, and there is also a shift in production patterns: an increased production of monogastric species, such as pigs and poultry, and a slowdown in the growth of ruminant production (cattle, sheep, goats). Since ruminants are raised extensively whereas monogastric animals require relatively small amounts of land, this could potentially relieve some land pressures, while at the same time producing less methane, a powerful GHG.

The livestock sector provides livelihoods for more than a billion people worldwide. For many poor farmers in developing countries livestock is a source of renewable energy and often the only source of fertilizer. However, the livestock sector is also contributing to deforestation, land degradation, unsustainable water use and eutrophication (FAO, 2006b). The increased consumption of meat and dairy products is also problematic from a climate change perspective; the livestock sector is responsible for 18 percent of global greenhouse gases (GHG), which is actually a higher share than global transport contributes. Some analysts argue that the GHG emissions from the livestock sector are actually much higher, if respiration and the land-intensive and resource-intensive nature of meat production and consumption are considered (Goodland and Anhang, 2009).

A considerable amount of land is also used to produce animal feed for export; some 11 million hectares are required for the soya cakes exported from Brazil to the EU for animal feed (FOE, 2008). One can compare this to the 7 million hectares that are required to produce all of Brazil's ethanol and sugar, which includes exports as well as meeting 55 percent of domestic demand for petrol. In terms of future land-use choices, one can conclude that a *'feed* vs fuel' dilemma presents just as significant a set of challenges as does 'food vs fuel', since the changes at the margin are potentially much more land-intensive due to the growing demand for meat in developing countries.

Transportation fuel and the demand for mobility

The demand for transport fuels is growing even faster than the demand for food or feed; during the period up to 2050 when population and food demand are expected to grow by 50 percent, the demand for transport fuels is expected to grow by 90 percent (Table 7.3). In East Asia alone,

Table 7.3 Transportation fuel demand (millions of toe)

	2000	2020	2030	2050	% change 2000–2050
North America	655	773	773	781	19%
Europe & Russia	519	658	652	609	17%
Pacific OECD	105	110	99	93	-11%
Africa, sub-Saharan	45	69	80	122	171%
Latin America	149	253	285	332	123%
Middle East & North Africa	108	214	259	342	217%
Asia, East	114	337	495	625	448%
Asia, South/South-East	111	224	322	544	390%
Developed	1,236	1,480	1,460	1,417	15%
Developing	576	1,174	1,529	2,068	259%
World	1,962	2,830	3,171	3,750	91%

Source: IEA, March 2009.
Note: World total is greater than sum since it includes bunker fuels and other industry-related consumption.

the phenomenal pace of economic growth in China is expected to result in a staggering five-fold-plus increase in fuel consumption! With the locus of global demand shifting to developing countries and especially to Asia, the structure of markets and distribution will also change considerably. As a major net importer of oil, China has energy security incentives to promote biofuels – and consequently the global impact of policy decisions taken in China on transport and biofuels will increase greatly in the coming decades. Stagnant demand growth in much of Europe and Russia means that the structural changes occurring at the margin will determine the direction of investment more so than in the past, when transport was part of general infrastructure and less directly tied to consumer demand.

Industrial agriculture and the bio-economy
The growing global demand for food, feed and bio-based renewable materials, such as biofuels, is changing the conditions for agricultural production worldwide, not least in developing countries. At the same time, the revolutionary achievements in the field of biosciences (see

below) are contributing to a transition whereby bio-based alternatives for energy and materials are becoming more economic and more mainstream. This has been called the development of a knowledge-based bio-economy, in which biological resources are transformed into new, sustainable, eco-efficient and value-added products (Eaglesham *et al.*, 2000). The development of a knowledge-based bio-economy is important for many reasons, including: (1) development of resource-efficient and productive agricultural systems able to adapt to climate change; (2) decreased dependence on fossil energy, thereby decreasing emission of greenhouse gases; (3) the possibility of revitalizing rural communities, increasing the production base and the opportunities for local value addition; and (4) increased capacity to recycle energy and material flows.

The central feature of a knowledge-based bio-economy is that agricultural systems are not only producing food and feed but to an increasing extent also agro-industrial products in applications spanning many sectors – pharmaceutical, industrial, chemical, and energy. As a consequence, we are seeing the development of agro-industrial systems producing not only biofuels but also things like novel fibres, specialized starch products, and 'green chemicals' such as biodegradable plastic, oil and lubricants. This process has been going on for a long time, but it is only during the last decade that we have seen a major shift in the momentum of the transition, fuelled by a number of important drivers:

- Increased demand for renewable resources including food and feed;
- An oil economy at its zenith – which in turn has led to an increased biofuel demand;
- Climate change, demanding both mitigation and adaptation strategies;
- The rapid increase of international trade and globalization;
- The bioscience revolution with its spectrum of technologies allowing for the development of tailor-made bio-resource produc-tions systems.

The production of agro-industrial products seems certain to be an increasingly important engine of economic growth for both the deve-loped and developing worlds. The transition to a bio-based economy is most rapid in the United States, where commercial petrochemical giants such as Dow Chemical and Dupont, major actors in the plastics revolution, are using recombinant DNA technology and other advanced biosciences to shift from the use of fossil-based raw material to agro-based raw material for their future products. Brazil is a good example of a knowledge-based bio-economy and increasingly so is China, which to a considerable extent is using agricultural innovation to generate growth in its agricultural sectors.

Industrial agriculture, with the emphasis on biofuels production, has been cited as a key factor in the increased competition for land and resources, and consequently in some cases as a cause of food insecurity. However, it can also be argued that increased demand and better prices for farm products would provide farmers with incentives to invest in their production and enable them to be more productive. This is particularly important in many developing countries where farmers are battling with weak market demand. Increased demand and subsequent improvements in farm incomes would enable these farmers to invest in agricultural inputs (fertilizers, improved seed, et cetera) and by doing so increase their overall production capacity and ability to feed themselves.

The bioscience revolution

The demand for increased crop productivity will be massive in the years to come: to meet it, farmers all over the world will have to produce more food, feed and industrial agricultural products on existing agricultural land under sustainable conditions. Achieving sustainable growth in farm production is a complex challenge. It calls for an integrated holistic approach, within which improved technology must be recognized as an important component. In most OECD countries farmers have been producing high-quality agriculture products in a resource-efficient and sustainable manner, thus minimizing impact. In regions such as Europe and the United States we have seen the development of precision farming, where advanced machinery and efficient production technology (including low-till agriculture) have reduced the use of fuel, fertilizer and other agro-inputs (World Bank, 2007). Organic farming is also on the rise in many countries, although crop productivity is lower in such systems in comparison with conventional farming. More advanced breeding and the use of improved varieties is also contributing to increased productivity, and will play a major role in the future. Overall, it is fair to say that while farming systems in most OECD countries are steadily becoming more sustainable, they are at the same time able to respond to an increased demand for food, feed and also industrial agricultural products.

The need for improved seeds and cultivars
In many developing countries in Africa and Asia, where increased food production is urgently needed, farmers face a host of difficulties – including lack of infrastructure, management and husbandry problems, ecosystem degradation, HIV/AIDS, weak markets and other socio-economic constraints. In many of these countries there is already a critical need for better land management and land tenure reforms, even as farmers are increasingly confronted with the impacts of climate change and resource constraints. Support is therefore needed at many different levels, but crop and animal genetics, effective breeding efforts, and dissemination of more productive seed and livestock remain the most effective means by which farmers can be assisted. This is recognized by institutions such as the FAO, the World Bank and the African Union (FAO, 2004; World Bank 2007; Juma and Seregeldin, 2007), who argue that one of the major constraints to increased food production, not least in sub-Saharan Africa, is the limited availability of improved seeds and livestock for poor and vulnerable farmers.

So, breeding of new, and more high-yielding crops for different agricultural sectors will therefore be of paramount importance in the years to come. The good news is that modern bioscience is revolutionizing the breeding sector all over the world and is providing an increasingly powerful innovation engine at a global scale for sustainable agricultural production, energy production, and development of a diverse range of novel bio-products (World Bank, 2007). In particular, agricultural biotechnology holds considerable promise for addressing breeding targets of great importance to farmers in all parts of the world:

- *Productivity*: To reach maturity, crops must be increasingly able to resist multiple stress factors such as drought and low soil fertility, often in combination with high disease stress. Agricultural biotechnology assists breeders to develop crops with increased tolerance to insect pests, diseases and climate stress.

- *Sustainability of agricultural practices*: Crop breeders can use agricultural biotechnology to develop crops tailored to lower degrees of pesticide inputs and to agricultural practices requiring less energy and labour input (such as low tillage and perennial grains). In the research pipeline are also crops that could make more efficient use of scarce resources such as water and crop nutrients.
- *Food and feed quality*: Crops are being developed with improved storage properties and nutritional characteristics (such as altered protein, mineral and vitamin content). Bio-fortified crops such as beans, rice and sorghum will soon be available to farmers and consumers in developing countries.
- *New production systems for crops with industrial applications* (such as biofuels, starch, fibre, oils). Metabolic pathways in agro-industrial crops could be altered and tailor-made to enhance the production of certain desirable compounds or components of the crop.

The impact of agricultural biotechnology

Genetic resources have long been important building blocks for agriculture and in the natural products industries. Today, with the arrival of modern biotechnology, a new chapter in the history of gene hunting has started. The field of agricultural biotechnology is expanding fast and ranges from the well-established techniques such as tissue culture and genetic characterization to the more novel, continuously evolving and converging fields of technologies such as DNA-marker-assisted breeding, genetic modification, and functional or synthetic genomics. The boundaries between various types of agricultural biotechnology are disappearing, and in general the whole system of technology applications is becoming increasingly valuable to agricultural breeding systems – in developing as well as developed countries. One of the most visible signs of the impact of agricultural biotechnology is the very rapid expansion in the cultivation of genetically modified (GM) crops (see Box 7.1).

The focus on GM food and feed crops has so far been on herbicide-

Box 7.1 GM crops to date

Biotechnology crops are today widely used globally by more than 10 million farmers. In 2008 GM crops covered more than 120 million hectares, which is roughly 10 percent of the total global cultivated land area. Most of the maize, soybean and cotton crops on the world commodity market today are genetically modified (James, 2008). Not only the biotech strongholds of the Americas (United States, Argentina and Brazil) but also China, India, Philippines, South Africa and Vietnam are investing heavily in agriculture based on biotechnology crops. The development has so far been focused on the more commercial crops and on already productive farmers in the North. The technology will probably increase in importance in the future as it is applied to crops other than the main food grains and legumes. Significant biotechnological crop-breeding efforts, particularly by the public breeding sector, are also being directed at small-scale farmers in developing countries – among these crops are genetically modified cassava, sorghum, banana, cowpea and beans. Biotechnology crops will also be an increasingly important tool for R&D efforts through the Consultative Group on International Agricultural Research (CGIAR) system.

and insect-tolerant maize, soybean, cotton and canola, but many more applications are in the R&D pipeline. Through the Africa Bio-fortified Sorghum project, funded by the Bill and Melinda Gates Foundation, a consortium of institutes is using advanced biosciences to develop a more nutritious and easily digestible sorghum that contains increased levels of essential amino acids, increased levels of Vitamins A and E, and more available iron and zinc (Biosorghum, 2010). Another very interesting project which may have a great impact on agriculture and breeding systems all over the world is the drought-tolerant GM maize technology developed by Monsanto, which may very well be a major breakthrough for GM breeding in its targeting of abiotic stress and crop yield (Fischer *et al.*, 2009). Of particular interest is the intent of the company to make this technology available for use in adapted maize in sub-Saharan Africa through the Water Efficient Maize for Africa (WEMA) project.

Future implications of modern biosciences

For industrial crops, including biofuels, modern biosciences will be increasingly important. The technologies used for food crops are also available for industrial and biofuel crops, making these crops more stress-tolerant and thereby enhancing total yield and yield stability. However, an even more attractive feature is that agro-biotechnology could also be used to alter metabolic pathways. Plants may offer an attractive alternative production system for proteins, oils, fibres and other compounds. Their use as a production system depends on their cost, quality, eco-efficiency and the time it takes to produce the desired compound, as well as on the uniqueness of the plants needed to produce that compound.

Today we see new types of GM maize, potatoes and canola producing modified plant oils. Researchers at Michigan State University have also engineered a 'second-generation biofuel crop' which already contains the necessary enzymes to break down cellulose and hemicellulose into simple sugars in their leaves, allowing for more cost-effective, efficient production of ethanol (*New Scientist*, 2008). Craig Venter, a well-known entrepreneurial scientist in the field of synthetic biology and genomics, has partnered with the Asiatic Centre for Genome Technology to sequence the genome of palm oil trees, which will lead to a crop that is more suitable for the biofuels industry. Another example of second-generation biofuels are those based on tree crops whose lignin content (the hard, 'woody' part of plants' cell walls) has been artificially weakened and reduced, and disintegrates easily under dedicated processing techniques. The energy crop grows normally, but is far easier to transform into bioproducts. Low-lignin hybrid trees (poplars) are being developed by several research organizations (Leplé *et al.*, 2007), among them the laboratory of the father of plant genetic engineering, Marc van Montagu of the University of Ghent, Belgium. Finally, the process of finding, characterizing and breeding new interesting biofuel crops can be greatly enhanced by modern biosciences.

Agricultural biotechnology is a relatively young technology and as it develops is likely to revolutionize agriculture as we know it today. For example, today there is extensive research on equipping crops (through genetic engineering) with more efficient photosynthetic machinery.

This involves transferring the more efficient C4 metabolism of maize into wheat and rice, and lowering photorespiration rates (competing with plant carbon storage) through modifying the key plant enzyme Rubisco. Research is also under way to make the widely successful hybrid maize technology for increasing stress tolerance commercially attractive for other cereals such as wheat (Fischer *et al.*, 2009). There are also futuristic research attempts aimed at making annual crops such as wheat, rice and maize into perennial crops, which could reduce the need for agricultural inputs. Another exciting area of research is to incorporate nitrogen fixation into crops such as rice, wheat and maize.

Undoubtedly, the new biosciences will be an increasingly important tool for the agricultural, forest and bioprocess sectors to tailor-make bioresource production systems to meet specific needs in terms of yield, quality characteristics and demands for resource efficiency. It is, however, important to point out that there is a wide gap between what agricultural biotechnology can do in principle and the extent to which the technology will improve the situation for farmers and farming systems in all parts of the world. This gap is particularly wide in many developing countries, and barriers to a successful use of agro-biotechnology in solving the productivity problems facing small-scale farmers are many – and beyond the scope of this chapter. Developing countries are, however, increasingly voicing awareness of the importance of participation in the bioscience revolution, with its spectrum of techniques and opportunities. Countries without the capacity to evaluate the rapidly expanding bioscience field critically from their own perspectives will be increasingly disadvantaged and continue to be dependent on the major global actors, thus missing the opportunity to adapt relevant parts of these technologies to their own local needs.

Future crops and feedstocks for biofuels

Nearly all of the biofuels crops used today are so-called 'first-generation' biofuels crops, including both the sugar and starch crops from which ethanol is made as well as the oilseed crops from which biodiesel is made. There is a fundamental transformation under way in the types of feedstocks used to produce biofuels, as the so-called first-generation biofuels crops are expected to give way to more advanced feedstocks.

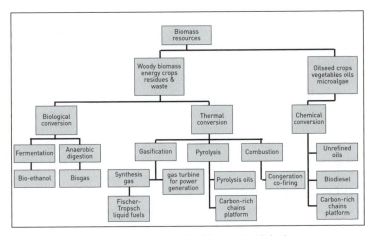

Figure 7.1 Various conversion routes for biomass to biofuels

The various routes can be summarized according to conversion plat-forms – thermal, biological and chemical – as shown in Figure 7.1.

The term 'second generation' when applied to biofuels crops has two interpretations in the general literature. One interpretation relates to the decreased reliance on food crops and less use of arable lands, which is accomplished through use of wastes and residues, non-edible plants or non-edible portions of plants, greater efficiency and/or the use of marginal lands. Another interpretation relates more to the conversion processes and energy carriers, which are advanced in that they use a much greater portion of the biomass, and thereby result in a much better energy balance and reduced environmental impacts. Third-generation biofuels are widely interpreted as those made from algae. In this section, we review the distinguishing characteristics of the various generations of biofuels, focusing on the prospects for increased market penetration of the more advanced biofuels and/or conversion processes.

What role for first-generation biofuels?
As explained elsewhere in this volume, first-generation biofuels include the sugar and starch crops that are converted into ethanol as well as the

oil-bearing crops that have been used to make biodiesel. In recent years, the logic of investing in first-generation biofuels has been questioned on many grounds, including basic economics but also food security and GHG impacts (see Chapter 6 in this volume). Consequently, the policy recommendations invariably consist of different strategies for phasing out first-generation biofuels in favour of the second generation of crops/feedstocks. The case of ethanol from sugarcane in Brazil and in regions with similar conditions is almost always cited as an exception to this rule, and is generally found to meet sustainability criteria (GBEP, 2008). Another first-generation crop that is expected to retain considerable interest in the coming years is jatropha: its ability to grow in marginal lands in semi-arid regions and the non-edible nature of the oil are characteristics that, taken together, minimize the conflict with food production.

Another caveat to predictions of the early demise of first-generation biofuels relates to the value of co-products and their close relation to provision of food and feed; failure to incorporate co-products leads to overestimates of impacts on food prices and land use. Using a comprehensive 'computable general equilibrium' (CGE) modelling approach, one study found that the expected cropland conversion from first-generation biofuel expansion due to the EU and US biofuel mandates is overestimated by 27 percent when by-product impacts are not included (Taheripour *et al.*, 2010). A related aspect is the attribution of indirect land-use change and GHG emissions to first-generation biofuels rather than apportioning these impacts to the food, fuel and feed components of these crops. A more holistic approach to biomass and agriculture would promote low tillage practices and land-use management practices that minimize the impacts from all uses rather than addressing only the fuel component (Kim *et al.*, 2009). In other words, the food–fuel connection that is inherently detrimental to the long-term sustainability of most first-generation biofuels crops is mitigated by the cascading utilization effect from animal feeds and other by-products. Consequently, first-generation biofuels crops will continue to play a limited role for many years to come, until second-generation biofuel technology platforms become commercially viable on a wide scale and can be deployed across a range of resource endowments in different world regions. Consequently, one can say that the transition to second-generation biofuels will occur not so much as a revolution but as more of an evolution.

Second-generation biofuels

As referenced elsewhere in this volume, the second-generation biofuels fall into two broad categories based on the choice of biochemical or thermo-chemical conversion platforms. The first category is lignocellulosic ethanol (LE), produced via hydrolysis of the woody or fibrous biomass, generally using enzyme catalysts. The second is the use of Fischer-Tropsch biomass-to-liquids (BTL) technologies to convert various biomass feedstocks into various fuels with varying properties. In addition to the physical difference in conversion platforms due to reliance on biological vs thermochemical methods, there are two key differences in the use of biomass and the resulting fuels. One difference is that the lignin is separated in biochemical conversion and can therefore be used separately for heat and power production, whereas with BTL the lignin is also converted into synthesis gas. A second difference lies in the fact that the biochemical route produces only ethanol, whereas BTL can produce a range of fuels with different properties, including aviation fuels as well as substitutes for petrol and diesel (Sims *et al.*, 2010). Projections of production cost tend to show a close equivalence for the two second-generation options, with BTL costs possibly requiring more time to achieve the cost reductions (see Table 7.4).

Table 7.4 IEA second-generation biofuel cost assumptions for 2010, 2030, and 2050

Fuel/year	2010	2030	2050
Biochemical ethanol	0.8 –0.90	0.55–0.65	0.55–0.60
BTL diesel	1.00–1.20	0.60–0.70	0.55–0.65

Note: Costs are expressed in dollars per litre of gasoline equivalent.
Source: IEA, 2009.

The versatility of BTL fuels is economically attractive and could contribute to an accelerated development in the next decade as both the public and private sector rush to bring advanced biofuels to the market. On the other hand, ethanol production from LE sources is a technology platform that can operate at scales and locations that are not so different from first-generation ethanol already being produced, making its deployment somewhat faster and less complicated. A key question that will determine the speed of market commercialization for second-generation biofuels is the relative pace of technological learning with its associated cost reductions. Of related importance is the timing of market introduction for second-generation biofuels and the distinction between scale-dependent and scale-independent cost reductions. In the European context, demand for diesel fuel is higher than petrol and, furthermore, the lower cost of oil crops compared to the starchy feed-stocks used for first-generation ethanol means that first-generation bio-diesel is cheaper in energy-equivalent terms than first-generation ethanol. Although the IEA projects slightly higher costs globally for BTL diesel, dynamic technological learning suggests that as second-generation fuels replace the first generation, there could be a cost advantage for BTL fuels from scale-learning effects, thus potentially rapidly increasing their market share. However, since the timing of market introduction remains uncertain, LE could gain a significant share in initial years (de Wit *et al.*, 2010). We therefore expect to see BTL diesel predominating in Europe, while LE might predominate in markets where petrol demand is higher, namely in North America.

Third-generation biofuels
The third generation of biofuels is generally defined as those derived from microalgae, which are either unicellular or simple multicellular organisms; not only do algae biofuels have much higher energy yields, but, since they are grown in water, they will avoid most of the land-use conflicts that characterize first- and second-generation biofuels. Algal-based biofuels also extend the versatility of end uses beyond those of second-generation biofuels because they can be used to create many different types of fuels, including not only substitutes for petrol or diesel, but also photobiological hydrogen gas (Brennan and Owende,

2010). Again, the versatility of end uses, fuels and energy carriers (gas, electricity, solid, hydrogen) represents another improvement over the previous generation of biofuels. Some researchers also classify genetically engineered biofuel crops as of the third generation, since the goal is similar to that of using algae – to improve the feedstocks themselves rather than improving conversion technologies, as is the goal of second-generation feedstocks (Kivits *et al.*, 2010). Other researchers consider these crops as a fourth generation, as discussed below.

Fourth-generation biofuels
The fourth generation of biofuels is not well defined, although most analysts and researchers would associate this class of biofuels with synthetic biology and more generally the use of biotechnology to 'design' biofuels with fairly specific technical characteristics to meet particular end-user needs or market demands. The fourth-generation biofuel technology platforms will combine genetically optimized feedstocks designed to capture large amounts of carbon with genomically synthesized microbes; these microbes will actually produce fuel and absorb CO_2. Consequently, fourth-generation biofuels would be truly *carbon-negative*, unlike their *carbon-neutral* predecessors (Kivits *et al.*, 2010).

It is difficult to speculate on the future impacts of fourth-generation biofuels, since their development is in its infancy, except to note that this special characteristic of being carbon-negative is the most significant in strategic terms, although more for addressing climate change than for food vs fuel conflicts *per se*. Assuming that current social reluctance to endorse biotechnology is gradually reduced over time, the fourth-generation biofuels could thus lead to a radical transformation in how fuels are developed and used, since they would increasingly be coupled to some form of carbon capture and storage system. Another element of this transformation is that they would have spin-offs in other sectors – health, industry, chemicals, and almost any sector that relies on resource inputs, whether renewable or non-renewable. Although such spin-offs are found in all generations of biofuels, it is likely that they would be more profound when genetic engineering is involved, since the possibilities increase exponentially.

Land and water use

Second- and third-generation biofuels will greatly reduce, although they will not eliminate, the competition for land with food crops. The competition becomes indirect rather than direct, and will depend considerably on the feedstocks used. Where residues are used, there is little or no competition with food, just as with first-generation biofuels. Where woody and fibrous biomass from dedicated sources is used, competition with food arises from the need for water, fertilizers and other inputs that may be scarce or in limited supply in some regions. Where the source is algae, the competition is even more remote, since it arises more from the different type of human and capital investment associated with maintaining the special conditions for algae growth, a rather different undertaking from the input-oriented nature of first- and second-generation biofuels crops.

This competition for resources gives rise, in economic terms, to a 'shadow price' for water and other inputs, indicating the cost for an additional unit of that input due to a binding constraint, such as water scarcity, in a particular region. With regional flexibility in bioenergy production and technical progress in yields, shadow prices for water scarcity will be considerably lower on average than previously expected; some analyses with projections until 2050 show relatively few areas where water scarcity becomes a constraint, since trade and yield improvements reduce the need for agricultural expansion and water removal (Lotze-Campen *et al.*, 2010).

Biomass resources in transition

The full potential of biomass resources remains largely untapped in many parts of the world, especially in the least-developed countries, where modern agricultural techniques have not penetrated and many farmers are operating at subsistence level. The same is true on the energy side of the equation, with nearly 100 percent of the rural poor continuing to rely on traditional biomass to meet their daily needs for cooking, heating and lighting. Modern agricultural and bioenergy systems offer the possibility of a major transformation in the entire food–fuel equation, along with all the other associated goods and services that arise from various local value-addition chains of biomass resources. The growing demand for various biomass resources, including food, feed and bio-based renewable materials such as biofuel, is transforming conditions for biomass utilization and production at both local and global levels. This transformation could help to revive rural economies in many developing countries and create new regional and international markets. A great deal of investment along with sound policies will be necessary, however, to achieve this transformation and make it a vehicle for sustainable economic growth.

Turning waste products into renewable resources
Biomass originating from crop residues of established agro-industrial production chains is currently often considered as waste material. This biomass can be redirected to new applications, both as a CO_2-neutral energy source as well as a variety of value-added products for both local and export markets. The tools to achieve these aims are to be found in the novel design of biorefineries (Kamm *et al.*, 2006).

The waste residues from agriculture, forestry, fishing, pulp and paper production, and many other 'bio-oriented' industries or agro-industries are often readily available for use as an energy source. In some industries, such as pulp and paper or sugar production, these residues have long provided energy for the manufacturing processes. More recently, it has been recognized that much more energy can be extracted by two interrelated adjustments: improving the energy efficiency in production of the primary product; and choosing more efficient conversion options and applications for the residues and other co-products. Contrary to the assumptions in standard neoclassical economic theory, transforming these waste products into renewable resources does not depend on prices alone, but also depends on the underlying institutions that raise or lower transaction costs and market barriers.

From single to multiple product(s)
Whereas an emphasis on bioenergy may have traditionally resulted in only one commercially valuable product, a bio-based economy will require a sustainable supply of large volumes of biomass feedstock for conversion into energy and many other products and services, adding versatility and stability. Demand for biomass from both industry and

energy plants will increase substantially in the coming years. These new demands for biomass will have serious implications for the agricultural and forestry sectors globally, requiring greater attention to key environmental policy issues such as the decline in biodiversity and the degradation of ecosystems. Concerns about food security in the poorer regions of the globe can be reversed and used as a stimulus for bio-economic development, creating a paradigm shift from more traditional economic development (van Dam *et al.*, 2005). The direct consequences of a bio-based economy are better utilization and recycling of forestry and agricultural residues, which might otherwise be wasted and result in environmental degradation, such as pollution of freshwater or the release of greenhouse gases such as methane.

From chemical to biological processes
Bioconversion and biotechnology will play key roles in the transition from a fossil-based to a bio-based society and are essential for the development of sensible uses of renewable resources. The application of industrial biotechnology to the processing and production of chemicals, materials and fuels provides the key multi-disciplinary knowledge system in the organization of technologies and incentives required in the implementation of (bio)economic and sustainable processes for converting bio-based materials (Carrez and Soetaert, 2005).

Fermentation processes to convert crops into food and beverages, or to extract medicines and fibres, have been known for thousands of years. Applied biotechnology is common practice these days in many industrial sectors ranging from pharmaceutical and chemical industries to food and non-food industries. In this context the complex technology for the conversion of biomass to materials and fuels is referred to as a 'biorefinery.' The chain of integrated processes for conversion of heterogeneous biomass to value-added products is woven into the key cluster of multi-disciplinary know-how that has to be developed and optimized (Kamm *et al.*, 2006).

Biofuels as global commodities
The rapid expansion of international trade during the past several decades has been a major factor in global economic growth, as different

world regions have sought to exploit comparative advantage in different sectors. Bioenergy trade is a more recent phenomenon, as it has only been in the last 5–10 years that countries such as Brazil have had a significant surplus for international markets – while, simultaneously, biofuels and biomass have emerged as more strategic international commodities under pressure from energy and climate concerns. Thus far, international trade in biofuels has been dominated by EU imports from Brazil and elsewhere.

At the same time, agricultural markets are still characterized by a significant degree of protectionism, especially due to the subsidies provided to farmers in the EU and the United States. Such protectionism has contributed to the dependence on cheap imports and food aid in a number of developing countries, which in turn has contributed to lower domestic investment in agriculture. Given the significant investments needed to meet future food demand, international trade will be one of several determining factors. Protectionist tendencies such as import bans can result in a 'starve thy neighbour' policy, which is neither morally acceptable nor economically efficient (Msangi and Rosengrant, 2009).

The direction of investments in bioenergy and agriculture will be more closely linked in the coming decades, as growing populations and changing diets result in greater land pressures for food, feed, fuel and fibre. Investments in first-generation crops in temperate climates will clearly face greater constraints under increasing demands for higher resource efficiency and greenhouse gas mitigation. Some of these first-generation biofuel crop productions schemes – those with poor energy and GHG balances – will thus probably be fairly short-lived.

The first-generation biofuel crops, however, will without doubt be an important stepping stone to second- and third-generation of biofuel crops. Indeed, the idea that first-generation biofuel crops should be quickly abandoned is a wasteful suggestion under any scenario that values the advanced biofuels, since these will build on similar infrastructure. Overall, agricultural value-added will benefit from biofuels investments under almost any scenario (Fischer *et al.*, 2009). However, the extent to which this affects food security is related to a number of factors such as the impact of higher food costs for urban consumers and the synergies that can be created between agro-food and agro-energy industries. Integrated biorefineries in the future could offer greater financial returns through a portfolio of products (Kamm *et al.*, 2006), with the possible risk-reducing advantage of being able to switch across different production strategies.

Linkages between food security and energy security
Expansion in the production and use of biofuels needs to be accomplished in a way that does not harm food security, an issue that is naturally much more complex than simply a matter of price and availability. The definition of food security agreed on at the 1996 World Food Summit was for people to have 'physical and economic access to sufficient safe and nutritious food to meet their dietary needs and food preferences for a healthy and active life'. Some measurements of food security do not necessarily address the general welfare that comes with improved living conditions through improved water, sanitation and health (Pinstrup-Anderson, 2009).

While food security is an issue for the developing world, energy security is generally viewed as an issue for the OECD countries, and is often closely associated with the availability of oil, a historical remnant of the so-called 'energy crises' of the 1970s, when high oil prices and/or shortages led to instability in transport fuel markets. However, the poor in developing countries face their own energy crisis in the form of high reliance on traditional biomass from wood fuels and agricultural residues; it is an energy crisis that amounts to a daily struggle in rural areas, where women and children walk long distances to gather wood, leading to significant health and safety impacts, as well as the opportunity costs associated with a time-consuming activity to access a low-quality energy source. There is a strong correlation between undernourishment and energy security viewed in such a context, especially among the rural poor. Non-oil-producing countries with a high global hunger index tend to have a high proportion of biomass use (Msangi and Ewing, 2009).

This linkage between food and fuel security arises from the poverty trap that can be created or exacerbated by the combination of subsistence farming and high biomass use. The interest in biofuels in many of the least-developed countries implicitly recognizes these linkages, particularly where biofuels are to be used locally for power generation or for running agricultural equipment. The choice of crop becomes a key variable in avoiding food–fuel conflicts, which is the reason many African countries have favoured non-edible crops such as jatropha that can grow on less favourable soils. It can be argued, however, that farmers who produce biofuels can generate incomes enabling them to increase their food crop productivity and/or buy food on the market.

Conclusions

A fundamental transformation is under way in the use of biomass resources for food, feed, fuel, fibre and many other uses. This transformation arises from the combination of three key drivers over the coming decades: the need to substitute renewable resources for the non-renewable ones on which economic growth has been predicated; the need to adapt to a changing climate by using resources more wisely and investing in the technology for carbon-negative biofuels; and the resource requirements of a growing world population with increasing demands for food, feed and fuel. There is wide scope for reconciling expanded biofuel production with food security, and even for deploying biofuels in a way that supports sustainable development and helps to revive rural economies. In order to realize the potential for synergies rather than conflicts between food and fuel, substantial investment in research and development is needed, as is a rejection of subsidies for unsustainable agricultural practices and a wide adoption of policies that support integrated and highly productive biomass platforms. Future trends in demand and supply reveal the importance of avoiding the view that food security and biofuel development are competing objectives: the biomass resources that support food and fuel – as well as feed, fibre, fertilizer and other uses – can and must be used synergistically to address the energy and climate challenge of the coming decades.

References

Biosorghum (2010) 'Africa biofortified sorghum project', <biosorghum.org>.
Brennan, L. and P. Owende (2010) 'Biofuels from microalgae – a review of technologies for production, processing, and extractions of biofuels and co-products', *Renewable and Sustainable Energy Reviews* 14: 557–77.

Bruinsma, J. (2009) 'The resource outlook to 2050: by how much do land, water and crop yields need to increase by 2050', in 'Proceedings of the FAO Expert Meeting on How to Feed the World in 2050', <www.fao.org>.

Carrez, D. and W. Soetaert (2005) 'Looking ahead in Europe: white biotech by 2025', *Industrial Biotechnology* 1 (2): 95–101.

de Wit, M., M. Junginger, S. Lensink, M. Londo and A. Faaij (2010) 'Competition between biofuels: modelling technological learning and cost reductions over time', *Biomass and Bioenergy* 34: 203–17.

Eaglesham, A., W. Brown and R. Hardy (2000) 'The bio-based economy of the twenty-first century: agriculture expanding into health, energy and chemicals', report, National Agricultural Biotechnology Council (NABC), Ithaca NY.

FAO (2004) *The State of Food and Agriculture 2003–2004: Agricultural Biotechnology: Meeting the Needs of the Poor,* FAO, Rome 2004.

—— (2006a) 'World agriculture: towards 2030/2050 – Interim report', FAO, Rome.

—— (2006b) 'Livestock's long shadow; environmental issues and options', report, FAO, Rome.

—— (2009) 'The state of food insecurity in the world,' report, FAO, Rome.

Fischer, R. A., D. Byerlee and G. O. Edmeades (2009) 'Can technology deliver on the yield challenge to 2050?', in 'Proceedings of the FAO Expert Meeting on How to Feed the World in 2050', <www.fao.org>.

FOE (2008) 'Soy consumption for feed and fuel in the European Union', research paper prepared for Milieudefensie (Friends of the Earth, Netherlands) Profundo Economic Research, 28 October.

GBEP (2008). 'A sustainable biofuels consensus', Global Bioenergy Partnership, March, <http://www.globalbioenergy.org/bioenergyinfo/global-initiativesbrbr/detail/en/news/4587/icode/1/>.

Goodland, R. and J. Anhang (2009) 'Livestock and climate change: what if the key actors in climate change are pigs, and chickens?' *World Watch* (November/December), <www.worldwatch.org>.

IEA (2009) *World Energy Outlook*, International Energy Agency, Paris, March 2009.

James, C. (2008) 'Global status of commercialized biotech/GM crops: 2008', report, International Service for the Acquisition of Agri-biotech Applications, Ithaca NY, 2008.

Juma, C. and I. Seregeldin (2007) 'Freedom to innovate: biotechnology in Africa's development', Report of the High Level African Panel on Modern Biotechnology, African Union, and New Partnership for Africa's Development (NEPAD), Addis Ababa and Pretoria.

Kamm, B., P. Gruber and M. Kamm (2006) 'Biorefineries – industrial processes and products: status quo and future directions', report, Wiley-VCH, Weinheim.

Kim, H., S. Kim and B. E. Dale (2009) 'Biofuels, land use change, and green-house gas emissions: some unexplored variables,' *Environmental Science and Technology* 43 (13): 4763–75.

Kivits, R., M. B. Charles and N. Ryan (2010) 'A post-carbon aviation future: air-ports and the transition to a cleaner aviation sector', *Futures* 42 (3): 199–211.

Leach, G. and F. Johnson (1999) 'Modern bioenergy – an overview of its pros-pects and potential,' *Renewable Energy for Development* 12 (4).

Leplé, J. C., R. Dauwe, K. Morreel, V. Storme, C. Lapierre, B. Pollet, A. Nau-mann, K. Y. Kang, H. Kim, K. Ruel, A. Lefebvre, J. P. Joseleau, J. Grima-Pettenati, R. de Rycke, S. Andersson-Gunnerås, A. Erban, I. Fehrle, M. Petit-Conil, J. Kopka, A. Polle, E. Messens, B. Sundberg, S. D. Mansfield, J. Ralph, G. Pilate and W. Boerjan (2007) 'Downregulation of cinnamoyl-coenzyme A reductase in poplar: multiple-level phenotyping reveals effects on cell wall polymer metabolism and structure', *The Plant Cell* 19: 3669–91.

Lotze-Campen, H., A. Popp, T. Beringer, C. Müller, A. Bondeau, S. Rost and W. Lucht (2010) 'Scenarios of global bioenergy production: the trade-offs between agricultural expansion, intensification and trade', *Ecological Modelling* 221 (18): 2188–96.

Msangi, S. and M. Ewing (2009) 'Biofuels production in developing countries: assessing tradeoffs in welfare and food security', *Environmental Science and Policy* 12 (2009) 520–8.

Msangi, S. and M. Rosengrant (2009) 'World agriculture in a dynamically-changing environment: IFPRI's long-term outlook for food and agriculture under additional demand and constraints', in 'Proceedings of the FAO Expert Meeting on How to Feed the World in 2050', <www.fao.org>.

New Scientist (2008) 'Biofuel corn makes cow bug enzyme to digest itself', <www.newscientist.com/article/dn13619>.

Pinstrup-Andersen, P. (2009) 'Food security: definition and measurement', *Food Security* 1: 5–7.

Sims, R., W. Mabee, J. N. Saddler and M. Taylor (2010) 'An overview of second generation biofuel technologies', *Bioresource Technology* 101: 1570–80.

Taheripour, F., T. W. Hertel, W. E. Tyner, J. F. Beckman and D. K. Birur (2010) 'Biofuels and their by-products: global economic and environmental implications', *Biomass and Bioenergy* 34: 278–89.

UN (2009) 'Population Projections', United Nations Statistical Office, Geneva, 2009.

van Dam, J. E. G., B. de Klerk-Engels, P. C. Struik and R. Rabbinge (2005) 'Securing renewable resources supplies for changing market demands in a biobased economy', *Industrial Crops and Products* 21: 129–44.

World Bank (2007) *Agriculture for Development* (World Development Report 2008), Washington DC, World Bank.

Food versus Fuel: Concluding Remarks

Francis X. Johnson and Frank Rosillo-Calle

The debate on food and fuel first arose in the 1970s when ethanol was made from corn in the US and from sugarcane in Brazil: it was the first time that government policy had envisioned a significant diversion of a food crop into energy. The main motivation for biofuels at the time was energy security, as high oil prices combined with political instability in the Middle East were viewed as a major constraint on economic growth and prosperity. The biofuel programme in Brazil had similar motivations, although it did not suffer from the 'food vs fuel' critique as much as the US programme did (see Chapter 1), since sugar was not a staple food crop in caloric and nutritional terms. Nor was there much expectation that food crops would be used for biofuels on any large scale outside of the US, as the costs were prohibitive: the conversion of starch to fermentable sugars was widely recognized as a costly process in energy and economic terms. The lower oil prices of the late 1980s dealt a further setback to biofuels development, and the food vs fuel issue generally receded from the public debate.

However, the need to develop renewable energy sources in the transport sector never went away. The accelerated pace of oil consumption globally, and especially in Asia, meant that consumption was outstripping supply even faster than expected; the long-term price trend can only be upward for a non-renewable resource with few substitutes in the modern economy. At the same time, two additional drivers of the interest in biofuels emerged in the past decade. One was climate change, as biofuels offered one of the few near-term mitigation options for the transport sector. The other factor was the role of biofuels in supporting investment in agriculture and rural development. These two factors, in combination with dwindling supplies of oil and the excessive reliance on petroleum products in the global economy, have endowed this second major phase of biofuels development – which began only in the past 5–10 years – with a different character compared to the short-lived first phase in the 1970s and early 1980s.

This development was naturally accompanied by a more rigorous public debate, since the potential scale was much greater and the stakes were higher for all the actors involved as well as the public at large. At this higher scale, there was much closer scrutiny of the potential negative social and environmental impacts of bioenergy, and especially biofuels, and the food vs fuel debate emerged as one of the key issues under contention. The debate reached its peak during 2008, tracing the same curve as the spike in agricultural commodity prices – which some attributed, rightly or wrongly, to the rise in production of biofuels. The discussion that subsequently emerged in the media has been driven not so much by scientific facts, but rather by moral, ethical and policy issues, along with the vested interests associated with traditional energy sources, some sectors of the agri-food industry, and the lobbying interests of NGOs. The confusion created by this debate gave rise to the need for an informed and accessible book, grounded in science rather than conjecture and controversy, so that both academic and professional specialists might share with the general public a more complete understanding of the issues.

Setting the scene

In Chapter 1 the three basic questions about the role of biofuels were introduced: (1) whether biofuel production is a choice between food or fuel; (2) whether biofuels have positive or negative effects on climate change and the broader environment; and, (3) whether biofuels contribute to socio-economic development, wealth generation and distribution. These questions were then covered in depth in the six chapters that form the body of this volume. Chapter 1 identified and explained a number of variables and drivers related to the three questions it introduced, covering political and social aspects as well as technical and economic characteristics. The chapter paid specific attention to the role of various lobbying groups; the objectives of climate policy and GHG reductions; the role of biofuels in wealth creation and poverty reduction; the relation between biofuels production and food prices;

impacts on land use; the role of subsidies and other policy instruments; how energy balances are determined; and the sustainability analyses aimed at market certification of biofuels.

Examining the pros and cons of the basic 'food vs fuel' debate, Chapter 1 came to the conclusion that the competing schools of thought both have compelling arguments in favour or against biofuels. This is partly because the debate has been rather premature, as there is still a considerable lack of scientific data to enable general conclusions in terms of the linkages between food and fuel in achieving the basic societal objectives of increasing welfare and sustainability.

Some people find it unethical to use land to produce biofuels which benefit mostly wealthy people, when almost one billion people are chronically undernourished in the world. However, the main reasons people go hungry are many and complex; they usually have little to do with food or land availability, but rather with poverty and income inequality. The impact of biofuels on food prices, a major concern, is the consequence of a complex web of factors that needs to be incorporated in any debate. Price increases related to *direct land competition* remain an insignificant factor in global market terms, since less than 1 percent of global agricultural land area is currently dedicated to biofuels.

On environmental impacts, it remains difficult to come up with any general conclusions, especially given the complexities associated with climate change and the difficulty of evaluating carbon sequestration in soils. Doubt over the GHG benefits of biofuels is partly due to the potentially large influence of land-use change on the carbon balance. In addition to *direct* land-use change, another phenomenon that has been evaluated is *indirect* land-use change (ILUC): this can occur when biofuels displace agricultural crops that are then produced by bringing additional land into agricultural use elsewhere in the world. The ILUC methodology relies on combining land-use data with economic modelling, which in some cases can lead to speculation that may not have much scientific content. The ILUC methodology requires considerable work if it is to be used for policy guidance.

Subsidies given to biofuels have also been strongly criticized by the anti-biofuels lobby. But this argument often ignores the point that governments around the world have been subsidizing the energy industries, both for fossil fuels and renewable energy, for many decades. The size of these subsidies varies considerably from country to country. Historically, subsidies given by governments to fossil fuels and nuclear energy have dwarfed those applied to biofuels. Even the comparison is unfair in many cases, since subsidies given to mature industries such as fossil fuels are generally inappropriate, whereas those given to emerging renewable industries are acknowledged as necessary to overcome the barriers associated with infrastructure and other underlying costs. Furthermore, diesel and gasoline are still heavily subsidized in many countries.

The energy balance (the amount of energy provided compared to the non-renewable energy inputs) has been the subject of considerable debate and still remains a contentious issue, particularly in the case of ethanol from corn. Oversimplifications of the energy balance analysis are frequently due to the complex web of economic, social and political factors that need to be taken into account: different assumptions and calculations can therefore lead to different results, as noted in Chapters 1 and 2. In some cases, underestimation of the energy balance is due to reliance on old data, a tendency not to include yield improvements, or to exclude the contribution of co-products. The energy balance can also be overestimated when land-use impacts or the use of inputs such as fertilizers are not properly incorporated into the analyses.

A considerable body of ongoing work is aimed at developing sustainability metrics and certification systems on bioenergy, but many questions remain unanswered. Principles, criteria and sustainability requirements are under consideration by many private and public groups, along with compliance mechanisms to assess performance and guide development of the sector.

The anti-biofuels arguments

The US surpassed Brazil in 2006 to become the world's largest producer of ethanol. Unfortunately the prime feedstock, corn, is not the most suitable for a combination of environmental, energy and economic reasons. This has resulted in considerable criticism and controversy in the US and beyond – which also takes in the role of the US as the world's largest exporter of maize. In Chapter 2, Pimentel *et al.* compiled and assessed a variety of data to support their case against biofuels, focusing primarily on the US but also addressing some global aspects.

They made the point that though it may seem beneficial to use renewable plant materials for biofuel, the use of crop residues and other biomass for biofuels raises many environmental and ethical concerns. They highlighted the fact that diverse conflicts exist in the use of land, water, energy and other environmental resources for food and biofuel production. And they paid special attention to two basic elements of the conflict: (1) uses and interdependencies among land, water and fossil energy resources in food and biofuel production; and (2) the characteristics of the resulting environmental impacts.

The use of water is of course a major concern. The authors made the point that producing 9 t/ha of corn, for example, requires annually about 7 million litres of water. Irrigation provides much of the water for world food production, but irrigation water is projected to decline significantly because of global warming.

On food and malnutrition, they made the point that cereal grains make up an alarming 80 percent of the world's food supply. And although grain yields per hectare in both developed and developing countries are still gradually increasing, the rate of increase is slowing, while the world population and its food needs are rising. The resulting decrease in food supply can result in widespread malnutrition, although the reasons are many and diverse.

On crop land and water resources, the authors provided considerable data to illustrate the point that, as the human population continues to increase rapidly, there has been an expansion of diverse human activities that has dramatically reduced available cropland and pasture land; most of the suitable cropland is already in use. The remaining land area is unsuitable for crops, pasture, and/or forests, because the soil is too infertile or shallow to support plant growth.

The total sustainable world biomass energy potential, including forests, has been estimated at about 27 percent of total global energy use. Of the total world land area in cropland, pasture, and forest, about 38 percent is cropland and pasture and about 30 percent is forests. Devoting a portion of this cropland and forest land to biofuels will stress both types of managed ecosystems and will not be sufficient to solve the world fuel problem.

With regard to energy resources and use, Pimentel *et al.* described the enormous amount of energy used since the industrial revolution, particularly by industrial countries. The huge consumption (and waste) of energy sources poses a serious challenge for mankind, particularly over our dependence on oil, and we may be about to reach the peak of oil production – followed by the inevitable decline marked by rising prices. The authors quoted ample sources to prove their point.

Ethanol from maize is problematic in the US from energy, economic and environmental perspectives. The authors stated that to make a litre of 99.5 percent ethanol requires 46 percent more fossil energy than the 'renewable' energy it produces when burned; the corn feedstock alone requires more than 33 percent of the total energy input. Not only does ethanol from corn have a negative energy balance, but it also receives huge subsidies (much greater than gasoline), although such figures remain contested. The authors also reviewed a large number of environmental impacts posed by ethanol from corn, primarily in the US.

The chapter also covered in considerable detail ethanol from grass and cellulose; biodiesel from soybean, rapeseed and canola; and oil produced from oil palm plantations and algae. And in all cases, after examining the pros and cons of each feedstock, their conclusions were negative.

Finally, the authors pointed out that using food crops to produce ethanol raises major nutritional and ethical concerns. Nearly 60 percent of humans in the world are currently malnourished, so the need for grains and other basic foods is critical. The basic conclusion is that growing crops for fuel squanders land, water, and energy resources vital for the production of food for people.

The pro-biofuels arguments

Chapter 3 (presenting the arguments of the pro-biofuels lobby) brought together two very different experiences, highlighted by two case studies. Luís Cortez and Manoel Regis Lima Verde Leal described the general case as well as a detailed analysis for Brazil, which is undoubtedly the world's most successful biofuel programme in economic and environmental terms. In the second case study, Thomas Sinkala considered the very different circumstances in Africa, the continent that is potentially the most exposed to the changes in resource pricing and availability associated with biofuels production. He used a specific example from Zambia – the case of jatropha oil production in that country – to illustrate possibilities for small-scale biofuels in support of rural and agricultural development.

Brazil has the world's more successful biofuel (ethanol) programme – an achievement that is often favourably contrasted with the more controversial US ethanol initiative. The Brazilian programme is based on sugarcane, one of the best crops for producing ethanol owing to its high productivity and the co-products that can be obtained, in addition to the fact that it can generate all the energy requirements of the plant and even provide a surplus for other uses.

Cortez and Regis began by explaining Brazil's ethanol experience during the twentieth Century and in particular the role of ProAlcool (the National Ethanol Programme, set up in 1975); they examined the causes that led to its creation and contrasted this programme with the other notable ethanol experiment in the US. Unique characteristics of the Brazilian case, they concluded, will make it difficult to replicate ethanol production on such a scale anywhere else in the world.

Their analysis of the scientific literature on the major questions posed by global large-scale production of ethanol – GHG and energy balance, food and fuel competition, land use, and social-economic impacts – illustrated the unique position of Brazil, which demonstrates the benefits of ethanol across all scenarios. The authors argued that the substitution of 10 percent of world gasoline consumption by ethanol from sugarcane is a target that Brazil could meet by cultivating an additional 25 Mha, mainly from low-productivity degraded and pasture lands: the expansion of ethanol production is currently under way.

It is obvious that the choice of the feedstock is crucial in terms not only of the overall GHG balance, but also of land requirements. Currently there are just under 8 Mha of sugarcane (about 45 percent for sugar production and 55 percent for ethanol), compared to 2 Mha in 1975; since that time, Brazil has become the world's largest producer of sugar and the second-largest producer of ethanol (behind the US). This has been possible thanks to continuous improvements in all production phases – for example, ethanol production in Brazil has increased from about 2,000 l/ha in the late 1970s to about 7,000 l/ha in 2008 (in some cases as much as 10,000 l/ha has been reported). With new technology such as the production of ethanol from bagasse, tops and leaves, productivities as high as 14,000 l/ha are possible. This will also require a more holistic approach to ethanol production – combining all aspects of agricultural production, transport and industrial processing.

There are, however, serious problems to overcome, such as the heavy concentration of sugarcane plantations in the State of São Paulo, and within this state in specific areas such as Reberao Prieto. The authors identified new potential areas for expansion without jeopardizing food production or incurring further land concentration.

As for socio-economic development, the authors argued that the introduction of energy crops will generate long-term impacts affecting such matters as land rights, income distribution, availability of finances, and skills training. However, it is important to remember that the main objective of biofuels is fossil fuel substitution, particularly gasoline and diesel, and the end product needs to be competitive with what is being substituted. So biofuels production is not the kind of activity in which one should expect high returns per hectare, as can be expected from other agricultural activities, largely because of the high cost of the feedstock – 60–70 percent of the total cost in case of ethanol, and 70–80 percent in the case of biodiesel.

On subsidies, the authors forcefully argued for initial support until biofuels reach maturity, and put the case of Brazil as a successful example. Once ProAlcool reached maturity, all subsidies were withdrawn and today the market is the sole regulator of the sector. This is generally the case with the development of the energy sector, which, as explained above, has been subsidized for many decades, with the overwhelming majority of those subsidies directed at fossil fuels and nuclear power.

Brazil is indeed a very successful case that may not be replicable elsewhere at such a large scale, but it is certainly a programme from which much can be learned. However, in Chapter 3 the authors recognized that, despite the success in Brazil, the present world energy and environment situation demands a new strategy. The Brazilian domestic market for gasoline is already 50 percent fulfilled with bioethanol from sugarcane, but when the world gasoline demand is analysed (about 1.2 trillion litres/year) it is clear that a major global effort will be required in many different areas. Obviously, it is unrealistic to expect all gasoline to be replaced by ethanol on a global basis; but replacing 10–20 percent is achievable – and would be a considerable achievement in light of the historical experiences.

What is important is to use the successful development of first-generation biofuels to pave the way for second and third generations. One important lesson is to prevent the concentration of sugarcane in sensitive areas of the country, in order to avoid endangering natural forests and food production. Another lesson is related to the significant Research and Development effort required to be successful with agronomics and breeding. In the case of sugarcane, it means developing cane varieties most suitable for ethanol rather than sugar production, and also the diversification of new varieties to meet climatic conditions. When the ProAlcool programme started, sugar and ethanol production basically depended on just a few varieties, whereas today there are more than 500 varieties of sugarcane, an impressive development that required painstaking analysis and a great deal of trial and error in the field and in the laboratory.

Despite the success of ProAlcool, future ethanol production requires new thinking. As the authors put it, to make the production of sugarcane bioethanol more sustainable, it is necessary to improve sugarcane productivity beyond what is expected using conventional technology: there is need for a strong genetic engineering and agronomic R&D programme to develop new sugarcane varieties, increase productivity, and improve utilization of cane residues and of by-products.

Food and fuel in the African context
The African context is quite different to the situation in Brazil for many reasons, including the prevalence of water scarcity, land degradation, food insecurity, the low level of infrastructure and the lack of opportunities for rural development. However, one similarity in the case of Zambia, which Thomson Sinkala used as his example in Chapter 3, is the low population density and a plentiful supply of agricultural land. The potential for biofuels in Zambia is therefore just as great as in Brazil

in terms of yields per hectare and the amount that can be made available *per capita*.

But there is a major qualitative difference in that Zambia does not have the infrastructure nor the large scale and market access of Brazil, and thus a strategy based primarily on large-scale biofuels is not possible without significant foreign investment and an enormous infrastructure-building effort. An alternative approach is to focus on biofuels crops that can be produced at smaller scale and can contribute to both the food security and the energy security of rural families. Sinkala's case study took the case of a family farm where jatropha can be grown on an intercropping basis that does not displace any food crops. The jatropha oil can substitute for expensive and polluting diesel-fuel electrical generators, while its by-products are used for soap, mosquito repellant and other useful items. Whatever the family does not need can often be sold to neighbouring communities or small businesses.

Agriculture and land use

In Chapter 4 Richard Hess *et al.* showed that land use is at the core of biofuels development. While world demand for energy continues to grow, the supply of cheap and clean energy is dwindling; at the same time, population continues to grow and so does the demand for improving living standards. What then could be the potential role of agriculture in meeting such demand without jeopardizing its primary role of providing food? What would be the economic, social, political, and environmental consequences? How this increasingly complex situation is managed will be crucial.

The authors, after analysing the pros and cons of land use and biofuels production, came to the conclusion that sufficient land is available for increased agricultural production – including crops for biofuel – but the land is disproportionately located in some areas, with large variations at global level.

Physical availability of land often means very little *per se* as other factors such as capital, market, technology, know-how and skills are key determinants. In addition, the development of sustainable agriculture, new crops capable of high productivity in marginal lands – and, in the case of biofuels, non-competition with food crops – will be the major conditional factors. Consequently, the authors call for an emphasis on much higher biomass productivity and a shift towards second- and third-generation biofuels. We need a holistic approach to agriculture and this is what the authors discuss in this chapter. The authors state that biofuels production will have some effect on land-use change, but other factors such as changing food consumption patterns are likely to be more detrimental than producing biofuel feedstocks.

The question is whether developing countries would be able to develop a modern and sustainable agricultural system when most of the prerequisites, such as capital investment and a strong domestic knowledge base, are missing? Countries or regions that already have a modern agricultural sector, such as the US and the EU, should be able to respond more easily to these changes, since they already possess the resources and infrastructure.

Determining the productive capacity of the world's agricultural sector requires addressing a complex and dynamic set of issues. Very simply, the first and most basic question becomes what is the aggregate productive capacity of agricultural lands under existing agronomic management scenarios. Of the world's 13.5 billion hectares of land surface area, roughly 61 percent is currently in grassland or forest and 12 percent is in cropland. After excluding forest land, protected areas, and land needed to meet increased demand for food crops and livestock, estimates of the amount of land potentially available for expanded crop production lie between 250 and 800Mha, most of which is found in tropical Latin America or Africa.

Changing diets will have a major impact on land availability. The authors state that an increased standard of living does not necessarily promote an increase in food consumption, but rather a shift towards more expensive foods that frequently require larger land areas to produce, such as higher-value meats, oils, cheese and other dairy products, and beverages such as beer, wine, coffee and tea. This will have a direct impact on land available for biofuels. Such issues cannot be ignored.

The case study in Chapter 4 demonstrates the need for a solid understanding and capability of determining and implementing sustainable practices relative to agricultural residue removal. The challenging reality is that implementing these criteria to determine good practices within current management scenarios generally leads to less resource being available for biofuels production. Maximizing the productive capacity of the land, while adhering to sustainability and ecosystem service constraints, will require a new approach to landscape management. This approach will advance a modern and dynamic agricultural sector that assembles the most advanced science and technologies to utilize each feature of the landscape in its most productive capacity.

The authors came to two main conclusions. First, there is abundant land available worldwide for agricultural production, including crops for biofuel. Several dynamic issues, such as changing diets, growing populations, and sustainability considerations will all place constraints on how this land will be used. The critical issue for ensuring that aggregate productive capacity of all agricultural products is maximized while meeting these constraints is determining the best productive use of each landscape feature, as previously described. Second, new commodity biomass feedstock supply system concepts will need to emerge that create accessible markets and provide economic viability while maximizing the quantity of resources that enter the system.

Establishing criteria, and mechanisms, for guiding sustainable agricultural management practices is critical for implementing the landscape vision. Creating accessible markets that facilitate highly integrated production management strategies through uniform-format supply system design concepts is equally critical, as a sustainable landscape vision will struggle to emerge without these markets.

Socio-economic objectives and impacts

In Chapter 5 Rocio Diaz-Chavez asked whether biofuels promote socio-economic development – another of the questions posed at the beginning of this book. This chapter dealt with this issue by highlighting themes such as job creation, health and gender, impacts on the poorest, livelihoods, infrastructure, investment, global trade, and policies to promote sustainable development – all in the context of the debate on whether biofuels can be produced and used sustainably, taking into consideration their wider environmental benefits and costs.

Job creation has often been over- or understated, depending on the source; a serious and detailed analysis of the pros and cons of job creation is still wanting, partly because it demands an analysis of the wider economic, social and political issues. Biofuels *per se* are not so different from any other sector of the economy. What the evidence does support is that biofuels, particularly in the feedstock production phase, require far more labour compared to fossils fuels, in some cases more than 100 times as many jobs per unit of energy produced. This is especially the case in most rural areas of developing countries, where there is a significant supply of low-cost labour available.

On health and gender, although much of the attention to the production of biofuels has assumed their use in the transport sector (mainly in developed countries), alternative uses in developing countries include electricity generation and cooking stoves. The main concerns on the traditional use of biomass are related to health, including indoor air pollution, the lifespan of women and children in rural areas of developing countries, and burns and injuries from carrying wood.

Some authors have investigated the benefits of bioenergy crops in terms of social and economic issues such as the increased availability and affordability of energy for household and commercial uses; or new markets and income for rural farmers supplying raw materials for bioenergy industries. Nevertheless, they consider that for this to be possible it is necessary to consider the gains for both men and women, as well as addressing the social constraints and cultural biases that limit women's access to education, training and decision-making processes, and restrict their rights to own land, borrow money, engage in business, and benefit from government programmes such as agricultural extension services.

As for poverty reduction, empirical evidence in support of this argument is available at the local level for small scales of production. A number of research networks have synthesized and analysed such evidence, as explained in the chapter. But the question is, with about a billion people undernourished around the world – caused by lack of access to land, water, energy and other resources – what can biofuels contribute? Poverty is a complex social and economic phenomenon, the dimensions and determinants of which are manifold. There is yet little evidence that biofuels production can reduce poverty directly. There is, however, a link to its role in creating local markets and local jobs.

In terms of infrastructure, investment and development, this is the Achilles heel of agricultural development in developing countries. Lack of capital, investment, education and skills have been a major conditioning factor for agricultural development. The main conclusions Diaz-Chavez reached were:

1   The global market for biofuels is still under development and will need to develop further in order to yield the socio-economic benefits – this will require policy mechanisms including necessary subsidies, various financial incentives and regulations on land use and infrastructure.
2   The social and economic impacts of biofuels production, both positive and negative, are in need of further research. There are no hard data to sustain many current assumptions, as some crops are still new in the market and the differences between production scales greatly influence the outcomes.
3   A global standard or certification scheme is under consideration but still far from being implemented worldwide. The reasons for this are varied and include the lack of national-level interpretation for many of the principles; a similar lack of local/national policies for renewable energy and agricultural production, especially in developing countries; and the need to embed such a scheme within international trading systems and WTO regulations.
4   Consideration of wider sustainability in agriculture production and what is important at each national level may help reduce the conflict, if any, between food production and bioenergy crops.

The debate on the sustainability of the production of biofuels has ignited a review of sustainability issues in associated sectors, notably food and feed production in agriculture. A similar analysis should be done for the fossil fuel industry, so that the comparisons made with renewable energy reflect the full impacts and costs of fossil fuel production and use.

Climate change implications

In Chapter 6 N. H. Ravindranath *et al.* showed that climate change is perhaps the key factor in determining the nature and pace of biofuels development, and hence the need to put biofuels within this context. This chapter assessed three major issues: (1) the CO_2 emissions from biofuels production in the context of climate change mitigation; (2) the implications of biofuels production for biodiversity; and (3) the potential impacts of climate change on sustainable biofuels production and possible adaptation options.

The authors argued that first-generation crops, which are noted in many cases for their high GHG burdens, are likely to dominate biofuels production for many years to come, since the technologies are well established and a large production programme exists. Furthermore, there is still considerable technological potential for increasing yields, although this depends upon crop variety, soil quality, rainfall and irrigation, nutrient supplement, and cultural practices. As for the next-generation biofuels, it was noted that lignocellulosic biomass will be harvested for its total biomass utilization, and is far more abundant around the world compared to the options for first-generation feedstocks.

Land area required and the land category for growing biofuels is at the heart of the debate on the environmental and economic impacts of biofuels production and this was covered in great detail by the authors. The chapter also looked at the implication for food production and the sources of GHG from biofuels in general, including land conversion, involving both direct and indirect land-use change (ILUC). The authors estimated CO_2 emissions associated with land conversion at the global level, considering first-generation biofuel crops under various yield assumptions. CO_2 emissions are estimated by considering a scenario of biofuels substituting 10 percent of the petroleum fuel used for transportation in 2030.

As for the sustainability of biofuels, the authors cited sustainable production practices involving high-diversity mixtures of native grassland perennials, which offer a range of ecosystem services along with reduced GHG emissions. The implications of expanded biofuels production on biodiversity would be heterogeneous, depending on the region under consideration. The use of next-generation grasses for expanding biofuel production is likely to have less impact on biodiversity than the replacement of tropical forests or grasslands by oil palm, soybean or maize.

There are no dedicated studies on the likely impacts of projected climate change on biofuel crops in different regions. There are annual (maize, sorghum and sugarcane) as well as perennial (jatropha and oil palm) biofuel crops. The projected impacts of climate change on food and cash crops are likely to provide an indication of the climate impacts on biofuel crops. The annual as well as the perennial biofuel crops are likely to be subjected to adverse impacts of climate change, particularly from warming, reduction in rainfall, water stress, droughts and increased occurrence of pests, leading to reduction in yield.

In the context of projected climate change and the likely adverse impacts, it is necessary to develop and implement adaptation strategies for sustained biofuel production. Currently, there is limited research on potential adaptation practices and strategies, even for food crops. Thus, only potential win-win adaptation strategies could be considered.

Biofuel production is likely to have direct as well as indirect effects on food security and water, particularly in developing countries where, as we have seen, the bulk of the future biofuel production is likely to occur. Cultivation of first-generation biofuel crops has also been shown to have adverse implications for biodiversity, through habitat conversion, agricultural intensification, the spread of invasive species, and pollution of soil and water.

Future trends

In Chapter 7 Francis Johnson and Ivar Virgin consider the main drivers for future food and fuel demand, and the supply to meet that demand. A major demand driver is the growing appetite in developing countries for more meat, which in turn requires more animal feed or more land for grazing. The demand for mobility is in many respects following closely on the demand for food and feed, since the ability of producers to get their products to market and the ability of people to adapt to changing labour needs and economic opportunities requires increasing mobility. Another major driver is that the geographical location of growth in demand has shifted to Asia, where the exponential growth in China and India will dwarf other regions in the coming decades because of their huge populations.

The bioscience revolution that has been taking place during the past several decades will need to continue to develop in order to meet changing demands for food, feed, fuel, fibre, fertilizer, and the many other goods and services provided by biomass resources through agriculture and changing patterns of land use. New cultivars are needed that address changes in quality and quantity across different markets, including industrial feedstocks and various health and materials applications. A much greater investment in research and development is needed to meet this challenge, and, in order to address undernourished regions in Africa, much greater agricultural productivity will be needed. Although biotechnology by itself cannot meet these challenges, it will certainly not be possible to meet them without an appropriate expansion of biotechnology applications and markets.

The advanced biofuels are needed in order to relieve extensive agriculture and improve land management so as to make better use of biomass resources in the future, as the twin pressures of dwindling fossil fuels and climate change begin to place strains on the provision of both food and fuel. Second-generation biofuels will address the need for improved conversion and better matching of applications and end uses, whereas third- and fourth-generation biofuels will go beyond immediate needs and allow for carbon negative energy options. The role of advanced bioenergy and biofuels thus provides a valuable climate mechanism in comparison to first-generation biofuels, which in some cases can become a climate liability, especially when grains such as maize are used for fuel production in temperate climates and result in land-use change that erases much of the GHG savings.

A fundamental transformation is thus under way in the use of biomass resources for food, feed, fuel, fibre and many other uses. There are ultimately three key drivers that will determine the production of food and fuel over the coming decades: the need to substitute renewable resources for non-renewable ones; the need to adapt to a changing climate; and the need to meet the resource requirements of a growing world population. There are opportunities for reconciling expanded biofuel production with food security so as to support sustainable development and revive rural economies. In order to realize the potential for synergies rather than conflicts between food and fuel, substantial investment in research and development is needed. Also needed are policies that stimulate more efficient bioenergy conversion platforms and reward innovation in both food and fuel provision through integrated biomass production systems that minimize waste, manage carbon wisely, and create a diversified landscape for agricultural development and the associated ecosystem services.

Index

Page numbers in *italics* refer to boxes, figures, and tables. A forward slash indicates continuous treatment of a topic that is interrupted by a full page table or figure.